ICD-10 Classification of Mental and Behavioural Disorders

For Churchill Livingstone

Commissioning Editor: Peter Richardson
Copy Editor: Jennifer Bew
Indexer: Jill Halliday
Design direction: Sarah Cape
Cover design: Keith Kail
Production: Mark Sanderson
Sales Promotion Executive: Caroline Boyd

ICD-10 Classification of Mental and Behavioural Disorders

with Glossary and Diagnostic Criteria for Research

Compilation and editorial arrangements by
J.E. Cooper

WORLD HEALTH ORGANIZATION GENEVA

Churchill Livingstone

EDINBURGH LONDON NEW YORK PHILADELPHIA ST LOUIS SYDNEY TORONTO 1994

CHURCHILL LIVINGSTONE
An imprint of Harcourt Publishers Limited

First published 1994
  Reprinted 1995
  Reprinted 1998
  Reprinted 1999
  Reprinted 2000
  Reprinted 2001 (twice)

ISBN 0-443-04909-2

British Library Cataloguing in Publication Data
A catalogue record for this book is available from the British Library

Library of Congress Cataloging in Publication Data
A catalog record for this book is available from the Library of Congress

The
publisher's
policy is to use
paper manufactured
from sustainable forests

Printed in China by RDC Group Limited

Contents

Foreword

Mental and behavioural disorders are frequent, can be grave in their consequences and cause suffering to hundreds of millions of people, worldwide. An improvement of the care which they receive – or should receive – depends on the better education of health workers (and of the general public) and on a more intensive commitment of governments to the development of services to the mentally ill and their communities. Both of these requirements, as well as the requirement for progress in the acquisition of knowledge, depend upon making information about mental illness available and comprehensible to those concerned. The materials which the world's scientific community, with WHO's leadership, has produced, such as the ICD-10 texts and their derivations including this Guide, can play a major role in this respect and help make a common language for psychiatry a reality.

Professor J.E. Cooper has been involved in the development of the classification of mental disorders incorporated in the International Classification of Diseases (ICD) since the 1960s, when he was one of the contributors to WHO's programme on the standardization of psychiatric diagnosis, classification and statistics which resulted in the 8th revision of the ICD. These activities included the production of the first internationally-accepted glossary of categories and the development of widely-accepted methods which allow the scientific exploration of the process of arriving at diagnoses and at their classification.[1,8*]

This process differed from previous related activities of the Organization in that it was supported by a co-operative agreement with the US National Institutes of Health and in that it added other activities to those aiming at the standardization of diagnosis and classification of psychiatric disorders,[2,1*,2*] including:

1. The development of a set of versions of the ICD classification of mental and behavioural disorders

prepared for different categories of users – a version for clinicians,[12*] a version for research,[15*] a version for use in primary health care and a multiaxial presentation. These have all been (or are in the process of being) tested extensively in a variety of countries; [14*]

2. the development of a series of internationally-applicable research instruments allowing an assessment of mental illness in comparable terms;

3. the development of a series of lexica[5*] which accompany the classification of mental disorders and the instruments for patient assessment;

4. the development of a network of research, training and reference centres working with WHO on the further development of instruments and classifications; and support of relevant research carried out by these and other centres;

5. a contribution to the recently-initiated revision process of the International Classification of Impairment, Disabilities and Handicap of the World Health Organization;

6. the production of a series of publications containing reviews of the world's literature,[2*] and other training materials which can be used in efforts to optimize the use of assessment tools and classifications.

These activities were carried out bearing in mind that an important future use of ICD-10 will be to facilitate the description and assessment of the quality of psychiatric services and of various interventions intended to help the mentally ill.

This pocket guide brings together parts of several products referred to particularly in paragraph 1 above. The main sources of the material presented here – in the production of which Professor Cooper has actively participated over the years – are the short definitions of categories (glossary notes) which are incorporated into the text of the International Classification of Diseases,[11*] the texts of the Clinical Descriptions and Diagnostic Guidelines,[12*] the text of the Diagnostic Criteria for Research,[15*] and the Crosswalks ICD-10/ICD-9.[10*] In addition to bringing these parts together for each category, Professor Cooper has added a series of notes on some of the main problems that are still unresolved with respect to this and other current classifications.

The *Pocket Guide* is thus a pragmatic compilation of

texts from several sources with which the user should be familiar. In particular, psychiatrists who use this book should be familiar with the WHO publication *Clinical Descriptions and Diagnostic Guidelines* which sets out the clinical context for the Diagnostic Criteria for Research. For those who are familiar with at least these two volumes, this pocket guide will undoubtedly be an invaluable additional aid to the correct and easy use of the diagnostic criteria and classification of mental disorders in the ICD-10.

Health service managers, administrators, data analysts and medical records staff should also find this pocket guide useful, since it contains the whole of Chapter V of ICD-10 (i.e. all of the category names plus code numbers), together with a conversion table between Chapters V of ICD-9 and ICD-10, and thus relates to the Psychiatric Adaptation of the ICD-10,[16*] which is in preparation and which is specifically designed for statistical and reporting purposes.

It is therefore with much pleasure that I recommend this book to psychiatrists, to those in postgraduate training in psychiatry and related disciplines, and to all others who need a quick and easy way to access the ICD-10 diagnostic and classification rules related to mental illness.

Norman Sartorius

REFERENCES
1. Shepherd M, Brooke E M, Cooper J E, Lin T 1968 An experimental approach to psychiatric diagnosis: an international study. *Acta Psychiatrica Scandinavica* **201**. Munksgaard, Copenhagen
2. Sartorius N 1993 WHO's work on the epidemiology of mental disorders. *Social Psychiatry and Psychiatric Epidemiology* **28**: 147–155

* These references can be found in the list on pages 401–402.

Preface

This volume is produced as a pocket book so as to be a convenient quick-reference guide to Chapter V of ICD-10 (referred to subsequently simply as Chapter V) for several types of user. The components of this volume are:–

1. All the titles and code numbers of the categories in the classification.
2. The text of the glossary to Chapter V that is given in the main ICD-10 volume, which contains all 21 chapters.
3. The diagnostic criteria for research of chapter V (DCR-10) plus Annexes 1 and 2.
4. Diagnostic notes and comments on points of special interest and importance. Some of these are unique to this volume, some are taken from the *Clinical descriptions and diagnostic guidelines* (CDDG) (WHO 1992), and some are from the basic DCR-10 volume (WHO 1993).
5. A conversion table between Chapter V of ICD-9 and Chapter V(F) of ICD-10.

Regarding titles and code numbers, the DCR-10 and their appendix contain some optional or provisional categories that are not included in the main classification. These are distinguished by a star ($\star$) on the code.

The text of the glossary to Chapter V from the main ICD volume is the description that has been agreed, after extensive consultation, as the internationally accepted description of the main features of each disorder. These descriptions are shorter than those in the CDDG, which are designed for use by psychiatrists and other mental health professionals. This shorter glossary facilitates the process of achieving maximum compatibility between ICD-10 and any future national or regional classifications. It also fulfils the need for a comparatively brief and simple description of the categories often voiced by records officers, clerical workers and administrators who are responsible for the collection and analysis of mental health service statistics. Other professionals who are not medically trained but who wish to learn something about the contents of Chapter V may also find these descriptions useful.

The diagnostic criteria for research of Chapter V have been developed directly from the CDDG. Statements about numbers and duration of symptoms have been added, together with other criteria required when choosing comparatively homogeneous groups of subjects for research. Clinicians should also find these criteria useful, since the presentation of the narrative glossary description alongside the DCR-10 will serve as a reminder of the main (and minimal) clinical features of the disorders expressed in a complementary manner. All users of the DCR-10 are nevertheless reminded that they are designed to be used in conjunction with the longer descriptions and comments to be found in the CDDG. Students and trainees should be particularly careful to base their studies on the more comprehensive descriptions and commentaries to be found in textbooks and other literary sources; they should not regard the DCR-10 or this volume as having sufficient content to form an adequate basis for clinical work.

Some of the diagnostic notes and comments on unsolved problems serve to remind the user of points included in various sections of both the CDDG and the DCR-10. An additional brief section of comments on unsolved problems and controversial points is included. These will remind the user that all classifications of psychiatric disorders are still temporary and incomplete statements, awaiting improvement as our knowledge progresses.

The dagger(†) and asterisk(*) system has now been extended to Chapter V. These symbols are used to indicate that two different aspects of the same disorder or disease are recorded in two different chapters of the ICD. One of these is regarded as the primary code, usually a disease process, and is marked with the dagger(†). The secondary code is in that part of the classification dealing with the organ system to which the manifestation or complication is related, and is marked with an asterisk(*). For instance, dementia in Pick's disease is recorded in Chapter V as:

F 02.0* Dementia in Pick's disease (G31.0†).

This indicates that category F02.0 is used to record the behavioural syndrome of dementia typical of Pick's disease, and that the presence of the pathological process itself is recorded by using category G31.0 (in Chapter 6(G)).

Users of this pocket book are strongly recommended to consult other sources about the content and development of ICD-10, such as the introduction and notes on selected categories that accompany the clinical descriptions and diagnostic guidelines to Chapter V (WHO 1992). Two additional and easily accessible publications are:

Sartorius N, Jablensky A, Cooper JE, Burke JD (eds) 1988 Psychiatric classification in an international perspective. *British Journal of Psychiatry* **152**: (Suppl. 1).

Sartorius N, Kaelber CT et al 1993 Progress towards achieving a common language in psychiatry: Results from the field trials of the clinical guidelines accompanying the WHO classification of Mental and Behavioural Disorders of ICD-10. *Archives of General Psychiatry* 50: 115–124.

References

WHO 1992 The ICD-10 classification of mental and behavioural disorders: clinical descriptions and diagnostic guidelines (CDDG). WHO, Geneva

WHO 1993 The ICD-10 classification of mental and behavioural disorders: diagnostic criteria for research (DCR-10). WHO, Geneva

Acknowledgements

The compilation of this pocket book has been made possible by the generous cooperation of the World Health Organization, Geneva, who gave permission to use the text of the DCR-10 and parts of other documents that comprise the ICD-10 'family'. Special thanks are due to the staff of the Division of Mental Health (Director Dr N. Sartorius) and to the staff of the Office of Publications (Chief Mr D.H. Thompson) for their help and guidance. A full list of the several hundred individuals in many countries who contributed in different ways to the development of Chapter V of ICD–10, including participating in the field trials, can be found in the volumes published by WHO Geneva that contain the Clinical Descriptions and Diagnostic Guidelines to Chapter V (WHO 1992), and the DCR–10 (WHO 1993).

WHO 1992 The ICD-10 classification of mental and behavioural disorders: clinical descriptions and diagnostic guidelines. WHO, Geneva.

WHO 1993 The ICD-10 classification of mental and behavioural disorders: diagnostic criteria for research. WHO, Geneva.

List of categories

Categories present only in the DCR-10 are
marked with a star ★

F00– Organic, including symptomatic,
F09 mental disorders

F00 Dementia in Alzheimer's disease
    F00.0 Dementia in Alzheimer's disease with early onset
    F00.1 Dementia in Alzheimer's disease with late onset
    F00.2 Dementia in Alzheimer's disease, atypical or mixed type
    F00.8 Dementia in Alzheimer's disease, unspecified

F01 Vascular dementia
    F01.0 Vascular dementia of acute onset
    F01.1 Multi-infarct dementia
    F01.2 Subcortical vascular dementia
    F01.3 Mixed cortical and subcortical vascular dementia
    F01.8 Other vascular dementia
    F01.9 Vascular dementia, unspecified

F02 Dementia in other diseases classified elsewhere
    F02.0 Dementia in Pick's disease
    F02.1 Dementia in Creutzfeldt–Jakob disease
    F02.2 Dementia in Huntington's disease
    F02.3 Dementia in Parkinson's disease
    F02.4 Dementia in human immunodeficiency virus [HIV] disease
    F02.8 Dementia in other specified diseases classified elsewhere

F03 Unspecified dementia
    A fifth character may be used to specify dementia in F00–F03, as follows:
    .x0 Without additional symptoms
    .x1 With other symptoms, predominantly delusional
    .x2 With other symptoms, predominantly hallucinatory
    .x3 With other symptoms, predominantly depressive
    .x4 With other mixed symptoms

* A sixth character may be used to indicate the
severity of the dementia:
  *.xx0 Mild
  *.xx1 Moderate
  *.xx2 Severe

F04 Organic amnesic syndrome, not induced by alcohol and other psychoactive substances

F05 Delirium, not induced by alcohol and other psychoactive substances
  F05.0 Delirium, not superimposed on dementia, so described
  F05.1 Delirium, superimposed on dementia
  F05.8 Other delirium
  F05.9 Delirium, unspecified

F06 Other mental disorders due to brain damage and dysfunction and to physical disease
  F06.0 Organic hallucinosis
  F06.1 Organic catatonic disorder
  F06.2 Organic delusional [schizophrenia-like] disorder
  F06.3 Organic mood [affective] disorder
    .30 Organic manic disorder
    .31 Organic bipolar disorder
    .32 Organic depressive disorder
    .33 Organic mixed affective disorder
  F06.4 Organic anxiety disorder
  F06.5 Organic dissociative disorder
  F06.6 Organic emotionally labile [asthenic] disorder
  F06.7 Mild cognitive disorder
    .70 Not associated with a physical disorder
    .71 Associated with a physical disorder
  F06.8 Other specified mental disorders due to brain damage and dysfunction and to physical disease
  F06.9 Unspecified mental disorder due to brain damage and dysfunction and to physical disease

F07 Personality and behavioural disorders due to brain disease, damage and dysfunction
  F07.0 Organic personality disorder
  F07.1 Postencephalitic syndrome

F07.2 Postconcussional syndrome
F07.8 Other organic personality and behavioural disorders due to brain disease, damage and dysfunction
F07.9 Unspecified mental disorder due to brain disease, damage and dysfunction

F09 Unspecified organic or symptomatic mental disorder

Mental and behavioural disorders due to psychoactive substance use

F10.– Mental and behavioural disorders due to use of alcohol

F11.– Mental and behavioural disorders due to use of opioids

F12.– Mental and behavioural disorders due to use of cannabinoids

F13.– Mental and behavioural disorders due to use of sedatives or hypnotics

F14.– Mental and behavioural disorders due to use of cocaine

F15.– Mental and behavioural disorders due to use of other stimulants, including caffeine

F16.– Mental and behavioural disorders due to use of hallucinogens

F17.– Mental and behavioural disorders due to use of tobacco

F18.– Mental and behavioural disorders due to use to volatile solvents

F19.– Mental and behavioural disorders due to multiple drug use and use of other psychoactive substances

Four-, five- and six-character categories are used to specify the clinical conditions as follows, and diagnostic criteria particular to each psychoactive substance are provided where appropriate for acute intoxication and withdrawal state:

F1x.0 Acute intoxication
    .00 Uncomplicated
    .01 With trauma or other bodily injury
    .02 With other medical complications
    .03 With delirium
    .04 With perceptual distortions
    .05 With coma
    .06 With convulsions
    .07 Pathological intoxication

F1x.1 Harmful use

F1x.2 Dependence syndrome
    .20 Currently abstinent
        .200 Early remission
        .201 Partial remission
        .202 Full remission
    .21 Currently abstinent, but in a protected environment
    .22 Currently on a clinically supervised maintenance or replacement regime [controlled dependence]
    .23 Currently abstinent, but receiving treatment with aversive or blocking drugs
    .24 Currently using the substance [active dependence]
        .240 Without physical features
        .241 With physical features
    .25 Continuous use
    .26 Episodic use [dipsomania]

F1x.3 Withdrawal state
    .30 Uncomplicated
    .31 With convulsions

F1x.4 Withdrawal state with delirium
    .40 Without convulsions
    .41 With convulsions

F1x.5 Psychotic disorder
    .50 Schizophrenia-like
    .51 Predominantly delusional
    .52 Predominantly hallucinatory
    .53 Predominantly polymorphic
    .54 Predominantly depressive psychotic symptoms
    .55 Predominantly manic psychotic symptoms
    .56 Mixed

F1x.6 Amnesic syndrome

F1x.7 Residual disorders and late-onset psychotic disorder
    .70 Flashbacks
    .71 Personality or behaviour disorder
    .72 Residual affective disorder
    .73 Dementia
    .74 Other persisting cognitive disorder
    .75 Late-onset psychotic disorder

F1x.8 Other mental and behavioural disorders

F1x.9 Unspecified mental and behavioural disorder

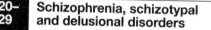

F20– F29 Schizophrenia, schizotypal and delusional disorders

F20 Schizophrenia
F20.0 Paranoid schizophrenia
F20.1 Hebephrenic schizophrenia
F20.2 Catatonic schizophrenia
F20.3 Undifferentiated schizophrenia
F20.4 Post-schizophrenic depression
F20.5 Residual schizophrenia
F20.6 Simple schizophrenia
F20.8 Other schizophrenia
F20.9 Schizophrenia, unspecified

A fifth character may be used to classify course:
.x0 Continuous
.x1 Episodic with progressive deficit
.x2 Episodic with stable deficit
.x3 Episodic remittent

.x4 Incomplete remission
.x5 Complete remission
.x8 Other
.x9 Course uncertain, period of observation too short

F21 Schizotypal disorder

F22 Persistent delusional disorders
F22.0 Delusional disorder
F22.8 Other persistent delusional disorders
F22.9 Persistent delusional disorder, unspecified

F23 Acute and transient psychotic disorders
F23.0 Acute polymorphic psychotic disorder without symptoms of schizophrenia
F23.1 Acute polymorphic psychotic disorder with symptoms of schizophrenia
F23.2 Acute schizophrenia-like psychotic disorder
F23.3 Other acute predominantly delusional psychotic disorder
F23.8 Other acute and transient psychotic disorders
F23.9 Acute and transient psychotic disorder, unspecified

A fifth character may be used to identify the presence or absence of associated acute stress:
.x0 Without associated acute stress
.x1 With associated acute stress

F24 Induced delusional disorder

F25 Schizoaffective disorders
F25.0 Schizoaffective disorder, manic type
F25.1 Schizoaffective disorder, depressive type
F25.2 Schizoaffective disorder, mixed type
F25.8 Other schizoaffective disorders
F25.9 Schizoaffective disorder, unspecified

*A fifth character may be used to classify the following subtypes:
*.x0 Concurrent affective and schizophrenic symptoms only
*.x1 Concurrent affective and schizophrenic symptoms, plus persistence of the

schizophrenic symptoms beyond the
duration of the affective symptoms

F28 Other non-organic psychotic disorders

F29 Unspecified non-organic psychosis

F30–F39	Mood [affective] disorders

F30 Manic episode
    F30.0 Hypomania
    F30.1 Mania without psychotic symptoms
    F30.2 Mania with psychotic symptoms
        .20 With mood-congruent psychotic
            symptoms
        .21 With mood-incongruent psychotic
            symptoms
    F30.8 Other manic episodes
    F30.9 Manic episode, unspecified

F31 Bipolar affective disorder
    F31.0 Bipolar affective disorder, current episode
           hypomanic
    F31.1 Bipolar affective disorder, current episode
           manic without psychotic symptoms
    F31.2 Bipolar affective disorder, current episode
           manic with psychotic symptoms
        .20 With mood-congruent psychotic
            symptoms
        .21 With mood-incongruent psychotic
            symptoms
    F31.3 Bipolar affective disorder, current episode
           mild or moderate depression
        .30 Without somatic syndrome
        .31 With somatic syndrome
    F31.4 Bipolar affective disorder, current episode
           severe depression without psychotic
           symptoms
    F31.5 Bipolar affective disorder, current episode
           severe depression with psychotic
           symptoms
        .50 With mood-congruent psychotic
            symptoms

.51 With mood-incongruent psychotic symptoms
- F31.6 Bipolar affective disorder, current episode mixed
- F31.7 Bipolar affective disorder, currently in remission
- F31.8 Other bipolar affective disorders
- F31.9 Bipolar affective disorder, unspecified

F32 Depressive episode
- F32.0 Mild depressive episode
  - .00 Without somatic syndrome
  - .01 With somatic syndrome
- F32.1 Moderate depressive episode
  - .10 Without somatic syndrome
  - .11 With somatic syndrome
- F32.2 Severe depressive episode without psychotic symptoms
- F32.3 Severe depressive episode with psychotic symptoms
  - .30 With mood-congruent psychotic symptoms
  - .31 With mood-incongruent psychotic symptoms
- F32.8 Other depressive episodes
- F32.9 Depressive episode, unspecified

F33 Recurrent depressive disorder
- F33.0 Recurrent depressive disorder, current episode mild
  - .00 Without somatic syndrome
  - .01 With somatic syndrome
- F33.1 Recurrent depressive disorder, current episode moderate
  - .10 Without somatic syndrome
  - .11 With somatic syndrome
- F33.2 Recurrent depressive disorder, current episode severe without psychotic symptoms
- F33.3 Recurrent depressive disorder, current episode severe with psychotic symptoms
  - *.30 With mood-congruent psychotic symptoms
  - *.31 With mood-incongruent psychotic symptoms

F33.4 Recurrent depressive disorder, currently in remission
F33.8 Other recurrent depressive disorders
F33.9 Recurrent depressive disorder, unspecified

F34 Persistent mood [affective] disorders
F34.0 Cyclothymia
F34.1 Dysthymia
F34.8 Other persistent mood [affective] disorders
F34.9 Persistent mood [affective] disorder, unspecified

F38 Other mood [affective] disorders
F38.0 Other single mood [affective] disorders
   .00 Mixed affective episode
F38.1 Other recurrent mood [affective] disorders
   .10 Recurrent brief depressive disorder
F38.8 Other specified mood [affective] disorders

F39 Unspecified mood [affective] disorder

F40– F48	Neurotic, stress-related and somatoform disorders

F40 Phobic anxiety disorders
F40.0 Agoraphobia
   .00 Without panic disorder
   .01 With panic disorder
F40.1 Social phobias
F40.2 Specific (isolated) phobias
F40.8 Other phobic anxiety disorders
F40.9 Phobic anxiety disorder, unspecified

F41 Other anxiety disorders
F41.0 Panic disorder [episodic paroxysmal anxiety]
   *.00 Moderate
   *.01 Severe
F41.1 Generalized anxiety disorder
F41.2 Mixed anxiety and depressive disorder
F41.3 Other mixed anxiety disorders
F41.8 Other specified anxiety disorders
F41.9 Anxiety disorder, unspecified

F42 Obsessive–compulsive disorder

    F42.0 Predominantly obsessional thoughts or
          ruminations
    F42.1 Predominantly compulsive acts
          [obsessional rituals]
    F42.2 Mixed obsessional thoughts and acts
    F42.8 Other obsessive–compulsive disorders
    F42.9 Obsessive–compulsive disorder,
          unspecified

F43 Reaction to severe stress, and adjustment disorders

    F43.0 Acute stress reaction
          *.00 Mild
          *.01 Moderate
          *.02 Severe
    F43.1 Post-traumatic stress disorder
    F43.2 Adjustment disorders
          .20 Brief depressive reaction
          .21 Prolonged depressive reaction
          .22 Mixed anxiety and depressive reaction
          .23 With predominant disturbance of
              other emotions
          .24 With predominant disturbance of
              conduct
          .25 With mixed disturbance of emotions
              and conduct
          .28 With other specified predominant
              symptoms
    F43.8 Other reactions to severe stress
    F43.9 Reaction to severe stress, unspecified

F44 Dissociative [conversion] disorders

    F44.0 Dissociative amnesia
    F44.1 Dissociative fugue
    F44.2 Dissociative stupor
    F44.3 Trance and possession disorders
    F44.4 Dissociative motor disorders
    F44.5 Dissociative convulsions
    F44.6 Dissociative anaesthesia and sensory loss
    F44.7 Mixed dissociative [conversion] disorders
    F44.8 Other dissociative [conversion] disorders
          .80 Ganser's syndrome
          .81 Multiple personality disorder
          .82 Transient dissociative [conversion]

disorders occurring in childhood and adolescence
.88 Other specified dissociative [conversion] disorders
F44.9 Dissociative [conversion] disorder, unspecified

F45 Somatoform disorders
F45.0 Somatization disorder
F45.1 Undifferentiated somatoform disorder
F45.2 Hypochondriacal disorders
F45.3 Somatoform autonomic dysfunction
.30 Heart and cardiovascular system
.31 Upper gastrointestinal tract
.32 Lower gastrointestinal tract
.33 Respiratory system
.34 Genitourinary system
.38 Other organ or system
F45.4 Persistent somatoform pain disorder
F45.8 Other somatoform disorders
F45.9 Somatoform disorder, unspecified

F48 Other neurotic disorders
F48.0 Neurasthenia
F48.1 Depersonalization–derealization syndrome
F48.8 Other specified neurotic disorders
F48.9 Neurotic disorder, unspecified

F50– F59	Behavioural syndromes associated with physiological disturbances and physical factors

F50 Eating disorders
F50.0 Anorexia nervosa
F50.1 Atypical anorexia nervosa
F50.2 Bulimia nervosa
F50.3 Atypical bulimia nervosa
F50.4 Overeating associated with other psychological disturbances
F50.5 Vomiting associated with other psychological disturbances
F50.8 Other eating disorders
F50.9 Eating disorder, unspecified

F51 Non-organic sleep disorders
  F51.0 Non-organic insomnia
  F51.1 Non-organic hypersomnia
  F51.2 Non-organic disorder of the sleep–wake schedule
  F51.3 Sleepwalking [somnambulism]
  F51.4 Sleep terrors [night terrors]
  F51.5 Nightmares
  F51.8 Other non-organic sleep disorders
  F51.9 Non-organic sleep disorder, unspecified

F52 Sexual dysfunction, not caused by organic disorder or disease
  F52.0 Lack or loss of sexual desire
  F52.1 Sexual aversion and lack of sexual enjoyment
    .10 Sexual aversion
    .11 Lack of sexual enjoyment
  F52.2 Failure of genital response
  F52.3 Orgasmic dysfunction
  F52.4 Premature ejaculation
  F52.5 Non-organic vaginismus
  F52.6 Non-organic dyspareunia
  F52.7 Excessive sexual drive
  F52.8 Other sexual dysfunction, not caused by organic disorder or disease
  F52.9 Unspecified sexual dysfunction, not caused by organic disorder or disease

F53 Mental and behavioural disorders associated with the puerperium, not elsewhere classified
  F53.0 Mild mental and behavioural disorders associated with the puerperium, not elsewhere classified
  F53.1 Severe mental and behavioural disorders associated with the puerperium, not elsewhere classified
  F53.8 Other mental and behavioural disorders associated with the puerperium, not elsewhere classified
  F53.9 Puerperal mental disorder, unspecified

F54 Psychological and behavioural factors associated with disorders or diseases classified elsewhere

F55 Abuse of non-dependence-producing substances

F55.0 Antidepressants
F55.1 Laxatives
F55.2 Analgesics
F55.3 Antacids
F55.4 Vitamins
F55.5 Steroids or hormones
F55.6 Specific herbal or folk remedies
F55.8 Other substances that do not produce dependence
F55.9 Unspecified

F59 Unspecified behavioural syndromes associated with physiological disturbances and physical factors

F60– F69 Disorders of adult personality and behaviour

F60 Specific personality disorders

F60.0 Paranoid personality disorder
F60.1 Schizoid personality disorder
F60.2 Dissocial personality disorder
F60.3 Emotionally unstable personality disorder
    .30 Impulsive type
    .31 Borderline type
F60.4 Histrionic personality disorder
F60.5 Anankastic personality disorder
F60.6 Anxious [avoidant] personality disorder
F60.7 Dependent personality disorder
F60.8 Other specific personality disorders
F60.9 Personality disorder, unspecified

F61 Mixed and other personality disorders

F61.0 Mixed personality disorder
F61.1 Troublesome personality changes

F62 Enduring personality changes, not attributable to brain damage and disease

F62.0 Enduring personality change after catastrophic experience
F62.1 Enduring personality change after psychiatric illness

F62.8 Other enduring personality changes
F62.9 Enduring personality change, unspecified

F63 Habit and impulse disorders
F63.0 Pathological gambling
F63.1 Pathological fire-setting [pyromania]
F63.2 Pathological stealing [kleptomania]
F63.3 Trichotillomania
F63.8 Other habit and impulse disorders
F63.9 Habit and impulse disorder, unspecified

F64 Gender identity disorders
F64.0 Transsexualism
F64.1 Dual-role transvestism
F64.2 Gender identity disorder of childhood
F64.8 Other gender identity disorders
F64.9 Gender identity disorder, unspecified

F65 Disorders of sexual preference
F65.0 Fetishism
F65.1 Fetishistic transvestism
F65.2 Exhibitionism
F65.3 Voyeurism
F65.4 Paedophilia
F65.5 Sadomasochism
F65.6 Multiple disorders of sexual preference
F65.8 Other disorders of sexual preference
F65.9 Disorder of sexual preference, unspecified

F66 Psychological and behavioural disorders associated with sexual development and orientation
F66.0 Sexual maturation disorder
F66.1 Egodystonic sexual orientation
F66.2 Sexual relationship disorder
F66.8 Other psychosexual development disorders
F66.9 Psychosexual development disorder, unspecified
A fifth character may be used to indicate association with:
.x0 Heterosexuality
.x1 Homosexuality
.x2 Bisexuality
.x8 Other, including prepubertal

F68 Other disorders of adult personality and behaviour
- F68.0 Elaboration of physical symptoms for psychological reasons
- F68.1 Intentional production of feigning of symptoms or disabilities, either physical or psychological [factitious disorder]
- F68.8 Other specified disorders of adult personality and behaviour

F69 Unspecified disorder of adult personality and behaviour

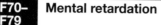

F70–F79 Mental retardation

F70 Mild mental retardation

F71 Moderate mental retardation

F72 Severe mental retardation

F73 Profound mental retardation

F78 Other mental retardation

F79 Unspecified mental retardation
A fourth character may be used to specify the extent of associated impairment of behaviour:
- F7x.0 No, or minimal, impairment of behaviour
- F7x.1 Significant impairment of behaviour requiring attention or treatment
- F7x.2 Other impairments of behaviour
- F7x.3 Without mention of impairment of behaviour

F80–F89 Disorders of psychological development

F80 Specific developmental disorders of speech and language
- F80.0 Specific speech articulation disorder

F80.1 Expressive language disorder
F80.2 Receptive language disorder
F80.3 Acquired aphasia with epilepsy [Landau–Kleffner syndrome]
F80.8 Other developmental disorders of speech and language
F80.9 Developmental disorder of speech and language, unspecified

F81 Specific developmental disorders of scholastic skills
F81.0 Specific reading disorder
F81.1 Specific spelling disorder
F81.2 Specific disorder of arithmetical skills
F81.3 Mixed disorder of scholastic skills
F81.8 Other developmental disorders of scholastic skills
F81.9 Developmental disorder of scholastic skills, unspecified

F82 Specific developmental disorder of motor function

F83 Mixed specific developmental disorder

F84 Pervasive developmental disorders
F84.0 Childhood autism
F84.1 Atypical autism
  *.10 Atypicality in age of onset
  *.11 Atypicality in symptomatology
  *.12 Atypicality in both age of onset and symptomatology
F84.2 Rett's syndrome
F84.3 Other childhood disintegrative disorder
F84.4 Overactive disorder associated with mental retardation and stereotyped movements
F84.5 Asperger's syndrome
F84.8 Other pervasive developmental disorders
F84.9 Pervasive developmental disorder, unspecified

F88 Other disorders of psychological development

F89 Unspecified disorder of psychological development

F90–F98 Behavioural and emotional disorders with onset usually occurring in childhood and adolescence

F90 Hyperkinetic disorder
- F90.0 Disturbance of activity and attention
- F90.1 Hyperkinetic conduct disorder
- F90.8 Other hyperkinetic disorders
- F90.9 Hyperkinetic disorder, unspecified

F91 Conduct disorders
- F91.0 Conduct disorder confined to the family context
- F91.1 Unsocialized conduct disorder
- F91.2 Socialized conduct disorder
- F91.3 Oppositional defiant disorder
- F91.8 Other conduct disorders
- F91.9 Conduct disorder, unspecified

F92 Mixed disorders of conduct and emotions
- F92.0 Depressive conduct disorder
- F92.8 Other mixed disorders of conduct and emotions
- F92.9 Mixed disorder of conduct and emotions, unspecified

F93 Emotional disorders with onset specific to childhood
- F93.0 Separation anxiety disorder of childhood
- F93.1 Phobic anxiety disorder of childhood
- F93.2 Social anxiety disorder of childhood
- F93.3 Sibling rivalry disorder
- F93.8 Other childhood emotional disorders
  *.80 Generalized anxiety disorder of childhood
- F93.9 Childhood emotional disorder, unspecified

F94 Disorders of social functioning with onset specific to childhood and adolescence
- F94.0 Elective mutism
- F94.1 Reactive attachment disorder of childhood
- F94.2 Disinhibited attachment disorder of childhood
- F94.8 Other childhood disorders of social functioning

F94.9 Childhood disorder of social functioning, unspecified

F95 Tic disorders

F95.0 Transient tic disorders
F95.1 Chronic motor or vocal tic disorder
F95.2 Combined vocal and multiple motor tic disorder [de la Tourette's syndrome]
F95.8 Other tic disorders
F95.9 Tic disorder, unspecified

F98 Other behavioural and emotional disorders with onset usually occurring in childhood and adolescence

F98.0 Nonorganic enuresis
   *.00 Nocturnal enuresis only
   *.01 Diurnal enuresis only
   *.02 Nocturnal and diurnal enureses
F98.1 Nonorganic encopresis
   *.10 Failure to acquire physiological bowel control
   *.11 Adequate bowel control with normal faeces deposited in inappropriate places
   *.12 Soiling that is associated with excessively fluid faeces, such as with retention with overflow
F98.2 Feeding disorder of infancy and childhood
F98.3 Pica of infancy and childhood
F98.4 Stereotyped movement disorders
   *.40 Non-self-injurious
   *.41 Self-injurious
   *.42 Mixed
F98.5 Stuttering [stammering]
F98.6 Cluttering
F98.8 Other specified behavioural and emotional disorders with onset usually occurring in childhood and adolescence
F98.9 Unspecified behavioural and emotional disorders with onset usually occurring in childhood and adolescence

F99 Unspecified mental disorder

F99 Mental disorder, not otherwise specified

Notes for users
of DCR-10

The following notes for users, like the texts in the shaded boxes headed DCR-10, have been reproduced from *The ICD-10 Classification of Mental and Behavioural Disorders: Diagnostic criteria for research* (Geneva, World Health Organization, 1993).

1. The content of *Diagnostic criteria for research* (DCR-10) is derived from Chapter V(F), Mental and behavioural disorders, of ICD-10. It provides specific criteria for the diagnoses contained in *Clinical descriptions and diagnostic guidelines* (CDDG), which was produced for general clinical and educational use by psychiatrists and other mental health professionals (WHO 1992).

2. Although completely compatible with both CDDG and Chapter V(F) of ICD-10, DCR-10 has a somewhat different style and layout. It is not designed to be used alone, and researchers should therefore make themselves familiar with CDDG. DCR-10 does not contain the descriptions of the clinical concepts upon which the research criteria are based, or any comments on commonly associated features which, although not essential for diagnosis, may well be relevant for both clinicians and researchers. These features are to be found in CDDG, the introductory chapters of which also contain information and comments that are relevant for both clinical and research uses of ICD-10. It is presumed that anyone using DCR-10 will have a copy of CDDG.

3. Certain other differences between DCR-10 and CDDG should be appreciated before DCR-10 can be used satisfactorily:

   (a) Like other published diagnostic criteria for research, the criteria of DCR-10 are deliberately restrictive: their use allows the selection of groups of individuals whose symptoms and other characteristics resemble each other in clearly stated ways. This tends to maximize the homogeneity of groups of patients but limits the generalizations that can be made. Researchers wishing to study the overlap of disorders or the best way to define boundaries between them may therefore need to supplement the criteria so as to allow the inclusion of atypical cases.

   (b) It is never appropriate to provide detailed criteria for the 'unspecified' (.9) categories of the overall

ICD-10 (Chapter V(F) classification, and rarely appropriate for the 'other' (.8) categories. Annex 1 (page 327) provides suggestions for criteria for some of the few exceptions; placement of these criteria in an annex implies that their present status is somewhat controversial or tentative and that further research is to be encouraged.

(c) Similarly, there is no requirement for extensive rules on mutual exclusions and co-morbidity in a set of diagnostic criteria for research, since different research projects have varied requirements for these, depending upon their objectives. Some of the more obvious and frequently used exclusion clauses have been included in DCR-10 as a reminder and for the convenience of users; more can be found in CDDG if required.

4. As a general rule, interference with the performance of social roles has not been used as a diagnostic criterion in ICD-10. This rule has been followed in DCR-10 as far as possible, but there are a few unavoidable exceptions, the most obvious being simple schizophrenia and dissocial personality disorder. Once the decision had been made to include these somewhat controversial disorders in the classification, it was considered best to do so without modifying the concepts; as a consequence it became necessary to include interference with social role in the diagnostic criteria for these disorders. Experience and further research should show whether these decisions were justified.

For many of the disorders of childhood and adolescence, some form of interference with social behaviour and relationships is included, among the diagnostic criteria. Initially, this appears to contravene the general ICD rule mentioned above. However, close examination of the disturbances classified in F80–F89 and F90–F98 shows that the need for social criteria is occasioned by the more complicated and interactive nature of the subject matter. Children often show general misery and frustration, but rarely produce specific complaints and symptoms equivalent to those that characterize the disorders of adults. Many of the disorders in F80–F89 and F90–F98 are joint disturbances that can be described only by indicating how roles within the family, school or peer group are affected.

5. For the same reasons given in 3(c) above, definitions of remission, relapse and duration of episodes have been provided in DCR-10 in only a limited number of instances. Further suggestions will be found in the lexicon of terms to Chapter V(F) of ICD-10 (WHO 1994).

6. The criteria are labelled with letters and/or numbers to indicate their place in a hierarchy of generality and importance. General criteria, which *must* be fulfilled by all members of a group of disorders (such as the general criteria for all varieties of dementia, or for the main types of schizophrenia), are labelled with a capital G plus a number. Obligatory criteria for individual disorders are distinguished by capital letters alone (A, B, C etc.). Numbers (1, 2, 3 etc.) and lower-case letters (a, b etc.) are used to identify further groups and subgroups of characteristics, of which only some are required for the diagnosis. To avoid the use of 'and/or', when it is specified that *either* of two criteria is required, it is always assumed that the presence of *both* criteria also satisfies the requirement.

7. When DCR-10 is used in research on patients who also suffer from neurological disorders, researchers may also wish to use the neurological application of ICD-10 (ICD-10NA) (WHO 1994) and the accompanying glossary.

8. The two annexes to DCR-10 are concerned with disorders of uncertain or provisional status. Annex 1 deals with some affective disorders that have been the subject of recent research, and certain personality disorders. Although the concepts are regarded as clinically useful in some countries, the disorders themselves are of uncertain status from an inter-

national viewpoint; it is hoped that their inclusion here will encourage research concerning their usefulness.

Annex 2 provides provisional descriptions of a number of disorders that are often referred to as 'culture-specific'. There are grounds for supposing that they might be better regarded as cultural variants of disorders already present in ICD-10 Chapter V(F), but reliable and detailed clinical information is still too scanty to allow definite conclusions to be drawn about them. The considerable practical difficulties involved in field studies of individuals with these disorders are recognized, but inclusion of the descriptions in DCR-10 may stimulate research by workers who are familiar with the languages and cultures of those affected. Information in Annex 2 will be supplemented by that in a lexicon of terms used in cross-cultural psychiatry that is expected to become available in 1994.

9. Note that 'and' in category titles stands for 'and/or'.

References

Application of the International Statistical Classification of Diseases and Related Health Problems, tenth revision, to neurology. Geneva, World Health Organization (in preparation).

WHO (1992) *The ICD-10 Classification of Mental and Behavioural Disorders. Clinical descriptions and diagnostic guidelines.* Geneva, World Health Organization.

WHO (1993) *The ICD-10 Classification of Mental and Behavioural Disorders: Diagnostic Criteria for Research.* Geneva, World Health Organization.

WHO (1994) *Lexicon of psychiatric and mental health terms. Volume 1, 2nd edn.* Geneva, World Health Organization (in preparation).

ICD-10 Chapter V: Mental and behavioural disorders, with glossary definitions, DCR-10 and diagnostic notes.

Organic, including symptomatic, mental disorders (F00–F09)

This block comprises a range of mental disorders grouped together on the basis of their having in common a demonstrable etiology in cerebral disease, brain injury or other insult leading to cerebral dysfunction. The dysfunction may be primary, as in diseases, injuries and insults that affect the brain directly and selectively, or secondary, as in systemic diseases and disorders that attack the brain only as one of the multiple organs or systems of the body that are involved.

Dementia (F00–F03) is a syndrome due to disease of the brain, usually of a chronic or progressive nature, in which there is disturbance of multiple higher cortical functions, including memory, thinking, orientation, comprehension, calculation, learning capacity, language and judgement. Consciousness is not clouded. The impairments of cognitive function are commonly accompanied, and occasionally preceded, by deterioration in emotional control, social behaviour or motivation. This syndrome occurs in Alzheimer's disease, in cerebrovascular disease and in other conditions primarily or secondarily affecting the brain.

Use additional code, if desired, to identify the underlying disease.

DCR-10 General criteria for dementia

G1.   There is evidence of each of the following:

(1)   A decline in memory, which is most evident in the learning of new information although in more severe cases the recall of previously learned information may also be affected. The impairment applies to both verbal and non-verbal material. The decline should be objectively verified by obtaining a reliable history from an informant, supplemented, if possible, by neuropsychological tests or

$\Rightarrow$

quantified cognitive assessments. The severity of the decline, with mild impairment as the threshold for diagnosis, should be assessed as follows:

Mild. The degree of memory loss is sufficient to interfere with everyday activities, though not so severe as to be incompatible with independent living. The main function affected is the learning of new material. For example, the individual has difficulty in registering, storing and recalling elements involved in daily living, such as where belongings have been put, social arrangements, or information recently imparted by family members.

Moderate. The degree of memory loss represents a serious handicap to independent living. Only highly learned or very familiar material is retained. New information is retained only occasionally and very briefly. Individuals are unable to recall basic information about their own local geography, what they have recently been doing, or the names of familiar people.

Severe. The degree of memory loss is characterized by the complete inability to retain new information. Only fragments of previously learned information remain. The individual fails to recognize even close relatives.

(2) A decline in other cognitive abilities characterized by deterioration in judgement and thinking, such as planning and organizing, and in the general processing of information. Evidence for this should ideally be obtained from an informant and supplemented, if possible, by neuropsychological tests or quantified objective assessments. Deterioration from a previously higher level of performance should be estab-

lished. The severity of the decline, with mild impairment as the threshold for diagnosis, should be assessed as follows:

Mild. The decline in cognitive abilities causes impaired performance in daily living, but not to a degree that makes the individual dependent on others. Complicated daily tasks or recreational activities cannot be undertaken.

Moderate. The decline in cognitive abilities makes the individual unable to function without the assistance of another in daily living, including shopping and handling money. Within the home, only simple chores can be performed. Activities are increasingly restricted and poorly sustained.

Severe. The decline is characterized by an absence, or virtual absence, of intelligible ideation.

The overall severity of the dementia is best expressed as the level of decline in memory *or* other cognitive abilities, whichever is the more severe (e.g. mild decline in memory *and* moderate decline in cognitive abilities indicate a dementia of moderate severity).

G2. Awareness of the environment (i.e. absence of clouding of consciousness (as defined in F05 – criterion A) is preserved during a period of time sufficiently long to allow the unequivocal demonstration of the symptoms in criterion G1). When there are superimposed episodes of delirium, the diagnosis of dementia should be deferred.

G3. There is decline in emotional control or motivation, or a change in social behaviour manifest as at least one of the following:

(1) emotional lability
(2) irritability

⇒

> (3) apathy
>
> (4) coarsening of social behaviour
>
> G4. For a confident clinical diagnosis, the symptoms in criterion G1 should have been present for at least 6 months; if the period since the manifest onset is shorter, the diagnosis can be only tentative.

Diagnostic notes

A debate is beginning as to whether the term dementia should be used only for irreversible states, as it is here. Current clinical terms and concepts will need to be revised if any successful therapeutic advances result from the present intense research efforts aimed at identifying the intracellular and genetic mechanisms involved in Alzheimer's and other forms of dementia.

Dementia is specified here as having a minimum duration of 6 months, to avoid confusion with clearly reversible states that initially have the same signs and symptoms. Subdural haemorrhage (S06.5), normal pressure hydrocephalus (G91.2) and some types of diffuse or local brain damage (S06.2 and S06.3) are important examples which may give rise to a chronic state of delirium (F05) for which 'subacute confusional state' used to be a commonly used term. Important points about the criteria for dementia and their relationship with impairment, personal disability and role handicap are contained on pages 8 and 9 of the Clinical descriptions and diagnostic guidelines to Chapter V (WHO 1992).

Judgements about independent living or the development of dependence upon others need to take account of the cultural expectations and context. The diagnosis may be further supported by evidence of damage to other higher cortical functions, such as aphasia, agnosia and apraxia.

A fifth character may be used to indicate the presence of additional symptoms for the categories F00–F03 (F00 Dementia in Alzheimer's disease, F01 Vascular dementia, F02 Dementia in diseases classified elsewhere, and F03 Unspecified dementia), as follows:

.x0 without additional symptoms
.x1 with other symptoms, predominantly delusional
.x2 with other symptoms, predominantly hallucinatory
.x3 with other symptoms, predominantly depressive
.x4 with other mixed symptoms

A sixth character may be used to indicate the severity of the dementia:

.xx0 mild
.xx1 moderate
.xx2 severe

As mentioned (page 30) the overall severity of the dementia depends on the level of memory or intellectual impairment, whichever is the more severe.

F00* Dementia in Alzheimer's disease (G30.–)

Alzheimer's disease is a primary degenerative cerebral disease of unknown aetiology with characteristic neuropathological and neurochemical features. The disorder is usually insidious in onset and develops slowly but steadily over a period of several years.

DCR-10

A. The general criteria for dementia (G1–G4) must be met.

B. There is no evidence from the history, physical examination or special investigations for any other possible cause of dementia (e.g. cerebrovascular disease, HIV disease, Parkinson's disease, Huntington's disease, normal pressure hydrocephalus), a systemic disorder (e.g. hypothyroidism, vitamin B_{12} or folic acid deficiency, hypercalcaemia), or alcohol or drug abuse.

Diagnostic notes

The diagnosis is confirmed by postmortem evidence of neurofibrillary tangles and neuritic plaques in excess of those found in normal ageing of the brain.

The following features support the diagnosis, but are not necessary elements: involvement of cortical functions as evidenced by aphasia, agnosia or apraxia; decrease of motivation and drive, leading to apathy and lack of spontaneity; irritability and disinhibition of social behaviour; evidence from special investigations that there is cerebral atrophy, particularly if this can be shown to be increasing over time. In severe cases there may be Parkinson-like extrapyramidal changes, logoclonia, and epileptic fits.

Specification of features for possible subtypes

Because of the possibility that subtypes exist, it is recommended that the following characteristics be ascertained as a basis for a further classification: age at onset; rate of progression; configuration of the clinical features, particularly the relative prominence (or lack) of temporal, parietal or frontal lobe signs; any neuropathological or neurochemical abnormalities, and their pattern.

The division of Alzheimer's disease into subtypes can at present be accomplished in two ways: first, by taking only the age of onset and labelling the disease as either early or late, with an approximate cut-off point at 65 years; or second, by assessing how well the individual conforms to one of the two putative syndromes of early- or late-onset type. It is unlikely that a sharp distinction exists between early- and late-onset types. The clinical features of the early-onset type may occur in late life, just as the features of the late-onset type may occasionally start under the age of 65. The following criteria may be used to differentiate F00.0 from F00.1, but it should be remembered that the status of this subdivision is still controversial.

F00.0* Dementia in Alzheimer's disease with early onset (G30.0)

Dementia in Alzheimer's disease with onset before the age of 65, with a relatively rapid deteriorating course and marked multiple disorders of the higher cortical functions.

Alzheimer's disease, type 2
Presenile dementia, Alzheimer's type
Primary degenerative dementia of the Alzheimer's type, presenile.

> **DCR-10**
>
> 1. The criteria for dementia in Alzheimer's disease (F00) must be met, and the age at onset must be below 65 years.
>
> 2. In addition, at least one of the following requirements must be met:
>
>   (a) evidence of a relatively rapid onset and progression;
>
>   (b) in addition to memory impairment, there must be aphasia (amnesic or sensory), agraphia, alexia, acalculia or apraxia (indicating the presence of temporal, parietal and/or frontal lobe involvement).

F00.1* Dementia in Alzheimer's disease with late onset (G30.1)

Dementia in Alzheimer's disease with onset after the age of 65, usually in the late 70s or thereafter, with a slow progression, and with memory impairment as the principal feature.

Alzheimer's disease, type 1
Primary degenerative dementia of the Alzheimer's type, senile onset
Senile dementia, Alzheimer's type

DCR-10

1. The criteria for dementia in Alzheimer's disease (F00) must be met and the age at onset must be 65 years or more.

2. In addition, at least one of the following requirements must be met:

   (a) evidence of a very slow, gradual onset and progression (the rate of the latter may be known only retrospectively after a course of 3 years or more);

   (b) predominance of memory impairment G1(1) over intellectual impairment G1(2) (see general criteria for dementia).

F00.2* Dementia in Alzheimer's disease, atypical or mixed type (G30.8)

Atypical dementia, Alzheimer's type
This term and code should be used for dementias that have important atypical features or that fulfil criteria for both early- and late-onset types of Alzheimer's disease. Mixed Alzheimer's and vascular dementia is also included here.

F00.9* Dementia in Alzheimer's disease, unspecified (G30.9)

F01 Vascular dementia

Vascular dementia is the result of infarction of the brain due to vascular disease, including hypertensive cerebrovascular disease. The infarcts are usually small but cumulative in their effect. Onset is usually in later life.

Includes: arteriosclerotic dementia.

DCR-10

G1. The general criteria for dementia (G1–G4) must be met.

G2. Deficits in higher cognitive function are unevenly distributed, with some functions affected and others relatively spared. Thus memory may be quite markedly affected while thinking, reasoning and information processing may show only mild decline.

G3. There is clinical evidence of focal brain damage, manifest as at least one of the following:

   (1) unilateral spastic weakness of the limbs

   (2) unilaterally increased tendon reflexes

   (3) an extended plantar response

   (4) pseudobulbar palsy.

G4. There is evidence from the history, examination or tests, of a significant cerebrovascular disease, which may reasonably be judged to be aetiologically related to the dementia (e.g. a history of stroke; evidence of cerebral infarction).

   The following criteria may be used to differentiate subtypes of vascular dementia, but it should be remembered that the usefulness of this subdivision may not be generally accepted.

F01.0 Vascular dementia of acute onset

Usually develops rapidly after a succession of strokes from cerebrovascular thrombosis, embolism or haemorrhage. In rare cases a single large infarction may be the cause.

DCR-10

A The general criteria for vascular dementia (F01) must be met.

B. The dementia develops rapidly (i.e. usually within 1 month, but within no longer than 3 months) after a succession of strokes or (rarely) after a single large infarction.

F01.1 Multi-infarct dementia

Gradual in onset, following a number of transient ischaemic episodes which produce an accumulation of infarcts in the cerebral parenchyma.
Predominantly cortical dementia.

DCR-10

A. The general criteria for vascular dementia (F01) must be met.

B. The onset of the dementia is gradual (i.e. within 3–6 months), following a number of minor ischaemic episodes.

Diagnostic notes

It is presumed that there is an accumulation of infarcts in the cerebral parenchyma. Between the ischaemic episodes there may be periods of actual clinical improvement.

F01.2 Subcortical vascular dementia

Includes cases with a history of hypertension and foci of ischaemic destruction in the deep white matter of the cerebral hemispheres. The cerebral cortex is usually preserved and this contrasts with the clinical picture, which may closely resemble that of dementia in Alzheimer's disease.

DCR-10

A. The general criteria for vascular dementia (F01) must be met.

B. There is a history of hypertension.

C. There is evidence from clinical examination and special investigations of vascular disease located in the deep white matter of the cerebral hemispheres, with preservation of the cerebral cortex.

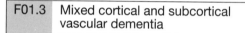

F01.3   Mixed cortical and subcortical vascular dementia

The mixed cortical and subcortical components of vascular dementia may be suspected from the clinical features, the results of investigations (including autopsy) or both.

F01.8   Other vascular dementia

F01.9   Vascular dementia, unspecified

F02*   Dementia in other diseases classified elsewhere

Cases of dementia due, or presumed to be due, to causes other than Alzheimer's disease or cerebrovascular disease. Onset may be at any time in life, though rarely in old age.

Diagnostic notes

The general rule in ICD-10 Chapter V is to give separate codes only to clinical states which have some individually identifying clinical characteristics. There is clinical evidence to justify this for dementia due to Pick's disease (G31.0), Creutzfeld–Jakob disease (A81.0) and in some cases of Huntingdon's disease (G10). This is not so for dementia occurring during the course of Parkinson's disease (G20) and human immunodeficiency virus (HIV) disease (B22.0), but exceptions have been made to the rule for these two disorders because of their clinical interest and their public health importance.

F02.0* Dementia in Pick's disease (G31.0)

A progressive dementia commencing in middle age, characterized by early, slowly progressing changes of character and social deterioration, followed by impairment of intellect, memory and language functions, with apathy, euphoria and, occasionally, extrapyramidal phenomena.

DCR-10

A The general criteria for dementia (G1–G4) must be met.

B. Onset is slow, with steady deterioration.

C. Predominance of frontal lobe involvement is evidenced by two or more of the following:

   (1) emotional blunting

   (2) coarsening of social behaviour

   (3) disinhibition

   (4) apathy or restlessness

   (5) aphasia.

D. In the early stages, memory and parietal lobe functions are relatively preserved.

F02.1* Dementia in Creutzfeldt–Jakob disease

A progressive dementia with extensive neurological signs, due to specific neuropathological changes that are presumed to be caused by a transmissible agent. Onset is usually in middle or later life, but may be at any adult age. The course is subacute, leading to death within 1–2 years.

DCR-10

A. The general criteria for dementia (G1–G4) must be met.

B. There is very rapid progression of the dementia, with disintegration of virtually all higher cerebral functions.

C. One or more of the following types of neurological symptoms and signs emerge, usually after or simultaneously with the dementia:

   (1) pyramidal symptoms

   (2) extrapyramidal symptoms

   (3) cerebellar symptoms

   (4) aphasia

   (5) visual impairment.

Diagnostic notes

An akinetic and mute state is the typical terminal stage. An amyotrophic variant may be seen where the neurological signs precede the onset of the dementia. A characteristic electroencephalogram (periodic spikes against a slow and low-voltage background), if present in association with the above clinical signs, will increase the probability of the diagnosis. However, the diagnosis can be confirmed only by neuropathological examination (neuronal loss, astrocytosis and spongiform changes). Because of the risk of infection, this should be carried out only under special protective conditions.

F02.2* Dementia in Huntington's disease
(G10)

A dementia occurring as part of a widespread degeneration of the brain. The disorder is transmitted by a single autosomal dominant gene. Symptoms typically emerge in the third and fourth decades. Progression is slow, leading to death usually within 10–15 days.

Dementia in Huntington's chorea.

DCR-10

A. The general criteria for dementia (G1–G4) must be met.

B. Subcortical functions are affected first and dominate the picture of dementia throughout, manifested by slowness of thinking or movement and personality alteration, with apathy or depression.

C. There are involuntary choreiform movements, typically of the face, hands or shoulders, or in the gait. The patient may attempt to conceal these by converting them into a voluntary action.

D. There is a history of Huntington's disease in one parent or a sibling, or a family history which suggests the disorder.

E. There are no clinical features that otherwise account for the abnormal movements.

Diagnostic notes

In addition to involuntary choreiform movements there may be development of extrapyramidal rigidity, or spasticity with pyramidal signs.

A dementia developing in the course of established Parkinson's disease.

No particular distinguishing clinical features have yet been demonstrated.

Dementia in:
- paralysis agitans
- parkinsonism

DCR-10

A. The general criteria for dementia (G1–G4) must be met.

B. A diagnosis of Parkinson's disease has been established.

C. None of the cognitive impairment is attributable to antiparkinsonian medication.

D. There is no evidence from the history, physical examination or special investigations for any other possible cause of dementia, including other forms of brain disease, damage or dysfunction (e.g. cerebrovascular disease, HIV disease, Huntington's disease, normal pressure hydrocephalus), a systemic disorder (e.g. hypothyroidism, vitamin B_{12} or folic acid deficiency, hypercalcaemia), or alcohol or drug abuse.

If criteria are also fulfilled for dementia in Alzheimer's disease with late onset (F00.1), category F001.1 should be used in combination with G20 (Parkinson's disease).

F02.4* Dementia in human immunodeficiency virus (HIV) disease (B22.0)

Dementia developing in the course of HIV disease, in the absence of a concurrent illness or condition other than HIV infection which could explain the clinical features.

DCR-10

A. The general criteria for dementia (G1–G4 must be met.

B. A diagnosis of HIV infection has been established.

C. There is no evidence from the history, physical examination or special investigations for any other possible cause of dementia, including other forms of brain disease, damage or dysfunction (e.g. Alzheimer's disease, cerebrovascular disease, Parkinson's disease, Huntington's disease, normal pressure hydrocephalus), a systemic disorder (e.g. hypothyroidism, vitamin B_{12} or folic acid deficiency, hypercalcaemia), or alcohol or drug abuse.

F02.8* Dementia in other specified diseases classified elsewhere

Dementia can occur as a consequence of a variety of cerebral and somatic conditions which are classified in other chapters of ICD-10. In such instances, and when the general criteria for dementia G1–G4 are met, this category should be used and the underlying condition identified by adding the ICD-10 code, for instance:

Dementia in:

cerebral lipidosis (E75.–)

epilepsy (G40.–)
hepatolenticular degeneration (E83.0)
hypercalcaemia (E83.5)
hypothyroidism, acquired (E01,E03.–)
intoxications (T36–T65)
multiple sclerosis (G35)
neurosyphilis (A52.1)
niacin deficiency (pellagra) (E52)
polyarteritis nodosa (M30.0)
systemic lupus erythematosus (M32.–)
trypanosomiasis (B56.–, B57.–)
vitamin B_{12} deficiency (E53.8)

F03　Unspecified dementia

This category should be used when the general criteria
for dementia (G1–G4) are met but when it is not possible
to identify one of the specific types (F00.0–F02.9).
Presenile:
• dementia NOS
• psychosis NOS
Primary degenerative dementia NOS
Senile:
• dementia:
• NOS
• depressed or paranoid type
• psychosis NOS

Excludes:　senile dementia with delirium or acute con-
　　　　　fusional state (F05.1)
　　　　　senility NOS (R54)

F04　Organic amnesic syndrome, not induced by alcohol and other psychoactive substances

A syndrome of prominent impairment of recent and
remote memory while immediate recall is preserved,
with reduced ability to learn new material and disorientation in time. Confabulation may be a marked
feature, but perception and other cognitive functions,
including the intellect, are usually intact. The prognosis
depends on the course of the underlying lesion.

Korsakov's psychosis or syndrome, non alcoholic

Excludes: amnesia:
• NOS (R41.3)
• anterograde (R41.1)
• dissociative (F44.0)
• retrograde (R41.2)
Korsakov's syndrome:
• alcohol-induced or unspecified (F10.6)
• induced by other psychoactive substances (F11–F19 with common fourth character 6)

DCR-10

A. There is memory impairment, manifest in both

 (1) a defect of recent memory (impaired learning of new material), to a degree sufficient to interfere with daily living; and

 (2) a reduced ability to recall past experiences.

B. There is an absence of

 (1) a defect in immediate recall (as tested, for example, by the digit span);

 (2) clouding of consciousness and disturbance of attention, as defined in F05.–, criterion A;

 (3) global intellectual decline (dementia).

C. There is objective evidence (from physical and neurological examination, laboratory tests) and/or history of an insult to, or a disease of the brain (especially involving bilaterally the diencephalic and medial temporal structures but other than alcoholic encephalopathy) that can reasonably be presumed to be responsible for the clinical manifestations described in criterion A.

Diagnostic notes

Associated features, including confabulations, emotional changes (apathy, lack of initiative) and lack of insight are useful additional pointers to the diagnosis but are not invariably present.

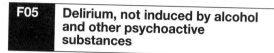

F05   Delirium, not induced by alcohol and other psychoactive substances

An aetiologically non-specific organic cerebral syndrome characterized by concurrent disturbances of consciousness and attention, perception, thinking, memory, psychomotor behaviour, emotion and the sleep–wake schedule. The duration is variable and the degree of severity ranges from mild to very severe.

Includes: acute or subacute:
• brain syndrome
• confusional state (nonalcoholic)
• psycho-organic syndrome
• infective psychosis
• organic reaction

Excludes: delirium tremens, alcohol-induced or unspecified (F10.4).

DCR-10

A. There is clouding of consciousness, i.e. reduced clarity of awareness of the environment, with reduced ability to focus, sustain or shift attention.

B. Disturbance of cognition is manifest by both:
  (1) impairment of immediate recall and recent memory, with relatively intact remote memory;

  (2) disorientation in time, place or person.

C. At least one of the following psychomotor disturbances is present:

⇒

    (1) rapid, unpredictable shifts from hypoactivity to hyperactivity;

    (2) increased reaction time;

    (3) increased or decreased flow of speech;

    (4) enhanced startle reaction.

D. There is disturbance of sleep or of the sleep–wake cycle, manifest by at least one of the following:

    (1) insomnia, which in severe cases may involve total sleep loss, with or without daytime drowsiness or reversal of the sleep–wake cycle;

    (2) nocturnal worsening of symptoms;

    (3) disturbing dreams and nightmares, which may continue as hallucinations or illusions after awakening.

E. Symptoms have rapid onset and show fluctuations over the course of the day.

F. There is objective evidence from history, physical and neurological examination or laboratory tests of an underlying cerebral or systemic disease (other than psychoactive substance-related) that can be presumed to be responsible for the clinical manifestations in criteria A–D.

Diagnostic notes

Emotional disturbances such as depression, anxiety or fear, irritability, euphoria, apathy or wondering perplexity, disturbances of perception (illusions or hallucinations, often visual) and transient delusions are typical but are not specific indications for the diagnosis.

A fourth character may be used to indicate whether or not the delirium is superimposed on dementia:

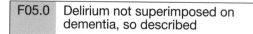

F05.0	Delirium not superimposed on dementia, so described

F05.1	Delirium superimposed on dementia

Conditions meeting the above criteria but developing in the course of a dementia (F00–F03)

F05.8	Other delirium

Delirium of mixed origin

F05.9	Delirium, unspecified

F06 Other mental disorders due to brain damage and dysfunction and to physical disease

Includes miscellaneous conditions causally related to brain disorder due to primary cerebral disease, to systemic disease affecting the brain secondarily, to exogenous toxic substances or hormones, to endocrine disorders, or to other somatic illnesses.

Excludes: associated with:
• delirium (F05.–)
• dementia as classified in F00–F03
resulting from use of alcohol and other psychoactive substances (F10–F19)

DCR-10

G1. There is objective evidence (from physical and neurological examination and laboratory tests) and/or history of cerebral disease, damage or dysfunction, or of systemic physical disorder known to cause cer- ⇒

ebral dysfunction, including hormonal disturbances (other than alcohol or other psychoactive substance-related) and non-psychoactive drug effects.

G2. There is a presumed relationship between the development (or marked exacerbation) of the underlying disease, damage or dysfunction and the mental disorder, the symptoms of which may have immediate onset or may be delayed.

G3. There is recovery from or significant improvement in the mental disorder following removal or improvement of the underlying presumed cause.

G4. There is insufficient evidence for an alternative causation of the mental disorder, e.g. a strong family history of a clinically similar or related disorder.

If criteria G1, G2 and G4 are met, a provisional diagnosis is justified; if, in addition, there is evidence of G3, the diagnosis can be regarded as certain.

Diagnostic notes

The terms 'cerebral disease, damage or dysfunction' in criterion G1 above are not intended to include marginal or non-specific findings such as slightly enlarged cerebral ventricles or minor degrees of cortical thinning that can be detected only by modern techniques such as CT scans or magnetic resonance (MR) imaging. The same also applies to the so-called 'soft' neurological signs.

Categories F06.0–F06.6 form an anomalous section of this classification, since they go against the basic classificatory rule that a particular clinical syndrome should have only one place allotted to it in the classification. In some other disorders in Chapter V, aetiology is also included as a defining characteristic, but only if the clinical syndrome is unique to that condition (for instance, F43: Reaction to severe stress, and adjustment disorders). The reason for the repetition of the clinical syndromes covered by F06.0–F06.6 but tied here to an organic aetiology is that many clinicians wish to be able to record knowledge of aetiology on the comparatively few occasions in practice when such knowledge is available. The gain is acceptability obtained by the inclusion of the anomalous group is likely to outweigh any complaints about the classification being inconsistent.

F06.0 Organic hallucinosis

A disorder of persistent or recurrent hallucinations, usually visual or auditory, which occur in clear consciousness and may or may not be recognized by the subject as such. Delusional elaboration of the hallucinations may occur, but delusions do not dominate the clinical picture; insight may be preserved.

Organic hallucinatory state (non-alcoholic)

Excludes: alcoholic hallucinosis (F10.5)
schizophrenia (F20.–)

> **DCR-10**
>
> A. The general criteria for F06 must be met.
>
> B. The clinical picture is dominated by persistent or recurrent hallucinations (usually visual or auditory).
>
> C. Hallucinations occur in clear consciousness.

Diagnostic notes

Delusional elaboration of the hallucinations, as well as full or partial insight, may or may not be present; these features are not essential for the diagnosis.

F06.1 Organic catatonic disorder

A disorder of diminished (stupor) or increased (excitement) psychomotor activity associated with catatonic symptoms. The extremes of psychomotor disturbance may alternate.

Excludes: catatonic schizophrenia (F20.2)
stupor:
• NOS (R40.1)
• dissociative (F44.2)

DCR-10

A. The general criteria for F06 must be met.

B. One of the following must be present:

(1) stupor, i.e. profound diminution or absence of voluntary movements and speech, and of normal responsiveness to light, noise and touch, but with normal muscle tone, static posture and breathing maintained (and often limited coordinated eye movements);

(2) negativism (positive resistance to passive movement of limbs or body or rigid posturing).

C. There is catatonic excitement (gross hypermotility of a chaotic quality with or without a tendency to assaultiveness).

D. There is rapid and unpredictable alternation of stupor and excitement.

Diagnostic notes

Confidence in the diagnosis will be increased if additional catatonic phenomena are present, e.g. stereotypies, waxy flexibility and impulsive acts. Care should be taken to exclude delirium; however, it is not known at present whether an organic catatonic state always occurs in clear consciousness or whether it represents an atypical manifestation of a delirium in which criteria A, B and D are only marginally met, while criterion C is prominent.

F06.2 Organic delusional [schizophrenia-like] disorder

A disorder in which persistent or recurrent delusions dominate the clinical picture. The delusions may be accompanied by hallucinations. Some features suggestive of schizophrenia, such as bizarre hallucinations or thought disorder, may be present.

Paranoid and paranoid–hallucinatory organic states
Schizophrenia-like psychosis in epilepsy

Excludes: disorder:
- acute and transient psychotic (F23.–)
- persistent delusional (F22.–)
  schizophrenia (F20.–)
- psychotic drug-induced (F11–F19) with common fourth character. 5)

DCR-10

A. The general criteria for F06 must be met.

B. The clinical picture is dominated by delusions (of persecution, bodily change, disease, death, jealousy) which may exhibit varying degrees of systematization.

C. Consciousness is clear and memory is intact.

Diagnostic notes

Further features that complete the clinical picture but which are not invariably present include hallucinations (in any modality); schizophrenic-type thought disorder; isolated catatonic phenomena such as stereotypies, negativism or impulsive acts.

The clinical picture may meet the symptomatic criteria for schizophrenia (F20.0–F20.3), persistent delusional disorder (F22) or acute and transient psychotic disorders (F23). However, if the state also meets the general criteria for a presumptive organic aetiology laid down in the introduction to F06, it should be classified here. The diagnostic notes about criterion G1 (page 48) are particularly important when considering this diagnosis.

F06.3 Organic mood [affective] disorders

Disorders characterized by a change in mood or affect, usually accompanied by a change in the overall level of activity – depressive, hypomanic, manic or bipolar (see F30–F32) – but arising as a consequence of an organic disorder.

Excludes: mood disorders, non-organic or unspecified (F30–F39)

> **DCR-10**
>
> A. The general criteria for F06 must be met.
>
> B. The condition must meet the criteria for one of the affective disorders, laid down in F30–F32.
>
> The type of the affective disorder may be specified by using a fifth character:
>
> F06.30 Organic manic disorder
> F06.31 Organic bipolar disorder
> F06.32 Organic depressive disorder
> F06.33 Organic mixed affective disorder

F06.4 Organic anxiety disorder

A disorder characterized by the essential descriptive features of a generalized anxiety disorder (F41.1), a panic disorder (F41.0) or a combination of both, but arising as a consequence of an organic disorder.

Excludes: anxiety disorders, non-organic or unspecified (F41.–)

> **DCR-10**
>
> A. The general criteria for F06 must be met.
>
> B. The condition must meet the criteria for either F41.0 or F41.1.

F06.5 Organic dissociative disorder

A disorder characterized by a partial or complete loss of the normal integration between memories of the past, awareness of identity and immediate sensations, and control of bodily movements (see F44.–), but arising as a consequence of an organic disorder.

Excludes: dissociative (conversion) disorders, non-organic or unspecified (F44.–)

DCR-10

A. The general criteria for F06 must be met.

B. The condition must meet the criteria for one of the subcategories F44.0–F44.8

F06.6 Organic emotionally labile [asthenic] disorder

A disorder characterized by emotional incontinence or lability, fatiguability and a variety of unpleasant physical sensations (e.g. dizziness) and pains, but arising as a consequence of an organic disorder.

Excludes: somatoform disorders, non-organic or unspecified (F45.–)

DCR-10

A. The general criteria for F06 must be met.

B. The clinical picture is dominated by emotional lability (uncontrolled, unstable and fluctuating expression of emotions).

C. There is a variety of unpleasant physical sensations such as dizziness or pains and aches.

Diagnostic notes

Fatiguability and listlessness (asthenia) are often present but are not essential for the diagnosis.

F06.7	Mild cognitive disorder

A disorder characterized by impairment of memory, learning difficulties and reduced ability to concentrate on a task for more than brief periods. There is often a marked feeling of mental fatigue when mental tasks are attempted, and new learning is found to be subjectively difficult even when objectively essential. None of these symptoms is so severe that a diagnosis of either dementia (F00–F03) or delirium (F05.–) can be made. This diagnosis should be made only in association with a specified physical disorder, and should not be made in the presence of any of the mental or behavioural disorders classified to F10–F99. The disorder may precede, accompany or follow a wide variety of infections and physical disorders, both cerebral and systemic, but direct evidence of cerebral involvement is not necessarily present. It can be differentiated from postencephalitic syndrome (F07.1) and postconcussional syndrome (F07.2) by its different aetiology, more restricted range of generally milder symptoms, and usually shorter duration.

Special note: The status of this construct is being examined. Special research criteria must be viewed as tentative. A main reason for its inclusion is to obtain further evidence allowing its differentiation from disorders such as dementia (F00–F03), organic amnesic syndrome (F04), delirium (F05.–) and several disorders in F07.–

DCR-10

A. The general criteria for F06 must be met.

B. There is a disorder in cognitive function for most of the time over a period of at least 2 weeks, as reported by the individual or a reliable informant. The disorder is exemplified by difficulties in any of the following areas: ⇒

(1) memory (particularly recall) or new learning

(2) attention or concentration

(3) thinking (e.g. slowing in problem-solving or abstraction)

(4) language (e.g. comprehension, word-finding)

(5) visual–spatial functioning.

C. There is an abnormality of or decline in performance in quantified cognitive assessments (e.g. neuropsychological tests or mental status examination).

D. None of the difficulties listed in criterion B (1) – (5) is such that a diagnosis can be made of dementia (F00 – F03), organic amnesic syndrome (F04), delirium (F05.–) post-encephalitic syndrome (F07.1), post-concussional syndrome (F07.2) or other persisting cognitive impairment due to psychoactive substance use (Flx.74)

Diagnostic notes

If general criterion G1 for F06 is fulfilled by the presence of central nervous system dysfunction, it is usually presumed that this is the cause of the mild cognitive disorder. If criterion G1 is fulfilled by the presence of a systemic physical disorder, it is often unjustified to assume that there is a direct causative relationship. Nevertheless, it may be useful in such instances to record the presence of the systemic physical disorder as 'associated' without implying a necessary causation. An additional fifth character may be used for this:

F06.70 not associated with a systemic physical disorder

F06.71 associated with a systemic physical disorder.

The systemic physical disorder should be recorded separately by its own ICD-10 code.

> ### F06.8 Other specified mental disorders due to brain damage and dysfunction and to physical disease

Epileptic psychosis NOS

Examples of this category are transient or mild abnormal mood states occurring during treatment with steroids or antidepressants which do not meet the criteria for organic mood disorder (F06.3).

> ### F06.9 Unspecified mental disorder due to brain damage and dysfunction and to physical disease

Organic:
• brain syndrome NOS
• mental disorder NOS

> ### F07 Personality and behavioural disorders due to brain disease, damage and dysfunction

Alteration of personality and behaviour can be a residual or concomitant disorder of brain disease, damage or dysfunction.

> G1. There must be objective evidence (from physical and neurological examination and laboratory tests) and/or history, of cerebral disease, damage or dysfunction.
>
> G2. There is no clouding of consciousness or significant memory deficit.
>
> G3. There is insufficient evidence for an alternative causation of the personality or behaviour disorder that would justify its placement in F60–F69.

F07.0 Organic personality disorder

A disorder characterized by a significant alteration of the habitual patterns of behaviour displayed by the subject premorbidly, involving the expression of emotions, needs and impulses. Impairment of cognitive and thought functions and altered sexuality may also be part of the clinical picture.

Organic:
• pseudopsychopathic personality
• pseudoretarded personality
Syndrome:
• frontal lobe
• limbic epilepsy personality
• lobotomy
• postleucotomy

Excludes: enduring personality change after:
• catastrophic experience (F62.0)
• psychiatric illness (F62.1)
postconcussional syndrome (F07.2)
postencephalitic syndrome (F07.1)
specific personality disorder (F60.–)

DCR-10

A. The general criteria for F07 must be met.

B. At least three of the following features must be present over a period of 6 months or more:

(1) consistently reduced ability to persevere with goal-directed activities, especially those involving relatively long periods of time and postponed gratification;

(2) one or more of the following emotional changes: (a) emotional lability (uncontrolled, unstable and fluctuating expression of emotions); (b) euphoria and shallow, inappropriate jocularity, unwarranted by the circumstances; (c) irritability and/or outbursts of anger and aggression; (d) apathy;

⇒

(3) disinhibited expression of needs or impulses without individual consideration of consequences or of social conventions (the individual may engage in dissocial acts such as stealing, inappropriate sexual advances, voracious eating, or exhibit extreme disregard for personal hygiene);

(4) cognitive disturbances, typically in the form of: (a) excessive suspiciousness and paranoid ideas; (b) excessive preoccupation with a single theme such as religion, or rigid categorization of other people's behaviour in terms of 'right' and 'wrong';

(5) marked alteration of the rate and flow of language production, with features such as circumstantiality, overinclusiveness, viscosity and hypergraphia.

Specification of features for possible sub-types

Option 1: A marked predominance of the symptoms in criteria (1) and (2)(d) is thought to define a pseudoretarded or apathetic type; a predominance of (1), (2)(c) and (3) is considered a pseudopsychopathic type; and the combination of (4), (5) and (6) is regarded as characteristic of the limbic epilepsy personality syndrome. None of these entities has yet been sufficiently validated to warrant a separate description.

Option 2: If desired, the following types may be specified: labile type, disinhibited type, aggressive type, apathetic type, paranoid type, mixed type and other.

| F07.1 | Postencephalitic syndrome |

Residual non-specific and variable behavioural change following recovery from either viral or bacterial encephalitis. The principal difference between this disorder and the organic personality disorders is that it is reversible.

Excludes: organic personality disorder (F07.0)

DCR-10

A. The general criteria for F07 must be met.

B. At least one of the following residual neuro-logical dysfunctions must be present:

(1) paralysis

(2) deafness

(3) aphasia

(4) constructional apraxia

(5) acalculia.

C. The syndrome is reversible and its duration rarely exceeds 24 months.

Diagnostic notes

Criterion C constitutes the main difference between this disorder and organic personality disorder (F07.0)

Residual symptoms and behavioural change following either viral or bacterial encephalitis are non-specific and do not provide a sufficient basis for a clinical diagnosis. They may include general malaise, apathy or irritability; some lowering of cognitive functioning (learning difficulties); disturbances in the sleep–wake pattern; or altered sexual behaviour.

F07.2	Postconcussional syndrome

A syndrome that occurs following head trauma (usually sufficiently severe to result in loss of consciousness) and includes a number of disparate symptoms such as headache, dizziness, fatigue, irritability, difficulty in concentration and in performing mental tasks, impairment of memory, insomnia and reduced tolerance to stress, emotional excitement or alcohol.

Postcontusional syndrome (encephalopathy)
Posttraumatic brain syndrome, nonpsychotic

Note: The nosological status of this syndrome is uncertain, and criterion G1 of the introduction to this rubric (page 57) is not always ascertainable. However, for those undertaking research into this condition, the following criteria are recommended:

DCR-10

A. The general criteria of F07 must be met.

B. There must be a history of head trauma with loss of consciousness preceding the onset of symptoms by a period of up to 4 weeks (objective EEG, brain imaging or oculonystagmographic evidence for brain damage may be lacking).

C. At least three of the following features must be present:

(1) complaints of unpleasant sensations and pains, such as headache, dizziness (usually lacking the features of true vertigo), general malaise and excessive fatigue or noise intolerance;

(2) emotional changes, such as irritability, emotional lability, both easily provoked or exacerbated by emotional excitement or stress, or some degree of depression and/or anxiety;

(3) subjective complaints of difficulty in concentration and in performing mental tasks, and of memory problems (without clear objective evidence, e.g. psychological tests, of marked impairment);

(4) insomnia;

(5) reduced tolerance to alcohol;

⇒

(6) preoccupation with the above symptoms
and fear of permanent brain damage, to
the extent of hypochondriacal overvalued
ideas and adoption of a sick role.

F07.8 Other organic personality and behavioural disorders due to brain disease, damage and dysfunction

Right hemispheric organic affective disorder

Brain disease, damage or dysfunction may produce a
variety of cognitive, emotional, personality and behavioural disorders, some of which may not be classifiable
under F07.0–F07.2. However, since the nosological
status of the tentative syndromes in this area is uncertain,
they should be coded as 'other'. A fifth character may
be added, if necessary, to identify presumptive individual
entities.

F07.9 Unspecified organic personality and behavioural disorder due to brain disease, damage and dysfunction

Organic psychosyndrome

F09 Unspecified organic or symptomatic mental disorder

This category should be used only for recording mental
disorders known to be of organic aetiology.

Psychosis:
• organic NOS
• symptomatic NOS

Excludes: psychosis NOS (F29)

Mental and behavioural disorders due to psychoactive substance use (F10–F19)

This block contains a wide variety of disorders that differ in severity and clinical form but which are all attributable to the use of one or more psychoactive substances, which may or may not have been medically prescribed. The third character of the code identifies the substance involved, and the fourth character specifies the clinical state. The codes should be used, as required, for each substance specified, but it should be noted that not all fourth-character codes are applicable to all substances.

Identification of the psychoactive substance should be based on as many sources of information as possible. These include self-report data, analysis of blood and other body fluids, characteristic physical and psychological symptoms, clinical signs and behaviour, and other evidence such as a drug being in the patient's possession or reports from informed third parties. Many drug users take more than one type of psychoactive substance. The main diagnosis should be classified, whenever possible, according to the substance or class of substances that has caused or contributed most to the presenting clinical syndrome. Other diagnoses should be coded when other psychoactive substances have been taken in intoxicating amounts (common fourth character .0) or to the extent of causing harm (common fourth character .1), dependence (common fourth character .2) or other disorders (common fourth character .3–9).

Only in cases in which patterns of psychoactive substance-taking are chaotic and indiscriminate, or in which the contributions of different psychoactive substances are inextricably mixed, should the diagnosis of disorders resulting from multiple drug use (F19.–) be used.

Excludes: abuse of non-dependence-producing substances (F55)

Chapter V: Mental and behavioural disorders
Mental and behavioural disorders due to psychoactive substance use

F10.– Mental and behavioural disorders due to use of alcohol

(see pages 65–69, 78–82, 86–91 for subdivisions)

F11.– Mental and behavioural disorders due to use of opioids

(see pages 65–67, 69, 78–83, 86–91 for subdivisions)

F12.– Mental and behavioural disorders due to use of cannabinoids

(see pages 65–67, 70, 78–83, 86–91 for subdivisions)

F13.– Mental and behavioural disorders due to use of sedatives or hypnotics

(see pages 65–67, 71, 78–82, 84, 86–91 for subdivisions)

F14.– Mental and behavioural disorders due to use of cocaine

(see pages 65–67, 72–73, 78–82, 84–91 for subdivisions)

F15.– Mental and behavioural disorders due to use of other stimulants, including caffeine

(see pages 65–67, 73–74, 78–82, 85–91 for subdivisions)

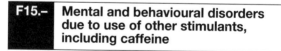

F16.– Mental and behavioural disorders due to use of hallucinogens

(see pages 65–67, 74–75, 78–82, 86–91 for subdivisions

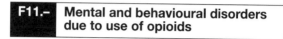

F17.– **Mental and behavioural disorders
due to use of tobacco**

(see pages 65–67, 76, 78–82, 86, 91 for subdivisions)

F18.– **Mental and behavioural disorders
due to use of volatile solvents**

(see pages 66–68, 77–83, 87–92 for subdivisions)

F19.– **Mental and behavioural disorders
due to multiple drug use and use of
other psychoactive substances**

(see pages 65–67, 77–82, 86–91 for subdivisions)

This category should be used when two or more psychoactive substances are known to be involved but it is
impossible to assess which substance is contributing
most to the disorders. It should also be used when
the exact identity of some or even all the psychoactive
substances being used is uncertain or unknown, since
many multiple drug users themselves often do not know
the details of what they are taking.

Includes: misuse of drugs NOS
The following fourth-character subdivisions are for use
with categories F10–F19.

F1x.0 Acute intoxication

A condition that follows the administration of a psychoactive substance, resulting in disturbances in level of
consciousness, cognition, perception, affect or behaviour, or other psychophysiological functions and
responses. The disturbances are directly related to the
acute pharmacological effects of the substance and
resolve with time with complete recovery except where
tissue damage or other complications have arisen. Complications may include trauma, inhalation of vomitus,
delirium, coma, convulsions and other medical com-

plications. The nature of these complications depends on the pharmacological class of substance and mode of administration.

Acute drunkenness in alcoholism

'Bad trips' (drugs)

Drunkenness NOS

Pathological intoxication

Trance and possession disorders in psychoactive substance intoxication

DCR-10

G1. There must be clear evidence of recent use of a psychoactive substance (or substances) at sufficiently high dose levels to be consistent with intoxication.

G2. There must be symptoms or signs of intoxication compatible with the known actions of the particular substance (or substances), as specified below, and of sufficient severity to produce disturbances in the level of consciousness, cognition, perception, affect or behaviour that are of clinical importance.

G3. Symptoms or signs present cannot be accounted for by a medical disorder unrelated to substance use and not better accounted for by another mental or behavioural disorder.

Acute intoxication frequently occurs in persons who have more persistent alcohol or drug-related problems in addition. Where there are such problems, e.g. harmful use (F1x.1), dependence syndrome (F1x.2) or psychotic disorder (F1x.5), they should also be recorded.

The following five-character codes may be used to indicate whether the acute intoxication was associated with any complications:

F1x.00	uncomplicated symptoms of varying severity, usually dose-dependent
F1x.01	with trauma or other bodily injury
F1x.02	with other medical complications (examples are haematemesis, inhalation of vomit)
F1x.03	with delirium
F1x.04	with perceptual distortions
F1x.05	with coma
F1x.06	with convulsions
F1x.07	pathological intoxication (applies only to alcohol).

F10.0 Acute intoxication due to use of alcohol

DCR-10

A. The general criteria for acute intoxication (f1x.0) must be met.

B. There must be dysfunctional behaviour, as evidenced by at least one of the following:

(1) disinhibition

(2) argumentativeness

(3) aggression

(4) lability of mood

(5) impaired attention

(6) impaired judgement

(7) Interference with personal functioning.

C. At least one of the following signs must be present:

(1) unsteady gait

(2) difficulty in standing

(3) slurred speech

$\Rightarrow$

> (4) nystagmus
>
> (5) decreased level of consciousness (e.g. stupor, coma)
>
> (6) flushed face
>
> (7) conjunctival injection.

Diagnostic notes

When severe, acute alcohol intoxication may be accompanied by hypotension, hypothermia and depression of the gag reflex. If desired, the blood alcohol level may be specified by using ICD-10 codes Y90.0–Y90.8. Code Y91.– may be used to specify the clinical severity of intoxication if the blood alcohol level is not available.

F10.07 Pathological intoxication

Note: The status of this condition is being examined. These research criteria must be regarded as tentative.

> **DCR-10**
>
> A. The general criteria for acute intoxication (F1x.0) must be met, with the exception that pathological intoxication occurs after drinking amounts of alcohol insufficient to cause intoxication in most people.
>
> B. There is verbally aggressive or physically violent behaviour that is not typical of the person when sober.
>
> C. The intoxication occurs very soon (usually a few minutes) after consumption of alcohol.
>
> D. There is no evidence of organic cerebral disorder or other mental disorders.

Diagnostic notes

This is an uncommon condition. The blood alcohol

levels found in this disorder are lower than those that would cause acute intoxication in most people, i.e. below 40 mg/100 ml.

| F11.0 | Acute intoxication due to use of opioids |

DCR-10

A. The general criteria for acute intoxication (F1x.0) must be met.

B. There must be dysfunctional behaviour, as evidenced by at least one of the following:

 (1) apathy and sedation

 (2) disinhibition

 (3) psychomotor retardation

 (4) impaired attention

 (5) impaired judgement

 (6) interference with personal functioning.

C. At least one of the following signs must be present:

 (1) drowsiness

 (2) slurred speech

 (3) pupillary constriction (except in anoxia from severe overdose, when pupillary dilatation occurs)

 (4) decreased level of consciousness (e.g. stupor, coma)

Diagnostic notes

When severe, acute opioid intoxication may be accompanied by respiratory depression (and hypoxia) and hypothermia.

DCR-10

A. The general criteria for acute intoxication (F1x.0) must be met.

B. There must be dysfunctional behaviour or perceptual disturbances including at least one of the following:

    (1) euphoria and disinhibition

    (2) anxiety or agitation

    (3) suspiciousness or paranoid ideation

    (4) temporal slowing (a sense that time is passing very slowly, and/or the person is experiencing a rapid flow of ideas)

    (5) impaired judgement

    (6) impaired attention

    (7) impaired reaction time

    (8) auditory, visual or tactile illusions

    (9) hallucinations, with preserved orientation

    (10) depersonalization

    (11) derealization

    (12) interference with personal functioning.

C. At least one of the following signs must be present:

    (1) increased appetite

    (2) dry mouth

    (3) conjunctival injection

    (4) tachycardia.

F13.0 Acute intoxication due to use of sedatives or hypnotics

DCR-10

A. The general criteria for acute intoxication (F1x.0) must be met.

B. There is dysfunctional behaviour, as evidenced by at least one of the following:

   (1) euphoria

   (2) apathy and sedation

   (3) abusiveness or aggression

   (4) lability of mood

   (5) impaired attention

   (6) anterograde amnesia

   (7) impaired psychomotor performance

   (8) interference with personal functioning.

C. At least one of the following signs must be present:

   (1) unsteady gait

   (2) difficulty in standing

   (3) slurred speech

   (4) nystagmus

   (5) decreased level of consciousness (e.g. stupor, coma)

   (6) erythematous skin lesions or blisters.

Diagnostic notes

When severe, acute intoxication from sedative or hypnotic drugs may be accompanied by hypotension, hypothermia and depression of the gag reflex.

F14.0	Acute intoxication due to use of cocaine

DCR-10

A. The general criteria for acute intoxication (F1x.0) must be met.

B. There must be dysfunctional behaviour or perceptual abnormalities, as evidenced by at least one of the following:

    (1) euphoria and sensation of increased energy

    (2) hypervigilance

    (3) grandiose beliefs or actions

    (4) abusiveness or aggression

    (5) argumentativeness

    (6) lability of mood

    (7) repetitive stereotyped behaviours

    (8) auditory, visual or tactile illusions

    (9) hallucinations, usually with intact orientation

    (10) paranoid ideation

    (11) interference with personal functioning.

C. At least two of the following signs must be present:

    (1) tachycardia (sometimes bradycardia)

    (2) cardiac arrhythmias

    (3) hypertension (sometimes hypotension)

    (4) sweating and chills

    (5) nausea or vomiting

    (6) evidence of weight loss

⇒

        (7) pupillary dilatation

        (8) psychomotor agitation (sometimes
            retardation)

        (9) muscular weakness

    (10) chest pain

    (11) convulsions.

Diagnostic notes

Interference with personal functioning is most readily apparent from the social interactions of the cocaine users, which range from extreme gregariousness to social withdrawal.

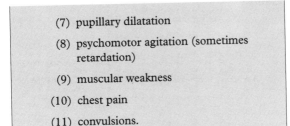

F15.0 Acute intoxication due to the use of other stimulants, including caffeine

DCR-10

A. The general criteria for acute intoxication (F1x.0) must be met.

B. There must be dysfunctional behaviour or perceptual abnormalities, as evidenced by at least one of the following:

    (1) euphoria and sensation of increased energy

    (2) hypervigilance

    (3) grandiose beliefs or actions

    (4) abusiveness or aggression

    (5) argumentativeness

    (6) lability of mood

    (7) repetitive stereotyped behaviours

    (8) auditory, visual or tactile illusions

⇒

   (9) hallucinations, usually with intact
       orientation

   (10) paranoid ideation

   (11) interference with personal functioning.

C. At least two of the following signs must be
   present:

   (1) tachycardia (sometimes bradycardia)

   (2) cardiac arrhythmias

   (3) hypertension (sometimes hypotension)

   (4) sweating and chills

   (5) nausea or vomiting

   (6) evidence of weight loss

   (7) pupillary dilatation

   (8) psychomotor agitation (sometimes
       retardation)

   (9) muscular weakness

   (10) chest pain

   (11) convulsions.

Diagnostic notes

Interference with personal functioning is most readily
apparent from the social interactions of the substance
users, which range from extreme gregariousness to social
withdrawal.

F16.0	Acute intoxication due to use of hallucinogens

DCR-10

A. The general criteria for acute intoxication
   (F1x.0) must be met.

⇒

B. There must be dysfunctional behaviour or perceptual abnormalities, as evidenced by at least one of the following:

(1) anxiety and fearfulness

(2) auditory, visual or tactile illusions or hallucinations occurring in a state of full wakefulness and alertness

(3) depersonalization

(4) derealization

(5) paranoid ideation

(6) ideas of reference

(7) lability of mood

(8) hyperactivity

(9) impulsive acts

(10) impaired attention

(11) interference with personal functioning

C. At least two of the following signs must be present:

(1) tachycardia

(2) palpitations

(3) sweating and chills

(4) tremor

(5) blurring of vision

(6) pupillary dilatation

(7) incoordination

F17.0 Acute intoxication due to use of tobacco [acute nicotine intoxication]

DCR-10

A. The general criteria for acute intoxication (F1x.0) must be met.

B. There must be dysfunctional behaviour or perceptual abnormalities, as evidenced by at least one of the following:

  (1) insomnia

  (2) bizarre dreams

  (3) lability of mood

  (4) derealization

  (5) interference with personal functioning.

C. At least one of the following signs must be present:

  (1) nausea or vomiting

  (2) sweating

  (3) tachycardia

  (4) cardiac arrhythmias.

F18.0 Acute intoxication due to use of volatile solvents

DCR-10

A. The general criteria for acute intoxication (F1x.0) must be met.

B. There must be dysfunctional behaviour, evidenced by at least one of the following:

⇒

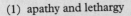

(1) apathy and lethargy

(2) argumentativeness

(3) abusiveness or aggression

(4) lability of mood

(5) impaired judgement

(6) impaired attention and memory

(7) psychomotor retardation

(8) interference with personal functioning.

C. At least one of the following signs must be present:

(1) unsteady gait

(2) difficulty in standing

(3) slurred speech

(4) nystagmus

(5) decreased level of consciousness (e.g. stupor, coma)

(6) muscle weakness

(7) blurred vision or diplopia.

Diagnostic notes

Acute intoxication from inhalation of substances other than solvents should also be coded here. When severe, acute intoxication from volatile solvents may be accompanied by hypotension, hypothermia and depression of the gag reflex.

| F19.0 | Acute intoxication due to multiple drug use, and use of other psychoactive substances |

This category should be used when there is evidence of intoxication caused by recent use of other psychoactive substances (e.g. phencyclidine) or of multiple psychoactive substances where it is uncertain which substance has predominated.

F1x.1 Harmful use

A pattern of psychoactive substance use that is causing damage to health. The damage may be physical (as in cases of hepatitis from the self-administration of injected psychoactive substances) or mental (e.g. episodes of depressive disorder secondary to heavy consumption of alcohol).

Psychoactive substance abuse

DCR-10

A. There must be clear evidence that the substance use was responsible for (or substantially contributed to) physical or psychological harm, including impaired judgement or dysfunctional behaviour.

B. The nature of the harm should be clearly identifiable (and specified).

C. The pattern of use has persisted for at least 1 month or has occurred repeatedly within a 12-month period.

D. The disorder does not meet the criteria for any other mental or behavioural disorder related to the same drug in the same time period (except for acute intoxication F1x.0).

F1x.2 Dependence syndrome

A cluster of behavioural, cognitive and physiological phenomena that develop after repeated substance use and that typically include a strong desire to take the drug, difficulties in controlling its use, persisting in its use despite harmful consequences, a higher priority given to drug use than to other activities and obligations, increased tolerance, and sometimes a physical withdrawal state.

The dependence syndrome may be present for a specific psychoactive substance (e.g. tobacco, alcohol or diazepam), for a class of substances (e.g. opioid drugs), or for a wider range of pharmacologically different psychoactive substances.

Chronic alcoholism

Dipsomania

Drug addiction.

DCR-10

A. Three or more of the following manifestations should have occurred together for at least 1 month or, if persisting for periods of less than 1 month, should have occurred together repeatedly within a 12-month period:

   (1) a strong desire or sense of compulsion to take the substance;

   (2) impaired capacity to control substance-taking behaviour in terms of its onset, termination, or levels of use, as evidenced by the substance being often taken in larger amounts or over a longer period than intended, or by a persistent desire or unsuccessful efforts to reduce or control substance use;

   (3) a physiological withdrawal state (see F1x.3 and F1x.4) when substance use is reduced or ceased, as evidenced by the characteristic withdrawal syndrome for the substance, or by use of the same (or closely related) substance with the intention of relieving or avoiding withdrawal symptoms;

   (4) evidence of tolerance to the effects of the

$\Rightarrow$

substance, such that there is a need for significantly increased amounts of the substance to achieve intoxication or the desired effect, or a markedly diminished effect with continued use of the same amount of the substance;

(5) preoccupation with substance use, as manifested by important alternative pleasures or interests being given up or reduced because of substance use; or a great deal of time being spent in activities necessary to obtain, take or recover from the effects of the substance;

(6) persistent substance use despite clear evidence of harmful consequences (see F1x.1), as evidenced by continued use when the individual is actually aware, or may be expected to be aware, of the nature and extent of harm.

Diagnosis of the dependence syndrome may be further specified by the following five- and six-character codes:

F1x.20   currently abstinent

    F1x.200   early remission

    F1x.201   partial remission

    F1x.202   full remission.

F1x.21   currently abstinent but in a protected environment (e.g. in hospital, in a therapeutic community, in prison etc.).

F1x.22   currently on a clinically supervised maintenance or replacement regime [controlled dependence] (e.g. with methadone, nicotine gum or nicotine patch).

F1x.23   currently abstinent, but receiving treatment with aversive or blocking

⇒

drugs (e.g. naltrexone or disulfiram).

F1x.24　currently using the substance [active dependence]

　　　　F1x.240　without physical features

　　　　F1x.241　with physical features.

The course of the dependence may be further specified, if desired, as follows:

F1x.25　continuous use

F1x.26　episodic use (dipsomania).

F1x.3　Withdrawal state

A group of symptoms of variable clustering and severity occurring on absolute or relative withdrawal of a psychoactive substance after persistent use of that substance. The onset and course of the withdrawal state are time-limited and are related to the type of psychoactive substance and the dose being used immediately before the cessation or reduction of use. The withdrawal state may be complicated by convulsions.

DCR-10

G1.　There must be clear evidence of recent cessation or reduction of substance use after repeated, and usually prolonged and/or high-dose, use of that substance.

G2.　Symptoms and signs are compatible with the known features of a withdrawal state from the particular substance or substances (see below).

G3.　Symptoms and signs are not accounted for by a medical disorder unrelated to substance use, and not better accounted for by another mental or behavioural disorder.

$\Rightarrow$

The diagnosis of withdrawal state may be further specified by using the following five-character codes:

F1x.30   uncomplicated

F1x.31   with convulsions.

F10.3   Alcohol withdrawal state

DCR-10

A.   The general criteria for withdrawal state (F1x.3) must be met.

B.   Any three of the following signs must be present:

(1) tremor of the tongue, eyelids or outstretched hands

(2) sweating

(3) nausea, retching or vomiting

(4) tachycardia or hypertension

(5) psychomotor agitation

(6) headache

(7) insomnia

(8) malaise or weakness

(9) transient visual, tactile or auditory hallucinations or illusions

(10) grand mal convulsions.

Diagnostic notes

If delirium is present, the diagnosis should be alcohol withdrawal state with delirium (delirium tremens) (F10.4).

F11.3 Opioid withdrawal state

DCR-10

A. The general criteria for withdrawal state (F1x.3) must be met. (Note than an opioid withdrawal state may also be induced by administration of an opioid antagonist after a brief period of opioid use.)

B. Any three of the following signs must be present:

(1) craving for an opioid drug

(2) rhinorrhoea or sneezing

(3) lacrimation

(4) muscle aches or cramps

(5) abdominal cramps

(6) nausea or vomiting

(7) diarrhoea

(8) pupillary dilatation

(9) piloerection, or recurrent chills

(10) tachycardia or hypertension

(11) yawning

(12) restless sleep.

F12.3 Cannabinoid withdrawal state

This is an ill-defined syndrome for which definitive diagnostic criteria cannot be established at present. It occurs following the cessation of prolonged high-dose use of cannabis. It has been reported variously as lasting from several hours to up to 7 days. Symptoms and signs include anxiety, irritability, tremor of the outstretched hands, sweating and muscle aches.

F13.3 Sedative or hypnotic withdrawal state

DCR-10

A. The general criteria for withdrawal state (F1x.3) must be met.

B. Any three of the following signs must be present:

    (1) tremor of the tongue, eyelids or outstretched hands

    (2) nausea or vomiting

    (3) tachycardia

    (4) postural hypotension

    (5) psychomotor agitation

    (6) headache

    (7) insomnia

    (8) malaise or weakness

    (9) transient visual, tactile or auditory hallucinations or illusions

    (10) paranoid ideation

    (11) grand mal convulsions.

Diagnostic notes

If delirium is present, the diagnosis of sedative or hypnotic withdrawal state with delirium (F13.4) should be made.

F14.3 Cocaine withdrawal state

DCR-10x

A. The general criteria for withdrawal state (F1x.3) must be met.

B. There is dysphoric mood (for instance, sadness or anhedonia).

C. Any two of the following signs must be present:

(1) lethargy and fatigue

(2) psychomotor retardation or agitation

(3) craving for cocaine

(4) increased appetite

(5) insomnia or hypersomnia

(6) bizarre or unpleasant dreams

F15.3 Withdrawal states from other stimulants, including caffeine

DCR-10

A. The general criteria for withdrawal state (F1x.3) must be met.

B. There is dysphoric mood (for instance, sadness or anhedonia).

C. Any two of the following signs must be present:

(1) lethargy and fatigue

(2) psychomotor retardation or agitation

(3) craving for stimulant drugs

(4) increased appetite

(5) insomnia or hypersomnia

(6) bizarre or unpleasant dreams.

Note: there is no recognised hallucinogen withdrawal state.

F17.3 Tobacco withdrawal states

DCR-10

A. The general criteria for withdrawal state (F1x.3) must be met.

B. Any two of the following signs must be present:

(1) craving for tobacco (or other nicotine-containing products

(2) malaise or weakness

(3) anxiety

(4) dysphoric mood

(5) irritability or restlessness

(6) insomnia

(7) increased appetite

(8) increased cough

(9) mouth ulceration

(10) difficulty in concentrating.

F18.3 Volatile solvents withdrawal state

Note: there is inadequate information on withdrawal states from volatile solvents for research criteria to be formulated.

F1x.4 Withdrawal state with delirium

A condition where the withdrawal state as defined by the common fourth character .3 is complicated by delirium as defined in F05.–. Convulsions may also occur. When organic factors are also considered to play a role in the aetiology, the condition should be classified to F05.8.

Delirium tremens (alcohol-induced)

DCR-10

A. The general criteria for withdrawal state (F1x.3) must be met.

B. The criteria for delirium (F05) must be met.

The diagnosis of withdrawal state with delirium may be further specified by using the following five-character codes:

F1x.40   without convulsions

F1x.41   with convulsions.

F1x.5   Psychotic disorder

A cluster of psychotic phenomena that occur during or following psychoactive substance use, but which are not explained on the basis of acute intoxication alone and do not form part of a withdrawal state. The disorder is characterized by hallucinations (typically auditory, but often in more than one sensory modality), perceptual distortions, delusions (often of a paranoid or persecutory nature), psychomotor disturbances (excitement or stupor) and an abnormal affect, which may range from intense fear to ecstasy. The sensorium is usually clear but some degree of clouding of consciousness, though not severe confusion, may be present.

Alcoholic:

- hallucinosis
- jealousy
- paranoia
- psychosis NOS

Excludes: alcohol- or other psychoactive substance-induced residual and late-onset psychotic disorder (F10–F19 with common fourth character .7).

DCR-10

A. Onset of psychotic symptoms must occur during or within 2 weeks of substance use.

B. The psychotic symptoms must persist for more than 48 hours.

C. Duration of the disorder must not exceed 6 months.

The diagnosis of psychotic disorder may be further specified by using the following five-character codes:

F1x.50 schizophrenia-like

F1x.51 predominantly delusional

F1x.52 predominantly hallucinatory

F1x.53 predominantly polymorphic

F1x.54 predominantly depressive symptoms

F1x.55 predominantly manic symptoms

F1x.56 mixed.

For research purposes it is recommended that change of the disorder from a non-psychotic to a clearly psychotic state be further specified as either abrupt (onset within 48 hours) or acute (onset in more than 48 hours but less than 2 weeks).

F1x.6	Amnesic syndrome

A syndrome associated with chronic prominent impairment of recent and remote memory. Immediate recall is usually preserved and recent memory is characteristically more disturbed than remote memory. Disturbances of time sense and ordering of events are usually evident, as are difficulties in learning new material. Confabulation may be marked but is not invariably present. Other cognitive functions are usually relatively well preserved and amnesic defects are out of proportion to other disturbances.

Amnestic disorder, alcohol- or drug-induced

Korsakov's psychosis or syndrome, alcohol- or other psychoactive substance-induced or unspecified

Excludes: non-alcoholic Korsakov's psychosis or syndrome (F04)

DCR-10

A. Memory impairment is manifest in both:
   (1) a defect of recent memory (impaired learning of new material) to a degree sufficient to interfere with daily living; and
   (2) a reduced ability to recall past experiences.

B. All of the following are absent (or relatively absent):
   (1) defect in immediate recall (as tested, for example, by the digit span);
   (2) clouding of consciousness and disturbance of attention, as defined in F05.-, criterion A;
   (3) global intellectual decline (dementia).

C. There is no objective evidence from physical and neurological examination, laboratory tests or history of a disorder or disease of the brain (especially involving bilaterally the diencephalic and medial temporal structures), other than that related to substance use, which can reasonably be presumed to be responsible for the clinical manifestations described under criterion A.

F1x.7 Residual and late-onset psychotic disorder

A disorder in which alcohol- or psychoactive substance-induced changes of cognition, affect, personality or behaviour persist beyond the period during which a direct psychoactive substance-related effect might reasonably be assumed to be operating. Onset of the disorder should be directly related to the use of the psychoactive substance. Cases in which initial onset of the state occurs later than episode(s) of such substance use should be coded here only where clear and strong evidence is available to attribute the state to the residual effect of the psychoactive substance. Flashbacks may be distinguished from psychotic states partly by their episodic nature, frequently of very short duration, and by their duplication of previous alcohol- or other psychoactive substance-related experiences.

DCR-10

A. Conditions and disorders meeting the criteria for the individual syndromes listed below should be clearly related to substance use. Where onset of the condition or disorder occurs subsequent to use of psychoactive substances, strong evidence should be provided to demonstrate a link.

Diagnostic notes

In view of the considerable variations in this category, the characteristics of such residual states or conditions should be clearly documented in terms of their type, severity and duration. For research purposes full descriptive details should be specified.

A fifth character may be used, if required as follows:

F1x.70 flashbacks

F1x.71   personality or behaviour disorder.

B. The general criteria for F07.– (personality and behavioural disorder due to brain disease, damage and dysfunction) must be met.

F1x.72   residual affective disorder

B. The criteria for F06.3 organic mood [affective] disorder, must be met

F1x.73   dementia

B. The general criteria for dementia (F00–F03) must be met.

F1x.74   other persisting cognitive impairment

B. The criteria for F06.7, mild cognitive disorder, must be met, except for the exclusion of psychoactive substance use in criterion D.

F1x.75   late-onset psychotic disorder

B. The general criteria for F1x.5, psychotic disorder, must be met, except with regard to the onset of the disorder, which is more than 2 weeks, but not more than 6 weeks after substance use.

| F1x.8 | Other mental and behavioural disorder |

| F1x.9 | Unspecified mental and behavioural disorders |

Schizophrenia, schizotypal and delusional disorders (F20–F29)

This block brings together schizophrenia, as the most important member of the group, schizotypal disorder, persistent delusional disorders and a larger group of acute and transient psychotic disorders. Schizoaffective disorders have been retained here in spite of their controversial nature.

F20 Schizophrenia

The schizophrenic disorders are characterized in general by fundamental and characteristic distortions of thinking and perception, and affects that are inappropriate or blunted. Clear consciousness and intellectual capacity are usually maintained, although certain cognitive deficits may evolve in the course of time. The most important psychopathological phenomena include thought echo; thought insertion or withdrawal; thought broadcasting; delusional perception and delusions of control; influence or passivity; hallucinatory voices commenting on or discussing the patient in the third person; thought disorders and negative symptoms.

The course of schizophrenic disorders can be either continuous or episodic with progressive or stable deficit, or there can be one or more episodes with complete or incomplete remission. The diagnosis of schizophrenia should not be made in the presence of extensive depressive or manic symptoms unless it is clear that schizophrenic symptoms antedate the affective disturbance. Nor should schizophrenia be diagnosed in the presence of overt brain disease or during states of drug intoxication or withdrawal. Similar disorders

⇒

developing in the presence of epilepsy or other brain disease should be classified under F06.2 and those induced by psychoactive substances under F10–F19, with common fourth character 5.

Excludes: schizophrenia:

- acute (undifferentiated) (F23.2)
- cyclic (F25.2)
  schizophrenic reaction (F23.2)
  schizotypal disorder (F21)

Diagnostic note

The general criteria for schizophrenia (G1 and G2) listed below apply, either at the time of the present diagnosis or at some time in the past, to all the disorders in F20 *with the exception of simple schizophrenia (F20.6)*; see note on page 103.

DCR-10

F20.0–F20.3 General criteria for paranoid, hebephrenic, catatonic and undifferentiated schizophrenia.

G1. Either at least one of the syndromes, symptoms and signs listed under (1) below or at least two of the symptoms and signs listed under (2) should be present for most of the time during an episode of psychotic illness lasting for at least 1 month (or at some time during most of the days).

   (1) At least one of the following must be present:

   (a) thought echo, thought insertion or withdrawal, or thought broadcasting;

   (b) delusions of control, influence or passivity, clearly referred to body or limb movements or specific

⇒

thoughts, actions or sensations; delusional perception;

(c) hallucinatory voices giving a running commentary on the patient's behaviour, or discussing the patient between themselves, or other types of hallucinatory voices coming from some part of the body;

(d) persistent delusions of other kinds that are culturally inappropriate and completely impossible (e.g. being able to control the weather, or being in communication with aliens from another world).

(2) Or at least two of the following:

(a) persistent hallucinations in any modality, when occurring every day for at least 1 month, when accompanied by delusions (which may be fleeting or half-formed) without clear affective content, or when accompanied by persistent overvalued ideas;

(b) neologisms, breaks or interpolations in the train of thought, resulting in incoherence or irrelevant speech;

(c) catatonic behaviour, such as excitement, posturing or waxy flexibility, negativism, mutism and stupor;

(d) 'negative' symptoms, such as marked apathy, paucity of speech and blunting or incongruity of emotional responses (it must be clear that these are not due to depression or to neuroleptic medication).

⇒

G2. *Most commonly used exclusion clauses*

> (1) If the patient also meets the criteria
> for manic episode (F30.) or
> depressive episode (F32.), the
> criteria listed under G1 (1) and
> G1 (2) above must have been met
> before the disturbance of mood
> developed.
>
> (2) The disorder is not attributable to
> organic brain disease (in the sense
> of F00–F09) or to alcohol- or
> drug-related intoxication (F1x.0),
> dependence (F1x.2) or withdrawal
> (F1x.3 and F1x.4).

Diagnostic notes

In evaluating the presence of these abnormal subjective experiences and behaviour, special care should be taken to avoid false-positive assessments, especially where culturally or subculturally influenced modes of expression and behaviour or a subnormal level of intelligence are involved.

Pattern of course

In view of the considerable variations in the course of schizophrenic disorders it may be desirable (especially for research) to specify the pattern of course by using a fifth character. Course should not usually be coded unless there has been a period of observation of at least 1 year. (For remission, see Note 5 in Notes for Users).

F20.x0 continuous (no remission of
psychotic symptoms throughout the
period of observation)

F20.x1 episodic with progressive deficit
(progressive development of
'negative' symptoms in the intervals
between psychotic episodes)

⇒

F20.x2	episodic with stable deficit (persistent but non-progressive 'negative' symptoms in the intervals between psychotic episodes)
F20.x3	episodic remittent (complete or virtually complete remissions between psychotic episodes)
F20.x4	incomplete remission
F20.x5	complete remission
F20.x8	other
F20.x9	course uncertain, period of observation too short.

F20.0 Paranoid schizophrenia

Paranoid schizophrenia is dominated by relatively stable, often paranoid, delusions, usually accompanied by hallucinations, particularly of the auditory variety, and perceptual disturbances. Disturbances of affect, volition and speech and catatonic symptoms are either absent or relatively inconspicuous.

Paraphrenic schizophrenia

Excludes: involutional paranoid state (F22.8)

paranoia (F22.0

DCR-10

A. The general criteria for schizophrenia (F20.0–F20.3) must be met.

B. Delusions or hallucinations must be prominent (such as delusions of persecution, reference, exalted birth, special mission, bodily change, or jealousy; threatening or commanding voices, hallucinations of smell or taste, sexual or other bodily sensations).

⇒

C. Flattening or incongruity of affect, catatonic symptoms or incoherent speech must not dominate the clinical picture, although they may be present to a mild degree.

F20.1 Hebephrenic schizophrenia

A form of schizophrenia in which affective changes are prominent, delusions and hallucinations fleeting and fragmentary, behaviour irresponsible and unpredictable and mannerisms common. The mood is shallow and inappropriate, thought is disorganized and speech is incoherent. There is a tendency to social isolation. Usually the prognosis is poor because of the rapid development of 'negative' symptoms, particularly flattening of affect and loss of volition. Hebephrenia should normally be diagnosed only in adolescents or young adults.

Disorganized schizophrenia

Hebephrenia

DCR-10

A. The general criteria for schizophrenia (F20.0–F20.3) must be met.

B. Either of the following must be present:

(1) definite and sustained flattening or shallowness of affect;

(2) definite and sustained incongruity or inappropriateness of affect;

C. Either of the following must be present:

(1) behaviour that is aimless and disjointed rather than goal-directed;

(2) definite thought disorder, manifesting as speech that is disjointed, rambling or incoherent;

D. Hallucinations or delusions must not dominate the clinical picture, although they may be present to a mild degree.

F20.2 Catatonic schizophrenia

Catatonic schizophrenia is dominated by prominent psychomotor disturbances, which may alternate between extremes such as hyperkinesis and stupor, or automatic obedience and negativism. Constrained attitudes and postures may be maintained for long periods.

Episodes of violent excitement may be a striking feature of the condition. The catatonic phenomena may be combined with a dream-like (oneiroid) state with vivid scenic hallucinations.

Catatonic stupor

Schizophrenic:

- catalepsy
- catatonia
- flexibilitas cerea

DCR-10

A. The general criteria for schizophrenia (F20.0–F20.3) must eventually be met, although this may not be possible initially if the patient is uncommunicative.

B. For a period of at least 2 weeks one or more of the following catatonic behaviours must be prominent:

(1) stupor (marked decrease in reactivity to the environment and reduction of spontaneous movements and activity) or mutism;

⇒

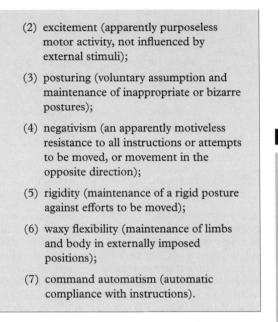

(2) excitement (apparently purposeless motor activity, not influenced by external stimuli);

(3) posturing (voluntary assumption and maintenance of inappropriate or bizarre postures);

(4) negativism (an apparently motiveless resistance to all instructions or attempts to be moved, or movement in the opposite direction);

(5) rigidity (maintenance of a rigid posture against efforts to be moved);

(6) waxy flexibility (maintenance of limbs and body in externally imposed positions);

(7) command automatism (automatic compliance with instructions).

F20.3 Undifferentiated schizophrenia

Psychotic conditions meeting the general diagnostic criteria for schizophrenia but not conforming to any of the subtypes in F20.0–F20.2, or exhibiting the features of more than one of them without a clear predominance of a particular set of diagnostic characteristics.

Atypical schizophrenia

Excludes: acute schizophrenia-like psychotic disorder (F23.2)

chronic undifferentiated schizophrenia (F20.5)

post-schizophrenic depression (F20.4)

DCR-10

A. The general criteria for schizophrenia (F20.0–F20.3) must be met.

⇒

B. Either of the following must apply:

   (1) insufficient symptoms to meet the criteria for any of the subtypes F20.0, F20.1, F20.4 or F20.5;

   (2) so many symptoms that the criteria for more than one of the subtypes listed in (1) above are met.

F20.4 Post-schizophrenic depression

A depressive episode, which may be prolonged, arising in the aftermath of a schizophrenic illness. Some schizophrenic symptoms, either 'positive' or 'negative', must still be present but they no longer dominate the clinical picture. These depressive states are associated with an increased risk of suicide. If the patient no longer has any schizophrenic symptoms, a depressive episode should be diagnosed (F32.–). If schizophrenic symptoms are still florid and prominent, the diagnosis should remain that of the appropriate schizophrenic subtype (F20.0–F20.3).

DCR-10

A. The general criteria for schizophrenia (F20.0–F20.3) must have been met within the previous 12 months, but are not met at the present time.

B. One of the conditions in criterion G1 (2) a,b,c or d for F20.0–F20.3 must still be present.

C. The depressive symptoms must be sufficiently prolonged, severe and extensive to meet criteria for at least a mild depressive episode (F32.0).

F20.5 Residual schizophrenia

A chronic stage in the development of a schizophrenic illness in which there has been a clear progression from an early stage to a later stage characterized by long-term, though not necessarily irreversible, 'negative', symptoms, e.g. psychomotor slowing; underactivity; blunting of affect; passivity and lack of initiative; poverty of quantity or content of speech; poor non-verbal communication by facial expression, eye contact, voice modulation and posture; poor self-care and social performance.

Chronic undifferentiated schizophrenia

Restzustand (schizophrenic)

Schizophrenic residual state

DCR-10

A. The general criteria for schizophrenia (F20.0–F20.3) must have been met at some time in the past, but are not met at the present time.

B. At least four of the following 'negative' symptoms have been present throughout the previous 12 months:

  (1) psychomotor slowing or underactivity

  (2) definite blunting of affect

  (3) passivity and lack of initiative

  (4) poverty of either the quantity or the content of speech

  (5) poor non-verbal communication by facial expression, eye contact, voice modulation or posture

  (6) poor social performance or self-care.

A disorder in which there is insidious but progressive development of oddities of conduct, inability to meet the demands of society and decline in total performance. The characteristic negative features of residual schizophrenia (e.g. blunting of affect and loss of volition) develop without being preceded by any overt psychotic symptoms.

DCR-10

A. There is slow but progressive development, over a period of at least 1 year, of all three of the following:

   (1) a significant and consistent change in the overall quality of some aspects of personal behaviour, manifest as loss of drive and interests, aimlessness, idleness, a self-absorbed attitude and social withdrawal;

   (2) gradual appearance and deepening of 'negative' symptoms such as marked apathy, paucity of speech, underactivity, blunting of affect, passivity and lack of initiative, and poor non-verbal communication (by facial expression, eye contact, voice modulation and posture);

   (3) marked decline in social, scholastic or occupational performance.

B. At no time are there any of the symptoms referred to in criterion G1 for F20.0–F20.3, nor are there hallucinations or well-formed delusions of any kind, i.e. the individual must never have met the criteria for any other types of schizophrenia, or for any other psychotic disorder.

C. There is no evidence of dementia or any other organic mental disorder listed in F00–F09.

Diagnostic notes

This controversial category has been retained because of its continued use in some countries. It is hoped that its presence here will stimulate investigations into its usefulness, and into its relationship with schizoid personality disorder and schizotypal disorder. Criterion A(3) above is one of the few exceptions in this classification to the general rule that the social consequences of disorders (that is, social role handicap) should not be included among the diagnostic criteria that define the disorders (see Note 4 in Notes for Users).

F20.8	Other schizophrenia

Cenesthopathic schizophrenia

Schizophreniform

• disorder NOS

• psychosis NOS

Excludes: brief schizophrenia-like disorders (F23.2)

F20.9	Schizophrenia, unspecified

F21	Schizotypal disorder

A disorder characterized by eccentric behaviour and anomalies of thinking and affect which resemble those seen in schizophrenia, although no definite and characteristic schizophrenic anomalies occur at any stage. The symptoms may include a cold or inappropriate affect; anhedonia; odd or eccentric behaviour; a tendency to social withdrawal; paranoid or bizarre ideas not amounting to true delusions; obsessive ruminations; thought disorder and perceptual disturbances; occasional transient quasipsychotic episodes with intense illusions, auditory or other hallucinations, and delusion-like ideas, usually occurring without external provocation. There is no definite onset, and evolution and course are usually those of a personality disorder.

Latent schizophrenic reaction
Schizophrenia:

- borderline

- latent

- prepsychotic

- prodromal

- pseudoneurotic

- pseudopsychopathic

Schizotypal personality disorder

Excludes: Asperger's syndrome (F84.5)

schizoid personality disorder (F60.1)

DCR-10

A. The subject must have manifested, either continuously or repeatedly over a period of at least 2 years, at least four of the following:

   (1) inappropriate or constricted affect, with the individual appearing cold and aloof;

   (2) behaviour or appearance that is odd, eccentric or peculiar;

   (3) poor rapport with others and a tendency to social withdrawal;

   (4) odd beliefs or magical thinking, influencing behaviour and inconsistent with subcultural norms;

   (5) suspiciousness or paranoid ideas;

   (6) ruminations without inner resistance, often with dysmorphophobic, sexual or aggressive contents;

   (7) unusual perceptual experiences, including somatosensory (bodily) or other illusions, depersonalization or derealization;

⇒

    (8) vague, circumstantial, metaphorical, overelaborate or often stereotyped thinking, manifested by odd speech or in other ways, without gross incoherence;

    (9) occasional transient quasipsychotic episodes with intense illusions, auditory or other hallucinations, and delusion-like ideas, usually occurring without external provocation.

B.   The subject must never have met the criteria for any disorder in F20.– (schizophrenia).

Diagnostic note

This disorder is placed here because there is some evidence that it is related to schizophrenia (as one of the 'schizophrenic spectrum' disorders). Schizoid personality disorder (F60.1) can be found on page 225.

F22   Persistent delusional disorders

Includes a variety of disorders in which long-standing delusions constitute the only, or the most conspicuous, clinical characteristic and which cannot be classified as organic, schizophrenic or affective. Delusional disorders that have lasted for less than a few months should be classified, at least temporarily, under F23.–.

F22.0   Delusional disorder

A disorder characterized by the development either of a single delusion or of a set of related delusions that are usually persistent and sometimes lifelong. The content of the delusion or delusions is very variable. Clear and persistent auditory hallucinations (voices), schizophrenic symptoms such as delusions of control and marked blunting of affect, and definite evidence of brain disease are all incompatible with this diagnosis.

However, the presence of occasional or transitory auditory hallucinations, particularly in elderly patients, does not rule out this diagnosis, provided that they are not typically schizophrenic and form only a small part of the overall clinical picture.

Paranoia

Paranoid:

- psychosis
- state

Paraphrenia (late)

Sensitiver Beziehungswahn

Excludes: paranoid:

- personality disorder (F60.0)
- psychosis, psychogenic (F23.3)
- reaction (F23.3)
- schizophrenia (F20.0

DCR-10

A. A delusion or a set of related delusions, other than those listed as typically schizophrenic in criterion G1 (1)(b) or (d) for F20.0–F20.3 (i.e. other than completely impossible or culturally inappropriate), must be present. The commonest examples are persecutory, grandiose, hypochondriacal, jealous (zelotypic) or erotic delusions.

B. The delusion(s) in criterion A must be present for at least 3 months.

C. The general criteria for schizophrenia (F20.0–F20.3) are not fulfilled.

D. There must be no persistent hallucinations in any modality (but there may be transitory or occasional auditory hallucinations that are not in the third person or giving a running commentary).

⇒

E. Depressive symptoms (or even a depressive episode (F32.–) may be present intermittently, provided that the delusions persist at times when there is no disturbance of mood.

F. *Most commonly used exclusion clause.* There must be no evidence of primary or secondary organic mental disorder as listed under F00–F09, or of a psychotic disorder due to psychoactive substance use (F1*x*.5).

Specification for possible subtypes

The following types may be specified if desired: persecutory; litiginous; self-referential; grandiose; hypochondriacal (somatic); jealous; erotomanic.

| F22.8 | Other persistent delusional disorders |

Disorders in which the delusion or delusions are accompanied by persistent hallucinatory voices or by schizophrenic symptoms that do not justify a diagnosis of schizophrenia (F20.–).

Delusional dysmorphophobia

Involutional paranoid state

Paranoia querulans

Diagnostic note

This is a residual category for persistent delusional disorders that do not meet the criteria for delusional disorder (F22.0). Disorders in which delusions are accompanied by persistent hallucinatory voices or by schizophrenic symptoms that are insufficient to meet the criteria for schizophrenia (F20.–) should be coded here. Delusional disorders that have lasted for less than 3 months should, however, be coded, at least temporarily, under F23.–.

F22.9	Persistent delusional disorder, unspecified

F23	Acute and transient psychotic disorders

A heterogeneous group of disorders characterized by the acute onset of psychotic symptoms such as delusions, hallucinations and perceptual disturbances, and by the severe disruption of ordinary behaviour. Acute onset is defined as a crescendo development of a clearly abnormal clinical picture in about 2 weeks or less. For these disorders there is no evidence of organic causation. Perplexity and puzzlement are often present but disorientation for time, place and person is not persistent or severe enough to justify a diagnosis of organically caused delirium (F05.–). Complete recovery usually occurs within a few months, often within a few weeks or even days. If the disorder persists, a change in diagnosis will be necessary. The disorder may or may not be associated with acute stress, defined as usually stressful events preceding the onset by 1–2 weeks.

> **DCR-10**
>
> G1. There is acute onset of delusions, hallucinations, incomprehensible or incoherent speech, or any combination of these. The time interval between the first appearance of any psychotic symptoms and the presentation of the fully developed disorder should not exceed 2 weeks.
>
> G2. If transient states of perplexity, misidentification or impairment of attention and concentration are present, they do not fulfil the criteria for organically caused clouding of consciousness as specified for F05.–, criterion A.
>
> G3. The disorder does not meet the symptomatic criteria for manic episode (F30.–),

⇒

depressive episode (F32.–), or recurrent depressive disorder (F33.–).

G4. There is insufficient evidence of recent psychoactive substance use to fulfil the criteria for intoxication (F1x.0), harmful use (F1x.1), dependence (F1x.2) or withdrawal states (F1x.3 and F1x.4). The continued moderate and largely unchanged use of alcohol or drugs in amounts or with the frequency to which the individual is accustomed does not necessarily rule out the use of F23; this must be decided by clinical judgement and the requirements of the research project in question.

G5. *Most commonly used exclusion clause.* There must be no organic mental disorder (F00–F09) or serious metabolic disturbances affecting the central nervous system (this does not include childbirth).

A fifth character should be used to specify whether the acute onset of the disorder is associated with acute stress (occurring 2 weeks or less before evidence of first psychotic symptoms):

F23.x0 without associated acute stress

F23.x1 with associated acute stress

For research purposes it is recommended that change of the disorder from a non-psychotic to a clearly psychotic state is further specified as either abrupt (onset within 48 hours) or acute (onset in more than 48 hours but less than 2 weeks).

F23.0 Acute polymorphic psychotic disorder without symptoms of schizophrenia

An acute psychotic disorder in which hallucinations, delusions or perceptual disturbances are obvious but markedly variable, changing from day to day or even from hour to hour. Emotional turmoil, with intense transient feelings of happiness or ecstasy, or anxiety and irritability, is also frequently present. The polymorphism and instability are characteristic for the overall clinical picture and the psychotic features do not justify a diagnosis of schizophrenia (F20.–). These disorders often have an abrupt onset, developing rapidly within a few days, and they frequently show a rapid resolution of symptoms, with no recurrence. If the symptoms persist the diagnosis should be changed to persistent delusional disorder (F22.–).

Boufée delirante without symptoms of schizophrenia, or unspecified

Cycloid psychosis without symptoms of schizophrenia, or unspecified

DCR-10

A. The general criteria for acute and transient psychotic disorders (F23) must be met.

B. Symptoms change rapidly in both type and intensity from day to day or within the same day.

C. Any type of either hallucinations or delusions occurs for at least several hours, at any time from the onset of the disorder.

D. Symptoms from at least two of the following categories occur at the same time:

(1) emotional turmoil, characterized by intense feelings of happiness or ecstasy, or overwhelming anxiety or marked irritability;

(2) perplexity, or misidentification of people or places;

(3) increased or decreased motility, to a marked degree

E. If any of the symptoms listed for schizo-

⇒

phrenia (F20.0–F20.3) criteria G1(1) and (2) are present, they are present only for a minority of the time from the onset, i.e. criterion B of F23.1 is not fulfilled.

F. The total duration of the disorder does not exceed 3 months.

F23.1 Acute polymorphic disorder with symptoms of schizophrenia

An acute psychotic disorder in which the polymorphic and unstable clinical picture is present, as described in F23.0; despite this instability, however, some symptoms typical of schizophrenia are also in evidence for the majority of the time. If the schizophrenic symptoms persist the diagnosis should be changed to schizophrenia (F20.–).

Bouffée delirante with symptoms of schizophrenia

Cycloid psychosis with symptoms of schizophrenia

DCR-10

A. Criteria A, B, C and D of acute polymorphic disorder (F23.0) must be met.

B. Some of the symptoms for schizophrenia (F20.0–F20.3) must have been present for the majority of the time since the onset of the disorder, although the full criteria need not be met, i.e. at least one of the symptoms in criteria G1(1)–G1(2).

C. The symptoms of schizophrenia in criterion B above do not persist for more than 1 month.

An acute psychotic disorder in which the psychotic symptoms are comparatively stable and justify a diagnosis of schizophrenia, but have lasted for less than about 1 month; the polymorphic unstable features, as described in F23.0, are absent. If the schizophrenic symptoms persist the diagnosis should be changed to schizophrenia (F20.–).

Acute (undifferentiated) schizophrenia

Brief schizophreniform:

- disorder
- psychosis

Oneirophrenia

Schizophrenic reaction

Excludes: organic delusional [schizophrenia-like] disorder (F06.2) schizophreniform disorder NOS (F20.8).

DCR-10

A. The general criteria for acute and transient psychotic disorder (F23) must be met.

B. The criteria for schizophrenia (F20.0–F20.3) are met, with the exception of the criterion for duration.

C. The disorder does not meet criteria B, C and D for acute polymorphic psychotic disorder (F23.0)

D. The total duration of the disorder does not exceed 1 month.

F23.3 Other acute predominantly delusional psychotic disorders

Acute psychotic disorders in which comparatively stable delusions or hallucinations are the main clinical features, but do not justify a diagnosis of schizophrenia (F20.–). If the delusions persist the diagnosis should be changed to persistent delusional disorder (F22.–).

Paranoid reaction

Psychogenic paranoid psychosis

DCR-10

A. The general criteria for acute and transient psychotic disorder (F23) must be met.

B. Relatively stable delusions and/or hallucinations are present but do not fulfil the symptomatic criteria for schizophrenia (F20.0-F20.3).

C. The disorder does not meet the criteria for acute polymorphic psychotic disorder (F23.0).

D. The total duration of the disorder does not exceed 3 months.

F23.8 Other acute and transient psychotic disorders

Any other specified acute psychotic disorders for which there is no evidence of organic causation and which do not justify classification to F23.0–F23.3.

Diagnostic note

Any other acute psychotic disorders that are not classifiable under any other category in F23 (such as acute psychotic states in which definite delusions or hallucinations occur but persist for only small proportions of the time) should be coded here. States of undifferentiated excitement should also be coded here if more detailed information about the patient's mental state is not available, provided that there is no evidence of an organic cause.

F23.9	Acute and transient psychotic disorder, unspecified

Brief reactive psychosis NOS

Reactive psychosis

F24	Induced delusional disorder

A delusional disorder shared by two or more people with close emotional links. Only one of the people suffers from a genuine psychotic disorder; the delusions are induced in the other(s) and usually disappear when the people are separated.

Folie à deux (trois, etc.)

Induced:

- paranoid disorder
- psychotic disorder

DCR-10

A. The individual(s) must develop a delusion or delusional system originally held by someone else with a disorder classified in F20–F23.

B. The people concerned must have an unusually close relationship with one another, and be relatively isolated from other people.

C. The individual(s) must not have held the belief in question before contact with the other person, and must not have suffered from any other disorder classified in F20–F23 in the past.

Episodic disorders in which both affective and schizophrenic symptoms are prominent but which do not justify a diagnosis of either schizophrenia or depressive or manic episodes. Other conditions in which affective symptoms are superimposed on a pre-existing schizophrenic illness, or coexist or alternate with persistent delusional disorders of other kinds, are classified under F20–F29. Mood-incongruent psychotic symptoms in affective disorders by themselves do not justify a diagnosis of schizoaffective disorder.

Diagnostic notes

The relationship of this group of disorders with both schizophrenia and the affective disorders are uncertain. Detailed criteria have been specified here in the hope of stimulating research into their aetiology and outcome. The diagnosis depends upon difficult clinical judgements about the approximate 'balance' between the number, severity and duration of the schizophrenic and the affective symptoms.

DCR-10

G1. The disorder meets the criteria for one of the affective disorders (F30.–, F31.–, F32.–) of moderate or severe degree, as specified for each category.

G2. Symptoms from at least one of the groups listed below must be clearly present for most of the time during a period of at least 2 weeks (these groups are almost the same as for schizophrenia (F20.0–F20.3):

   (1) thought echo, thought insertion or withdrawal, thought broadcasting (criterion G1(1)a for F20.0–F20.3);

   (2) delusions of control, influence or passivity, clearly referred to body or limb movements or specific thoughts,

$\Rightarrow$

actions or sensations (criterion G1(1)b
for F20.0–F20.3);

(3) hallucinatory voices giving a running
commentary on the patient's
behaviour or discussing the patient
between themselves, or other types of
hallucinatory voices coming from some
part of the body (criterion G1(1)c for
F20.0–F20.3);

(4) persistent delusions of other kinds that
are culturally inappropriate and
completely impossible, but not merely
grandiose or persecutory (criterion
G1(1)d for F20.0–F20.3), e.g. has
visited other worlds; can control the
clouds by breathing in and out; can
communicate with plants or animals
without speaking;

(5) grossly irrelevant or incoherent speech,
or frequent use of neologisms (a
marked form of criterion G1(2)b for
F20.0–F20.3);

(6) intermittent but frequent appearance
of some forms of catatonic behaviour,
such as posturing, waxy flexibility and
negativism (criterion G1(2)c for F20.0–
F20.3);

G3. Criteria G1 and G2 above must be met
within the same episode of the disorder, and
concurrently for at least part of the episode.
Symptoms from both G1 and G2 must be
prominent in the clinical picture.

G4. *Most commonly used exclusion clause.* The disorder is not attributable to organic mental
disorder (in the sense of F00–F09) or to
psychoactive substance-related intoxication, dependence or withdrawal (F10–
F19).

F25.0 Schizoaffective disorder, manic type

A disorder in which both schizophrenic and manic symptoms are prominent so that the episode of illness does not justify a diagnosis of either schizophrenia or a manic episode. This category should be used for both a single episode and a recurrent disorder in which the majority of episodes are schizoaffective, manic type.

Schizoaffective psychosis, manic type

Schizophreniform psychosis, manic type

> **DCR-10**
>
> A. The general criteria for schizoaffective disorder (F25) must be met.
>
> B. Criteria for a manic disorder (F30.1 or F31.1) must be met.

F25.1 Schizoaffective disorder, depressive type

A disorder in which both schizophrenic and depressive symptoms are prominent so that the episode of illness does not justify a diagnosis of either schizophrenic or a depressive episode.

This category should be used for both a single episode and a recurrent disorder in which the majority of episodes are schizoaffective, depressive type.

Schizoaffective psychosis, depressive type

Schizophreniform psychosis, depressive type

> **DCR-10**
>
> A. The general criteria for schizoaffective disorder (F25) must be met.

$\Rightarrow$

B. The criteria for a depressive disorder of at
    least moderate severity (F31.3, F31.4, F32.1,
    F32.2) must be met.

F25.2   Schizoaffective disorder, mixed type

Cyclic schizophrenia

Mixed schizophrenic and affective psychosis

DCR-10

A. The general criteria for schizoaffective dis-
    order (F25) must be met.

B. The criteria for mixed bipolar affective dis-
    order (F31.6) must be met.

F25.8   Other schizoaffective disorders

F25.9   Schizoaffective disorder, unspecified

Schizoaffective psychosis NOS

If desired, further subtypes of schizoaffective disorder may be specified, according to the longitudinal development of the disorder, as follows:

F25.x0 concurrent affective and
        schizophrenic symptoms only
        (symptoms as defined in criterion G2
        for F25);

F25.x1 concurrent affective and
        schizophrenic symptoms, plus
        persistence of schizophrenic
        symptoms beyond the duration of
        affective symptoms.

F28 Other non-organic psychotic disorders

Delusional or hallucinatory disorders that do not justify a diagnosis of schizophrenia (F20.–), persistent delusional disorders (F22.–), acute and transient psychotic disorders (F23.–), psychotic types of manic episode (F30.2) or severe depressive episode (F32.3).

Chronic hallucinatory psychosis

Diagnostic note

Any other combinations of symptoms not covered by the previous categories F20–F25, such as delusions other than those listed as typically schizophrenic under criterion G1(1)b or d for F20.0–F20.3 (i.e. other than completely impossible or culturally inappropriate) plus catatonia, should also be included here.

F29 Unspecified non-organic psychosis

Psychosis NOS

Excludes: mental disorder NOS (F99)
          organic or symptomatic psychosis NOS (F09)

Mood (affective) disorders (F30–F39)

This block contains disorders in which the fundamental disturbance is a change in affect or mood to depression (with or without associated anxiety) or to elation. The mood change is usually accompanied by a change in the overall level of activity; most of the other symptoms are either secondary to, or easily understood in the context of, the change in mood and activity. Most of these disorders tend to be recurrent and the onset of individual episodes can often be related to stressful events or situations.

Diagnostic notes

Mood disorders arising in childhood or adolescence should be recorded by using categories in this section, so long as they meet the descriptions given (but see also F92, Mixed disorders of conduct and emotions).

This classification allows for the diagnosis of single first episodes of mania and hypomania without the implication that there is a necessary overall diagnosis of bipolar affective disorder; this is because substantial proportions of patients have only one episode of illness.

It is acknowledged that the symptoms referred to here as 'somatic' could have equally well been called 'melancholic', 'vital', 'biological' or 'endogenomorphic'. The status of this syndrome is still uncertain, but it has been included because many clinicians believe that the concept is useful.

F30 Manic episodes

All the subdivisions of this category should be used only for a single episode. Hypomanic or manic episodes in individuals who have had one or more previous affective episodes (depressive, hypomanic, manic or mixed) should be coded as bipolar affective disorder (F31.–).

Includes: bipolar disorder, single manic episode.

F30.0   Hypomania

A disorder characterized by a persistent mild elevation of mood, increased energy and activity, and usually marked feelings of well-being and both physical and mental efficiency. Increased sociability, talkativeness, over-familiarity, increased sexual energy and a decreased need for sleep are often present, but not to the extent that they lead to severe disruption of work or result in social rejection. Irritability, conceit and boorish behaviour may take the place of the more usual euphoric sociability. The disturbances of mood and behaviour are not accompanied by hallucinations or delusions.

DCR-10

A.   The mood is elevated or irritable to a degree that is definitely abnormal for the individual concerned and sustained for at least 4 consecutive days.

B.   At least three of the following signs must be present, leading to some interference with personal functioning in daily living:

(1)   increased activity or physical restlessness

(2)   increased talkativeness

(3)   difficulty in concentration or distractability

(4)   decreased need for sleep

(5)   increased sexual energy

(6)   mild overspending, or other types of reckless or irresponsible behaviour

(7)   increased sociability or overfamiliarity.

C.   The episode does not meet the criteria for mania (F30.1 and F30.2), bipolar affective disorder (F31.–), depressive episode (F32.–), cyclothymia (F34.0) or anorexia nervosa (F50.0).

⇒

D. *Most commonly used exclusion cause*. The episode is not attributable to psychoactive substance use (F10–F19) or to any organic mental disorder (in the sense of F00–F09).

F30.1   Mania without psychotic symptoms

Mood is elevated out of keeping with the patient's circumstances and may vary from carefree joviality to almost uncontrollable excitement. Elation is accompanied by increased energy, resulting in over-activity, pressure of speech and a decreased need for sleep. Attention cannot be sustained and there is often marked distractability. Self-esteem is often inflated, with grandiose ideas and overconfidence. Loss of normal social inhibitions may result in behaviour that is reckless, foolhardy or inappropriate to the circumstances and out of character.

Diagnostic notes

In some manic episodes the mood is one of irritability or suspiciousness rather than elation.

DCR-10

A. Mood must be predominantly elevated, expansive or irritable, and definitely abnormal for the individual concerned. The mood change must be prominent and sustained for at least 1 week (unless it is severe enough to require hospital admission).

B. At least three of the following signs must be present (four if the mood is merely irritable), leading to severe interference with personal functioning in daily living:

   (1) increased activity or physical restlessness

   (2) increased talkativeness ('pressure of speech')

⇒

(3) flight of ideas or the subjective experience of thoughts racing

(4) loss of normal social inhibitions, resulting in behaviour that is inappropriate to the circumstances

(5) decreased need for sleep

(6) inflated self-esteem or grandiosity

(7) distractibility or constant changes in activity or plans

(8) behaviour that is foolhardy or reckless and whose risks the individual does not recognize, e.g. spending sprees, foolish enterprises, reckless driving

(9) marked sexual energy or sexual indiscretions

C. There are no hallucinations or delusions, although perceptual disorders may occur (e.g. subjective hyperacusis, appreciation of colours as especially vivid).

D. *Most commonly used exclusion clause.* The episode is not attributable to psychoactive substance use (F10–F19) or to any organic mental disorder (in the sense of F00–F09).

F30.2   Mania with psychotic symptoms

In addition to the clinical picture described in F30.1, delusions (usually grandiose) or hallucinations (usually of voices speaking directly to the patient) are present, or the excitement, excessive motor activity and flight of ideas are so extreme that the subject is incomprehensible or inaccessible to ordinary communications.

Mania with:

- mood-congruent psychotic symptoms

- mood-incongruent psychotic symptoms

Manic stupor

Diagnostic notes

Differentiation of mania from schizophrenia is a common diagnostic problem, particularly if the patient is seen for the first time at the height of the illness. Partial response to medication may also create diagnostic problems, since overactivity often responds to medication before delusions and hallucinations.

DCR-10

A. The episode meets the criteria for mania without psychotic symptoms (F30.1), with the exception of criterion C.

B. The episode does not simultaneously meet the criteria for schizophrenia (F20.0–F20) or schizoaffective disorder, manic type (F25.0).

C. Delusions or hallucinations are present, other than those listed as typically schizophrenia – criterion G1(1) b, c and d for F20.0–F20.3 (i.e. delusions other than those that are completely impossible or culturally inappropriate, and hallucinations that are not in the third person or giving a running commentary). The commonest examples are those with grandiose, self-referential, erotic or persecutory content.

D. *Most commonly used exclusion clause.* The episode is not attributable to psychoactive substance use (F10–F19) or to any organic mental disorder (in the sense of F00–F09).

   A fifth character may be used to specify whether the hallucinations or delusions are congruent or incongruent with the mood:

   F30.20 with mood-congruent psychotic symptoms (such as grandiose delusions or voices telling the subject that he has superhuman powers)

$\Rightarrow$

> F30.21 with mood-incongruent psychotic
> symptoms (such as voices speaking
> to the subject about affectively
> neutral topics, or delusions of
> reference or persecution).

| F30.8 | Other manic episodes |

| F30.9 | Manic episode, unspecified |

Mania NOS

| F31 | Bipolar affective disorder |

A disorder characterized by two or more episodes in which the patient's mood and activity levels are significantly disturbed, this disturbance consisting on some occasions of an elevation of mood and increased energy and activity (hypomania or mania) and on others of a lowering of mood and decreased energy and activity (depression). Repeated episodes of hypomania or mania only are classified as bipolar (F31.8).

Includes: manic-depressive:

- illness
- psychosis
- reaction

Excludes: bipolar disorder, single manic episode (F30.–)

cyclothymia (F34.0)

Diagnostic notes

Episodes are demarcated by a switch to an episode of opposite or mixed type, or by a remission.

F31.0 Bipolar affective disorder, current episode hypomanic

The patient is currently hypomanic, and has had at least one other affective episode (hypomanic, manic, depressive or mixed) in the past.

DCR-10

A. The current episode meets the criteria for hypomania (F30.0).

B. There has been at least one other affective episode in the past, meeting the criteria for hypomanic or manic episode (F30.–), depressive episode (F32.–) or mixed affective episode (F38.00).

F31.1 Bipolar affective disorder, current episode manic without psychotic symptoms

The patient is currently manic, without psychotic symptoms (as in F30.1), and has had at least one other affective episode (hypomanic, manic depressive or mixed) in the past.

DCR-10

A. The current episode meets the criteria for mania without psychotic symptoms (F30.1)

B. There has been at least one other affective episode in the past, meeting the criteria for hypomanic or manic episode (F30.–), depressive episode (F32.–) or mixed affective episode (F38.00).

F31.2 Bipolar affective disorder, current episode manic with psychotic symptoms

The patient is currently manic, with psychotic symptoms (as in F30.2), and has had at least one other affective episode (hypomanic, manic, depressive or mixed) in the past.

DCR-10

A. The current episode meets the criteria for mania with psychotic symptoms (F30.2).

B. There has been at least one other affective episode in the past, meeting the criteria for hypomanic or manic episode (F30.–), depressive episode (F32.–) or mixed affective episode (F38.00).

A fifth character may be used to specify whether the psychotic symptoms are congruent or incongruent with the mood:

F31.20 with mood-congruent psychotic symptoms

F31.21 with mood-incongruent psychotic symptoms.

F31.3 Bipolar affective disorder, current episode mild or moderate depression

The patient is currently depressed, as in a depressive episode of either mild or moderate severity (F32.0 or F32.1) and has had at least one authenticated hypomanic, manic or mixed affective episode in the past.

DCR-10

A. The current episode meets the criteria for a depressive episode of either mild (F32.0) or moderate (F32.1) severity.

⇒

B. There has been at least one other affective episode in the past, meeting the criteria for hypomanic or manic episode (F30.–) or mixed affective episode (F38.00).

A fifth character may be used to specify the presence of the 'somatic syndrome', as defined in F32.–, in the current episode of depression:

F31.30 without somatic syndrome

F31.31 with somatic syndrome.

F31.4 Bipolar affective disorder, current episode severe depression without psychotic symptoms

The patient is currently depressed, as in severe depressive episode without psychotic symptoms (F32.2), and has had at least one authenticated hypomanic, manic or mixed affective episode in the past.

DCR-10

A. The current episode meets the criteria for a severe depressive episode without psychotic symptoms (F32.2).

B. There has been at least one well authenticated hypomanic or manic episode (F30.–) or mixed affective episode (F38.00) in the past.

F31.5 Bipolar affective disorder, current episode severe depression with psychotic symptoms

The patient is currently depressed, as in severe depressive episode with psychotic symptoms (F32.3), and has had at least one authenticated hypomanic, manic or mixed affective episode in the past.

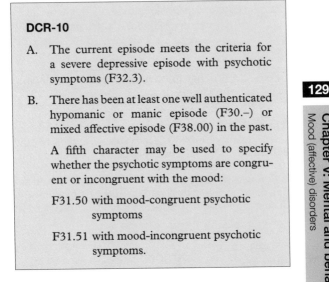

DCR-10

A. The current episode meets the criteria for a severe depressive episode with psychotic symptoms (F32.3).

B. There has been at least one well authenticated hypomanic or manic episode (F30.–) or mixed affective episode (F38.00) in the past.

A fifth character may be used to specify whether the psychotic symptoms are congruent or incongruent with the mood:

F31.50 with mood-congruent psychotic symptoms

F31.51 with mood-incongruent psychotic symptoms.

| F31.6 | Bipolar affective disorder, current episode mixed |

The patient has had at least one authenticated hypomanic, manic, depressive or mixed affective episode in the past, and currently exhibits either a mixture or a rapid alteration of manic and depressive symptoms.

Excludes: single mixed affective episode (F38.0)

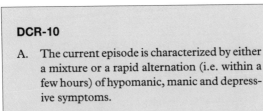

DCR-10

A. The current episode is characterized by either a mixture or a rapid alternation (i.e. within a few hours) of hypomanic, manic and depressive symptoms.

B. Both manic and depressive symptoms must be prominent most of the time during a period of at least 2 weeks.

⟹

C. There has been at least one well authenticated hypomanic or manic episode (F30.–), depressive episode (F32.–) or mixed affective episode (F38.00) in the past.

F31.7 Bipolar affective disorder, currently in remission

The patient has had at least one authenticated hypomanic, manic or mixed affective episode in the past, and at least one other affective episode (hypomanic, manic, depressive or mixed) in addition, but is not currently suffering from any significant mood disturbance and has not done so for several months. Periods of remission during prophylactic treatment should be coded here.

DCR-10

A. The current state does not meet the criteria for depressive or manic episode of any severity, or for any other mood disorder in F30–F39 (possibly because of treatment to reduce the risk of future episodes).

B. There has been at least one well authenticated hypomanic or manic episode (F30.–) in the past and in addition at least one other affective episode, hypomanic or manic (F30.–), depressive (F32.–) or mixed (F38.00).

F31.8 Other bipolar affective disorders

Bipolar II disorder

Recurrent manic episodes

| F31.9 | Bipolar affective disorder, unspecified |

| F32 | Depressive episode |

In typical mild, moderate or severe depressive episodes the patient suffers from lowering of mood, reduction of energy and decrease in activity. Capacity for enjoyment, interest and concentration is reduced, and marked tiredness after even minimum effort is common. Sleep is usually disturbed and appetite diminished. Self-esteem and self-confidence are almost always reduced and, even in the mild form, some ideas of guilt or worthlessness are often present. The lowered mood varies little from day to day, is unresponsible to circumstances and may be accompanied by so-called 'somatic' symptoms, such as loss of interest and pleasurable feelings, waking in the morning several hours before the usual time, depression worst in the morning, marked psychomotor retardation, agitation, loss of appetite, weight loss and loss of libido. Depending upon the number and severity of the symptoms, a depressive episode may be specified as mild, moderate or severe.

Includes: single episodes of:

- depressive reaction

- psychogenic depression

- reactive depression

Excludes: adjustment disorder (F43.2)

recurrent depressive disorder (F33.–)

when associated with conduct disorders in F91.– (F92.0)

DCR-10

G1. The depressive episode should last for at least 2 weeks.

G2. There have been no hypomanic or manic symptoms sufficient to meet the criteria for hypomanic or manic episode (F30.–) at any time in the individual's life.

⇒

G3. *Most commonly used exclusion clause*. The episode is not attributable to psychoactive substance use (F10–F19) or to any organic mental disorder (in the sense of F00–F09).

Somatic syndrome

Some depressive symptoms are widely regarded as having special clinical significance and are here called 'somatic'. (Terms such as biological, vital, melancholic or endogenomorphic are used for this syndrome in other classifications.)

A fifth character (as indicated in F31.3; F32.0 and F32.1; F33.0 and F33.1) may be used to specify the presence or absence of the somatic syndrome. To qualify for the somatic syndrome, four of the following symptoms should be present:

(1) marked loss of interest or pleasure in activities that are normally pleasurable;

(2) lack of emotional reactions to events or activities that normally produce an emotional response;

(3) waking in the morning 2 hours or more before the usual time;

(4) depression worse in the morning;

(5) objective evidence of marked psychomotor retardation or agitation (remarked on or reported by other people);

(6) marked loss of appetite;

(7) weight loss (5% or more of body weight in the past month);

(8) marked loss of libido.

Diagnostic notes

In the *ICD-10 Classification of mental and behavioural disorders: clinical descriptions and diagnostic guidelines*, the presence or absence of the somatic syndrome is not specified for severe depressive episode, since it is presumed to be present in most cases. For research purposes, however, it may be advisable to allow for the coding of the absence of the somatic syndrome in severe depressive episode.

F32.0 Mild depressive episode

Two or three of the symptoms (noted under F32 above and also listed below) are usually present. The patient is usually distressed by these but will probably be able to continue with most activities.

DCR-10

A. The general criteria for depressive episode (F32) must be met.

B. At least two of the following three symptoms must be present:

(1) depressed mood to a degree that is definitely abnormal for the individual, present for most of the day and almost every day, largely uninfluenced by circumstances, and sustained for at least 2 weeks;

(2) loss of interest or pleasure in activities that are normally pleasurable;

(3) decreased energy or increased fatiguability.

C. An additional symptom or symptoms from the following list should be present, to give a total of at least four:

(1) loss of confidence or self esteem;

(2) unreasonable feelings of self-reproach or excessive and inappropriate guilt;

(3) recurrent thoughts of death or suicide, or any suicidal behaviour;

$\Rightarrow$

    (4) complaints or evidence of diminished
        ability to think or concentrate, such as
        indecisiveness or vacillation;

    (5) change in psychomotor activity, with
        agitation or retardation (either
        subjective or objective);

    (6) sleep disturbance of any type;

    (7) change in appetite (decrease or increase)
        with corresponding weight change.

A fifth character may be used to specify the presence or absence of the 'somatic syndrome'
(defined on page 132):

    F.32.00 without somatic syndrome

    F32.01 with somatic syndrome.

F32.1   Moderate depressive episode

Four or more of the symptoms (noted under F32 above
and also listed below) are usually present and the patient
is likely to have great difficulty in continuing with ordinary activities.

DCR-10

A. The general criteria for depressive episode
    (F32) must be met.

B. At least two of the three symptoms listed for
    F32.0, criterion B, must be present.

C. Additional symptoms from F32.0, criterion
    C, must be present, to give a total of at least
    six.

A fifth character may be used to specify the presence or absence of the 'somatic syndrome'
(defined on page 132):

$\Rightarrow$

F32.10 without somatic syndrome

F32.11 with somatic syndrome.

F32.2 Severe depressive episode without psychotic symptoms

An episode of depression in which several of the above symptoms are marked and distressing, typically loss of self-esteem and ideas of worthiness or guilt. Suicidal thoughts and acts are common and a number of 'somatic' symptoms are usually present.

Agitated depression ⎤
Major depression ⎬ single episode without psychotic symptoms
Vital depression ⎦

Diagnostic notes

If important symptoms such as agitation or retardation are marked, the patient may be unwilling or unable to describe many symptoms in detail. An overall grading of severe episode may still be justified in such a case.

DCR-10

A. The general criteria for depressive episode (F32) must be met.

B. All three of the symptoms in criterion B, F32.0, must be present.

C. Additional symptoms from F32.0, criterion C, must be present, to give a total of at least eight.

D. There must be no hallucinations, delusions or depressive stupor.

F32.3 Severe depressive episode with psychotic symptoms

An episode of depression as described in F32.2, but with the presence of hallucinations delusions, psychomotor retardation or stupor so severe that ordinary social activities are impossible; there may be danger to life from suicide, dehydration or starvation. The hallucinations and delusions may or may not be mood-congruent. Single episodes of:

- major depression with psychotic symptoms
- psychogenic depressive psychosis
- psychotic depression
- reactive depressive psychosis

DCR-10

A. The general criteria for depressive episode (F32) must be met.

B. The criteria for severe depressive episode without psychotic symptoms (F32.2) must be met with the exception of criterion D.

C. The criteria for schizophrenia (F20.0–F20.3) or schizoaffective disorder, depressive type (F25.1) are not met.

D. Either of the following must be present:

(1) delusions or hallucinations, other than those listed as typically schizophrenic in criterion G1(1)b, c and d for F20.0–F20.3 (i.e. delusions other than those that are completely impossible or culturally inappropriate, and hallucinations that are not in the third person or giving a running commentary); the commonest examples are those with depressive, guilty, hypochondriacal, nihilistic, self-referential or persecutory content;

(2) depressive stupor.

⇒

A fifth character may be used to specify whether the psychotic symptoms are congruent or incongruent with mood:

> F32.30 With mood-congruent psychotic symptoms (i.e. delusions of guilt, worthlessness, bodily disease or impending disaster, derisive or condemnatory auditory hallucinations)

> F32.31 With mood-incongruent psychotic symptoms (i.e. persecutory or self-referential delusions and hallucinations without an affective content).

F32.8 Other depressive episodes

Atypical depression

Single episodes of 'masked' depression NOS

Diagnostic notes

Episodes should be included here which do not fit the descriptions given for depressive episodes in F32.0–F32.3, but for which the overall diagnostic impression indicates that they are depressive in nature. Examples include fluctuating mixtures of depressive symptoms (particularly those of the somatic syndrome) with non-diagnostic symptoms such as tension, worry and distress, and mixtures of somatic depressive symptoms with persistent pain or fatigue not due to organic causes (as sometimes seen in general hospital services).

F32.9 Depressive episode, unspecified

Depression NOS

Depressive disorder NOS

F33   Recurrent depressive disorder

A disorder characterized by repeated episodes of depression as described for depressive episode (F32.–), without any history of independent episodes of mood elevation and increased energy (mania). There may, however, be brief episodes of mild mood elevation and overactivity (hypomania) immediately after a depressive episode, sometimes precipitated by antidepressant treatment. The more severe forms of recurrent depressive disorder (F33.2 and F33.3) have much in common with earlier concepts, such as manic–depressive depression, melancholia, vital depression and endogenous depression. The first episode may occur at any age from childhood to old age, the onset may be either acute or insidious, and the duration varies from a few weeks to many months. The risk that a patient with recurrent depressive disorder will have an episode of mania never disappears completely, however many depressive episodes have been experienced. If such an episode does occur, the diagnosis should be changed to bipolar affective disorder (F31.–).

Includes: recurrent episodes of:

- depressive reaction
- psychogenic depression
- reactive depression

seasonal depressive disorder

Excludes: recurrent brief depressive episodes (F38.1)

DCR-10

G1.   There has been at least one previous episode, mild (F32.0), moderate (F32.1) or severe (F32.2 or F32.3), lasting a minimum of 2 weeks and separated from the current episode by at least 2 months free from any significant mood symptoms.

G2.   At no time in the past has there been an episode meeting the criteria for hypomanic or manic episode (F30.–).

⇒

G3. *Most commonly used exclusion clause.* The episode is not attributable to psychoactive substance use (F10–F19) or to any organic mental disorder (in the sense of F00–F09).

It is recommended that the predominant type of previous episodes is specified (mild, moderate, severe, uncertain).

F33.0 Recurrent depressive disorder, current episode mild

A disorder characterized by repeated episodes of depression, the current episode being mild, as in F32.0, and without any history of mania.

DCR-10

A. The general criteria for recurrent depressive disorder (F33) are met.

B. The current episode meets the criteria for mild depressive episode (F32.0). A fifth character may be used to specify the presence or absence of the somatic syndrome, as defined in F32.–, in the current episode:

F33.00 without somatic syndrome

F33.01 with somatic syndrome.

F33.1 Recurrent depressive disorder, current episode moderate

A disorder characterized by repeated episodes of depression, the current episode being of moderate severity, as in F32.1, and without any history of mania.

DCR-10

A. The general criteria for recurrent depressive disorder (F33) are met.

B. The current episode meets the criteria for moderate depressive episode (F32.1). A fifth character may be used to specify the presence or absence of the somatic syndrome, as defined in F32.–, in the current episode:

F33.10 without somatic syndrome

F33.11 with somatic syndrome.

F33.2 Recurrent depressive disorder, current episode severe without psychotic symptoms

A disorder characterized by repeated episodes of depression, the current episode being severe without psychotic symptoms, as in F32.2, and without any history of mania.

Endogenous depression without psychotic symptoms

Major depression, current without psychotic symptoms

Manic–depressive psychosis, depressed type without psychotic symptoms

Vital depression, recurrent without psychotic symptoms

DCR-10

A. The general criteria for recurrent depressive disorder (F33) are met.

B. The current episode meets the criteria for severe depressive episode without psychotic symptoms (F32.2).

F33.3 Recurrent depressive disorder, current episode severe with psychotic symptoms

A disorder characterized by repeated episodes of depression, the current episode being severe with psychotic symptoms, as in F32.3, and with no previous episodes of mania.

Endogenous depression with psychotic symptoms

Manic–depressive psychosis, depressed type with psychotic symptoms

Recurrent severe episodes of:

- major depression with psychotic symptoms
- psychogenic depressive psychosis
- psychotic depression
- reactive depressive psychosis

DCR-10

A. The general criteria for recurrent depressive disorder (F33) are met.

B. The current episode meets the criteria for severe depressive episode with psychotic symptoms (F32.3).

   A fifth character may be used to specify whether the psychotic symptoms are congruent or incongruent with the mood:

   F33.30 with mood-congruent psychotic symptoms

   F33.31 with mood-incongruent psychotic symptoms.

F33.4 Recurrent depressive disorder, currently in remission

The patient has had two or more depressive episodes as described in F33.0–F33.3 in the past, but has been free from depressive symptoms for several months.

DCR-10

A. The general criteria for recurrent depressive disorder (F33) have been met in the past.

B. The current state does not meet the criteria for a depressive episode F32.– of any severity, or for any other disorder in F30–F39.

Diagnostic notes

This category can still be used if the patient is receiving treatment to reduce the risk of further episodes.

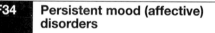

F33.8   Other recurrent depressive disorders

F33.9   Recurrent depressive disorder, unspecified

Monopolar depression NOS

F34   Persistent mood (affective) disorders

Persistent and usually fluctuating disorders of mood in which the majority of the individual episodes are not sufficiently severe to warrant being described as hypomanic or mild depressive episodes. Because they last for many years, and sometimes for the greater part of the patient's adult life, they involve considerable distress and disability. In some instances, recurrent or single manic or depressive episodes may become superimposed on a persistent affective disorder.

F34.0   Cyclothymia

A persistent instability of mood involving numerous periods of depression and mild elation, none of which is sufficiently severe or prolonged to justify a diagnosis of bipolar affective disorder (F31.–) or recurrent depressive disorder (F33.–). This disorder is frequently found in the relatives of patients with biopolar affective disorder. Some patients with cyclothymia eventually develop bipolar affective disorder.

Affective personality disorder

Cycloid personality

Cyclothymic personality

DCR-10

A. There must have been a period of at least 2 years of instability of mood involving several periods of both depression and hypomania, with or without intervening periods of normal mood.

B. None of the manifestations of depression or hypomania during such a 2-year period should be sufficiently severe or long-lasting to meet the criteria for manic episode or depressive episode (moderate or severe); however, manic or depressive episode(s) may have occurred before, or may develop after, such a period of persistent mood instability.

C. During at least some of the periods of depression at least three of the following should be present:

(1) reduced energy or activity

(2) insomnia

(3) loss of self-confidence or feelings of inadequacy

(4) difficulty in concentrating

(5) social withdrawal

(6) loss of interest in or enjoyment of sex and other pleasurable activities

⇒

(7) reduced talkativeness

(8) pessimism about the future or brooding over the past.

D. During at least some of the periods of mood elevation at least three of the following should be present:

(1) increased energy or activity

(2) decreased need for sleep

(3) inflated self-esteem

(4) sharpened or unusually creative thinking

(5) increased gregariousness

(6) increased talkativeness or wittiness

(7) increased interest and involvement in sexual and other pleasurable activities

(8) over-optimism or exaggeration of past achievements

Diagnostic notes

If desired, time of onset may be specified as early (in late teenage or the 20s) or late (usually between age 30 and 50 years, following an affective episode).

| F34.1 | Dysthymia |

A chronic depression of mood, lasting at least several years, which is not sufficiently severe, or in which individual episodes are not sufficiently prolonged, to justify a diagnosis of severe, moderate or mild recurrent depressive disorder (F33.–).

Depressive:

- neurosis

- personality disorder

Neurotic depression

Persistent anxiety–depression

Excludes: anxiety–depression (mild or not persistent) (F41.2).

Diagnostic notes

Although the current symptoms must not justify a diagnosis of depressive disorder, a diagnosis of dysthymia can still be made if this has been so in the past, particularly at the onset of the disorder. The balance between individual phases of mild depression and intervening periods of comparative normality is very variable. Dysthymia has much in common with the concepts of depressive neurosis and neurotic depression.

DCR-10

A. There must be a period of at least 2 years of constant or constantly recurring depressed mood. Intervening periods of normal mood rarely last for longer than a few weeks and there are no episodes of hypomania.

B. None, or very few, of the individual episodes of depression within such a 2-year period should be sufficiently severe or long-lasting to meet the criteria for recurrent mild depressive disorder (F33.0).

C. During at least some of the periods of depression at least three of the following should be present:

    (1) reduced energy or activity

    (2) insomnia

    (3) loss of self-confidence or feelings of inadequacy

    (4) difficulty in concentrating

    (5) frequent tearfulness

    (6) loss of interest in enjoyment of sex and other pleasurable activities

⇒

(7) feelings of hopelessness or despair

(8) perceived inability to cope with the routine responsibilities of everyday life

(9) pessimism about the future or brooding over the past

(10) social withdrawal

(11) reduced talkativeness

Diagnostic notes

If desired, time of onset may be specified as early (in late teenage or the 20s) or late (usually between age 30 and 50 years following an affective episode).

F34.8	Other persistent mood (affective) disorders

Diagnostic notes

This is a residual category for persistent affective disorders that are not sufficiently severe or long-lasting to fulfil the criteria for cyclothymia (F34.0) or dysthymia (F34.1) but which are nevertheless clinically significant. Some types of depression previously called 'neurotic' are included here, provided that they do not meet the criteria for either cyclothymia (F34.0) or dysthymia (F34.1) or for depressive episodes of mild (F32.0) or moderate (F32.1) severity.

F34.9	Persistent mood (affective) disorder, unspecified.

F38	**Other mood (affective) disorders**

Any other mood disorders that do not justify classification to F30–F34, because they are not of sufficient severity or duration.

Diagnostic notes

There are so many possible disorders that could be listed under F38 that no attempt has been made to specify criteria, except for mixed affective episode (F38.00) and recurrent brief depressive disorder (F38.10). Investigators requiring criteria more exact than those available in *Clinical descriptions and diagnostic guidelines* should construct them according to the requirements of their studies.

F38.0 Other single mood (affective) disorders

F38.00 Mixed affective episode

DCR-10

A. The episode is characterized by either a mixture or a rapid alternation (i.e. within a few hours) of hypomanic, manic and depressive symptoms.

B. Both manic and depressive symptoms must be prominent most of the time during a period of at least 2 weeks.

C. There is no history of previous hypomanic, depressive or mixed episodes.

F38.1 Other recurrent mood (affective) disorders

F38.10 Recurrent brief depressive disorder

DCR-10

A. The disorder meets the symptomatic criteria for mild (F32.0), moderate (F32.1) or severe (F32.2) depressive episode.

⇒

B. The depressive episodes have occurred about once a month over the past year.

C. The individual episodes last less than 2 weeks (typically 2–3 days).

D. The episodes do not occur solely in relation to the menstrual cycle.

F38.8 Other specified mood (affective) disorders

This is a residual category for affective disorders that do not meet the criteria for any other categories F30–F38 above.

F39 Unspecified mood (affective) disorder

Affective psychosis NOS

Neurotic, stress-related and somatoform disorders (F40–F48)

Excludes: when associated with conduct disorders in F91.– (F92.8)

Diagnostic notes

In ICD-10 Chapter V, the concept of neurosis has not been used as a major principle of classification. Nevertheless, neurotic, stress-related and somatoform disorders have been brought together here in one large group because of their historical inter-relationships and the association of many of them with psychological stress.

Mixtures of symptoms are common (particularly coexistent depression and anxiety) but it is usually best to try to decide which is the predominant symptom for diagnostic purposes. A new category of mixed anxiety and depression (F41.2) is provided for those cases in which neither type of symptom reaches diagnostic significance in its own right, and for which it would be artificial to force a decision between the two.

F40 Phobic anxiety disorders

A group of disorders in which anxiety is evoked only, or predominantly, in certain well-defined situations that are not currently dangerous. As a result these situations are characteristically avoided or endured with dread. The patient's concern may be focused on individual symptoms like palpitations or feeling faint, and is often associated with secondary fears of dying, losing control or going mad. Contemplating entry to the phobic situation usually generates anticipatory anxiety. Phobic anxiety and depression often coexist. Whether two diagnoses – phobic anxiety and depressive episode – are needed, or only one, is determined by the time course of the two conditions and by therapeutic considerations at the time of consultation.

Diagnostic notes

The situations or objects that are the focus of the anxiety must be external to the subject. This means that fears relating to the presence in the subject of disease (nosophobia) and disfigurement (dysmorphophobia) should be classified under F45.2 (hypochondriacal disorder); if such ideas are delusional, then a category in F22 (persistent delusional disorders) should be considered.

In this classification, a panic attack occurring in an established phobic situation is regarded as an expression of the severity of the phobia, which should be given diagnostic precedence and recorded as the main diagnosis. In such cases the panic may, of course, be recorded as an additional or secondary diagnosis if required, so long as the criteria for F41.0 (panic disorder) are fulfilled.

| F40.0 | Agoraphobia |

A fairly well-defined cluster of phobias embracing fears of leaving home, entering shops, crowds and public places, or travelling alone in trains, buses or planes. Panic disorder is a frequent feature of both present and past episodes. Depressive and obsessional symptoms and social phobias are also commonly present as subsidiary features. Avoidance of the phobic situation is often prominent, and some agoraphobics experience little anxiety because they are able to avoid their phobic situations.

Agoraphobia without history of panic disorder

Panic disorder with agoraphobia

DCR-10

A. There is marked and consistently manifest fear in, or avoidance of, at least two of the following situations:

⇒

    (1) crowds

    (2) public places

    (3) travelling alone

    (4) travelling away from home.

B. At least two symptoms of anxiety in the feared situation must have been present together, on at least one occasion since the onset of the disorder, and one of the symptoms must have been from items (1)–(4) listed below:

Autonomic arousal symptoms

    (1) palpitations or pounding heart or accelerated heart rate

    (2) sweating

    (3) trembling or shaking

    (4) dry mouth (not due to medication or dehydration).

Symptoms involving chest and abdomen

    (5) difficulty in breathing

    (6) feeling of choking

    (7) chest pain or discomfort

    (8) nausea or abdominal distress (e.g. churning in stomach).

Symptoms involving mental state

    (9) feeling dizzy, unsteady, faint or lightheaded

    (10) feeling that objects are unreal (derealization), or that self is distant or 'not really here' (depersonalization)

    (11) fear of losing control, 'going crazy' or passing out

    (12) fear of dying.

⇒

General symptoms

    (13) hot flushes or cold chills

    (14) numbness or tingling sensations.

C. Significant emotional distress is caused by the avoidance or by the anxiety symptoms and the individual recognizes that these are excessive or unreasonable.

D. Symptoms are restricted to, or predominate in, the feared situations or contemplation of the feared situations.

E. *Most commonly used exclusion clause.* Fear or avoidance of situations (criterion A) is not the result of delusions, hallucinations or other disorders, such as organic mental disorder (F00–F09), schizophrenia and related disorders (F20–F29), mood [affective] disorders (F30–F39) or obsessive–compulsive disorder (F42.–), and is not secondary to cultural beliefs. The presence or absence of panic disorder (F41.0) in a majority of agoraphobic situations may be specified by using a fifth character:

F40.00 agoraphobic without panic disorder

F40.01 agoraphobia with panic disorder.

Options for rating of severity. Severity in F40.00 may be rated by indicating the degree of avoidance, taking into account the specific cultural setting. Severity in F40.01 may be rated by counting the number of panic attacks.

F40.1   Social phobias

Fear of scrutiny by other people, leading to avoidance of social situations. More pervasive social phobias are usually associated with low self-esteem and fear of criticism. These may present as a complaint of blushing, hand tremor, nausea or urgency of micturition, the patient sometimes being convinced that one of these secondary manifestations of their anxiety is the primary problem. Symptoms may progress to panic attacks.

Anthropophobia

Social neurosis

DCR-10

A. Either of the following must be present:

   (1) marked fear of being the focus of attention, or fear of behaving in a way that will be embarrassing or humiliating;

   (2) marked avoidance of being the focus of attention, or of situations in which there is fear of behaving in an embarrassing or humiliating way. These fears are manifested in social situations, such as eating or speaking in public, encountering known individuals in public, or entering or enduring small group situations (e.g. parties, meetings, classrooms).

B. At least two symptoms of anxiety in the feared situation, as defined in F40.0 criterion B, must have been manifest at some time since the onset of the disorder, together with at least one of the following symptoms:

   (1) blushing or shaking

   (2) fear of vomiting

   (3) urgency or fear of micturition or defaecation.

C. Significant emotional distress is caused by the symptoms or by the avoidance, and the individual recognizes that these are excessive or unreasonable.

D. Symptoms are restricted to, or predominate ⇒

in, the feared situations or contemplation of the feared situations.

E. *Most commonly used exclusion clause.* The symptoms listed in criteria A and B are not the result of delusions, hallucinations or other disorders, such as organic mental disorders (F00–F09), schizophrenia and related disorders (F20–F29), mood [affective] disorders (F30–F39) or obsessive–compulsive disorder (F42.–), and are not secondary to cultural beliefs.

F40.2 Specific (isolated) phobias

Phobias restricted to highly specific situations, such as proximity to particular animals, heights, thunder, darkness, flying, closed spaces, urinating or defaecating in public toilets, eating certain foods, dentistry, or the sight of blood or injury. Though the triggering situation is discrete, contact with it can evoke panic as in agoraphobia or social phobia.

Acrophobia

Animal phobias

Claustrophobia

Simple phobia

Excludes: dysmorphophobia (non-delusional) (F45.2), nosophobia (F45.2)

DCR-10

A. Either of the following must be present:

   (1) marked fear of a specific object or situation not included in agoraphobia (F40.0) or social phobia (F40.1);

   (2) marked avoidance of a specific object or situation not included in agoraphobia (F40.0) or social phobia (F40.1).

⇒

Among the most common objects and situations are animals, birds, insects, heights, thunder, flying, small enclosed spaces, the sight of blood or injury, injections, dentists and hospitals.

B. Symptoms of anxiety in the feared situation as defined in F40.0, criterion B, must have been manifest at some time since the onset of the disorder.

C. Significant emotional distress is caused by the symptoms or by the avoidance, and the individual recognizes that these are excessive or unreasonable.

D. Symptoms are restricted to the feared situation or contemplation of the feared situation.

If desired, the specific phobias may be subdivided as follows:

- animal type (e.g. insects, dogs)

- nature-forces type (e.g. storms, water)

- blood, injection and injury type

- situational type (e.g. elevators, tunnels)

- other type.

F40.8 Other phobic anxiety disorders

F40.9 Phobic anxiety disorder, unspecified

Phobia NOS

Phobic state NOS

F41	**Other anxiety disorders**

Disorders in which manifestation of anxiety is the major symptom and is not restricted to any particular environmental situation. Depressive and obsessional symptoms, and even some elements of phobic anxiety, may also be present, provided that they are clearly secondary or less severe.

F41.0	**Panic disorder (episodic paroxysmal anxiety)**

The essential feature is recurrent attacks of severe anxiety (panic), which are not restricted to any particular situation or set of circumstances and are therefore unpredictable. As with other anxiety disorders, the dominant symptoms include sudden onset of palpitations, chest pain, choking sensations, dizziness and feelings of unreality (depersonalization or derealization). There is often also a secondary fear of dying, losing control or going mad. Panic disorder should not be given as the main diagnosis if the patient has a depressive disorder at the time the attacks start; in these circumstances the panic attacks are probably secondary to depression.

Panic:

- attack
- state

Excludes: panic disorder with agoraphobia (F40.0)

DCR-10

A. The individual experiences recurrent panic attacks that are not consistently associated with a specific situation or object, and which often occur spontaneously (i.e. the episodes are unpredictable). The panic attacks are not associated with marked exertion or with exposure to dangerous or life-threatening situations.

⇒

B. A panic attack is characterized by all of the following:

(1) it is a discrete episode of intense fear of discomfort;

(2) it starts abruptly;

(3) it reaches a maximum within a few minutes and lasts at least some minutes;

(4) at least four of the symptoms listed below must be present, one of which must be from items (a)–(d):

Autonomic arousal symptoms

(a) palpitations or pounding heart, or accelerated heart rate

(b) sweating

(c) trembling or shaking

(d) dry mouth (not due to medication or dehydration).

Symptoms involving chest and abdomen

(e) difficulty breathing

(f) feeling of choking

(g) chest pain or discomfort

(h) nausea or abdominal distress (e.g. churning in stomach).

Symptoms involving mental state

(i) feeling dizzy, unsteady, faint or lightheaded

(j) feelings that objects are unreal (derealization) or that the self is distant or 'not really here' (depersonalization)

(k) fear of losing control, 'going crazy' or passing out

(l) fear of dying.

⇒

General symptoms

(m) hot flushes or cold chills

(n) numbness or tingling sensations.

C. *Most commonly used exclusion clause.* Panic attacks are not due to a physical disorder, organic mental disorder (F00–F09) or other mental disorders such as schizophrenia and related disorders (F20–F29), mood [affective] disorders (F30–F39) or somatoform disorders F45.–).

The range of individual variation in both content and severity is so great that two grades, moderate and severe, may be specified, if desired, with a fifth character:

F41.00 panic disorder, moderate (at least four panic attacks in a 4-week period)

F41.01 panic disorder, severe (at least four panic attacks per week over a 4-week period).

F41.1 Generalized anxiety disorder

Anxiety that is generalized and persistent but not restricted to, or even strongly predominating in, any particular environmental circumstances (i.e. it is 'free-floating'). The dominant symptoms are variable but include complaints of persistent nervousness, trembling, muscular tensions, sweating, lightheadedness, palpitations, dizziness and epigastric discomfort. Fears that the patient or a relative will shortly become ill or have an accident are often expressed.

Anxiety:

• neurosis

- reaction
- state

Excludes: neurasthenia (F48.0)

Diagnostic notes

For children, different criteria may be applied (see F93.80).

In children and adolescents the range of complaints by which the general anxiety is manifest is often more limited than in adults, and the specific symptoms of autonomic arousal are often less prominent. For these individuals, an alternative set of criteria is provided for use in F93.80 (generalized anxiety disorder of child), if preferred.

DCR-10

A. There must have been a period of at least 6 months with prominent tension, worry and feelings of apprehension about everyday events and problems.

B. At least four of the symptoms listed below must be present, at least one of which must be from items (1)–(4):

Autonomic arousal symptoms

(1) palpitations or pounding heart, or accelerated heart rate

(2) sweating

(3) trembling or shaking

(4) dry mouth (not due to medication or dehydration).

Symptoms involving chest and abdomen

(5) difficulty breathing

(6) feeling of choking

(7) chest pain or discomfort

⇒

    (8) nausea or abdominal distress (e.g. churning in stomach).

Symptoms involving mental state

    (9) feeling dizzy, unsteady, faint or lightheaded

  (10) feelings that objects are unreal (derealization) or that the self is distant or 'not really here' (depersonalization)

  (11) fear of losing control, 'going crazy' or passing out

  (12) fear of dying.

General symptoms

  (13) hot flushes or cold chills

  (14) numbness or tingling sensations

  (15) muscle tension or aches and pains

  (16) restlessness and inability to relax

  (17) feeling keyed up, on edge or mentally tense

  (18) a sensation of a lump in the throat, or difficulty in swallowing.

Other non-specific symptoms

  (19) exaggerated response to minor surprises or being startled

  (20) difficulty in concentrating, or mind 'going blank', because of worrying or anxiety

  (21) persistent irritability

  (22) difficulty in getting to sleep because of worrying.

C. The disorder does not meet the criteria for panic disorder (F41.0), phobic anxiety disorders (F40.–), obsessive–compulsive dis-

⇒

order (F42.–) or hypochondriacal disorder (F45.2).

D. *Most commonly used exclusion clause.* The anxiety disorder is not due to a physical disorder, such as hyperthyroidism, an organic mental disorder (F00–F09) or a psychoactive substance-related disorder (F10–F19), such as excess consumption of amphetamine-like substances or withdrawal from benzodiazepines.

F41.2 Mixed anxiety and depressive disorder

This category should be used when symptoms of anxiety and depression are both present, but neither is clearly predominant, and neither type of symptom is present to the extent that justifies a diagnosis if considered separately. When both anxiety and depressive symptoms are present and severe enough to justify individual diagnoses, both diagnoses should be recorded and this category should not be used.

Anxiety depression (mild or not persistent)

Diagnostic notes

There are so many possible combinations of comparatively mild symptoms for these disorders that specific criteria are not given, other than those already in the diagnostic guidelines. It is suggested that researchers wishing to study patients with these disorders should arrive at their own criteria within the guidelines, depending upon the setting and purpose of their studies.

F41.3 Other mixed anxiety disorders

Symptoms of anxiety mixed with features of other disorders in F42–F48. Neither type of symptom is severe enough to justify a diagnosis if considered separately.

| F41.8 | Other specified anxiety disorders |

Anxiety hysteria

| F41.9 | Anxiety disorder, unspecified |

Anxiety NOS

| F42 | Obsessive–compulsive disorder |

The essential feature is recurrent obsessional thoughts or compulsive acts. Obsessional thoughts are ideas, images or impulses that enter the patient's mind again and again in a stereotyped form. They are almost invariably distressing and the patient often tries, unsuccessfully, to resist them. They are, however, recognized as his or her own thoughts, even though they are involuntary and often repugnant. Compulsive acts or rituals are stereotyped behaviours that are repeated again and again. They are not inherently enjoyable, nor do they result in the completion of inherently useful tasks. Their function is to prevent some objectively unlikely event, often involving harm to or caused by the patient, which he or she fears might otherwise occur. Usually, this behaviour is recognized by the patient as pointless or ineffectual and repeated attempts are made to resist. Anxiety is almost invariably present. If compulsive acts are resisted the anxiety gets worse.

Includes: anankastic neurosis
obsessive–compulsive neurosis

Excludes: obsessive–compulsive personality
(disorder) (F60.5)

DCR-10

A. Either obsessions or compulsions (or both) are present on most days for a period of at least 2 weeks.

⇒

B. Obsessions (thoughts, ideas or images) and compulsions (acts) share the following features, all of which must be present:

   (1) they are acknowledged as originating in the mind of the patient, and are not imposed by outside persons or influences;

   (2) they are repetitive and unpleasant, and at least one obsession or compulsion that is acknowledged as excessive or unreasonable must be present;

   (3) The patient tries to resist them (but resistance to very long-standing obsessions or compulsions may be minimal). At least one obsession or compulsion that is unsuccessfully resisted must be present;

   (4) Experiencing the obsessive thought or carrying out the compulsive act is not in itself pleasurable. (This should be distinguished from the temporary relief of tension or anxiety.)

C. The obsessions or compulsions cause distress or interfere with the patient's social or individual functioning, usually by wasting time.

D. *Most commonly used exclusion clause.* The obsessions or compulsions are not the result of other mental disorders, such as schizophrenia and related disorders (F20–F29) or mood [affective] disorders (F30–F39).

The diagnosis may be further specified by the following four-character codes:

F42.0   Predominantly obsessional thoughts or ruminations

These may take the form of ideas, mental images or impulses to act, which are nearly always distressing to the subject. Sometimes the ideas are an indecisive, endless consideration of alternatives, associated with an inability to make trivial but necessary decisions in day-to-day living. The relationship between obsessional ruminations and depression is particularly close and a diagnosis of obsessive–compulsive disorder should be preferred only if ruminations arise or persist in the absence of a depressive episode.

F42.1   Predominantly compulsive acts (obsessional rituals)

The majority of compulsive acts are concerned with cleaning (particularly handwashing), repeated checking to ensure that a potentially dangerous situation has not been allowed to develop, or orderliness and tidiness. Underlying the overt behaviour is a fear, usually of danger either to or caused by the patient, and the ritual is an ineffectual or symbolic attempt to avert that danger.

F42.2   Mixed obsessional thoughts and acts

F42.8   Other obsessive–compulsive disorders

F42.9   Obsessive–compulsive disorder, unspecified

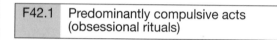

F43   Reaction to severe stress, and adjustment disorders

This category differs from others in that it includes disorders identifiable on the basis of not only symptoms and course but also the existence of one or other of two causative influences: an exceptionally stressful life event producing an acute stress reaction, or a significant life change leading to continued unpleasant circumstances that result in an adjustment disorder. Although less severe psychosocial stress ('life events') may precipitate the onset or contribute to the presentation of a very wide range of disorders classified elsewhere in this chapter, its aetiological importance is not always clear, and in each case will be found to depend on individual, often idiosyncratic, vulnerability, i.e. the life events are neither necessary nor sufficient to explain the occurrence and form of the disorder. In contrast, the disorders brought together here are thought to arise always as a direct consequence of acute severe stress or continued trauma. The stressful events or the continuing unpleasant circumstances are the primary and overriding causal factor, and the disorder would not have occurred without their impact. The disorders in this section can thus be regarded as maladaptive responses to severe or continued stress, in that they interfere with successful coping mechanisms and therefore lead to problems of social functioning.

Diagnostic notes

Acts of self-harm, most commonly self-poisoning by prescribed medication, that are associated closely in time with the onset of either a stress reaction or an adjustment disorder, should be recorded by means of an additional *x* code from Chapter XX of ICD-10. These codes do not allow differentiation between attempted suicide and 'parasuicide', both being included in the general category of self-harm.

F43.0 Acute stress reaction

A transient disorder that develops in an individual without any other apparent mental disorder in response to exceptional physical and mental stress, and which usually subsides within hours or days. Individual vulnerability and coping capacity play a role in the occurrence and severity of acute stress reactions. The symptoms show a typically mixed and changing picture, and include an initial state of 'daze' with some constriction of the field of consciousness and narrowing of attention, inability to comprehend stimuli and disorientation. This state may be followed either by further withdrawal from the surrounding situation (to the extent of a dissociative stupor (F44.2)), or by agitation and overactivity (flight reaction or fugue). Autonomic signs of anxiety (tachycardia, sweating, flushing) are commonly present. The symptoms usually appear within minutes of the impact of the stressful stimulus or event, and disappear within 2–3 days (often within hours). Partial or complete amnesia (F44.0) for the episode may be present. If the symptoms persist, a change in diagnosis should be considered.

Acute:

- crisis reaction
- reaction to stress

combat fatigue

crisis state

psychic shock

DCR-10

A. The patient must have been exposed to an exceptional mental or physical stressor.

B. Exposure to the stressor is followed by an immediate onset of symptoms (within 1 hour).

C. Two groups of symptoms are given; the acute stress reaction is graded as:

F43.00 mild; only criterion (1) below is fulfilled

F43.01 moderate; criterion (1) is met and there are any two symptoms from criterion (2)

F43.02 severe; either criterion (1) is met and there are any four symptoms

⇒

from criterion (2), or there is dissociative stupor (see F44.2).

(1) criteria B, C and D for generalized anxiety disorder (F41.1) are met

(2) (a) withdrawal from expected social interaction

(b) narrowing of attention

(c) apparent disorientation

(d) anger or verbal aggression

(e) despair or hopelessness

(f) inappropriate or purposeless overactivity

(g) uncontrollable and excessive grief (judged by local cultural standards).

D. If the stressor is transient or can be relieved, the symptoms must begin to diminish after not more than 8 hours. If exposure to the stressor continues, the symptoms must begin to diminish after not more than 48 hours.

E. *Most commonly used exclusion clause.* The reaction must occur in the absence of any other concurrent mental or behavioural disorder in ICD-10 (except F41.1 (generalized anxiety disorder), and F60.– (personality disorders)), and not within 3 months of the end of an episode of any other mental or behavioural disorder.

F43.1 Post-traumatic stress disorder

Arises as a delayed or protracted response to a stressful event or situation (of either brief or long duration) of an exceptionally threatening or catastrophic nature, which is likely to cause pervasive distress in almost anyone.

Predisposing factors, such as personality traits (e.g. compulsive, asthenic) or previous history of neurotic illness may lower the threshold for the development of the syndrome or aggravate its course, but they are neither necessary nor sufficient to explain its occurrence. Typical features include episodes of repeated reliving of the trauma in intrusive memories ('flashbacks'), dreams or nightmares, occurring against the persisting background of a sense of 'numbness' and emotional blunting, detachment from other people, unresponsiveness to surroundings, anhedonia and avoidance of activities and situations reminiscent of the trauma. There is usually a state of autonomic hyperarousal, with hypervigilance, an enhanced startle reaction and insomnia. Anxiety and depression are commonly associated with the above symptoms and signs, and suicidal ideation is not infrequent. The onset follows the trauma with a latency period that may range from a few weeks to months. The course is fluctuating but recovery can be expected in the majority of cases. In a small proportion of cases the condition may follow a chronic course over many years, with eventual transition to an enduring personality change (F62.0).

Traumatic neurosis

DCR-10

A. The patient must have been exposed to a stressful event or situation (either short- or long-lasting) of exceptionally threatening or catastrophic nature, which would be likely to cause pervasive distress in almost anyone.

B. There must be persistent remembering of 'reliving' of the stressor in intrusive 'flash-backs', vivid memories or recurring dreams, or in experiencing distress when exposed to circumstances resembling or associated with the stressor.

C. The patient must exhibit an actual or pre-ferred avoidance of circumstances resem-bling or associated with the stressor which

⇒

was not present before exposure to the stressor.

D. Either of the following must be present:

   (1) inability to recall, either partially or completely, some important aspects of the period of exposure to the stressor;

   (2) persistent symptoms of increased psychological sensitivity and arousal (not present before exposure to the stressor), shown by any two of the following:

   (a) difficulty in falling or staying asleep

   (b) irritability or outbursts of anger

   (c) difficulty in concentrating

   (d) hypervigilance

   (e) exaggerated startle response.

E. Criteria B, C and D must all be met within 6 months of the stressful event or of the end of a period of stress. (For some purposes, onset delayed more than 6 months may be included, but this should be clearly specified.)

F43.2 Adjustment disorders

States of subjective distress and emotional disturbance, usually interfering with social functioning and performance, arising in the period of adaption to a significant life change or a stressful life event. The stressor may have affected the integrity of an individual's social network (bereavement, separation, experiences) or the wider system of social supports and values (migration, refugee status), or represented a major developmental transition or crisis (going to school, becoming a parent, failure to attain a cherished personal goal, retirement). Individual predisposition or vulnerability plays an important role in the risk of occurrence and the shaping of the manifestations of adjustment disorders, but it is nevertheless assumed that the condition would not have arisen without the stressor. The manifestations vary and include depressed mood, anxiety or worry (or a mixture of these), a feeling of inability to cope, plan ahead or continue in the present situation, as well as some degree of disability in the performance of daily routine. Conduct disorders may be an associated feature, particularly in adolescents. The predominant feature may be a brief or prolonged depressive reaction, or a disturbance of other emotions and conduct.

Culture shock

Grief reaction

Hospitalism in children

Excludes: separation anxiety disorder of childhood (F93.0)

Diagnostic notes

In children, regressive phenomena such as a return to bed-wetting, babyish speech or thumb-sucking are frequently part of the symptom pattern. If these features predominate, F43.23 should be used.

Normal bereavement reactions. Contacts with medical and psychiatric services because of normal bereavement reactions, appropriate to the culture of the individual concerned and not usually exceeding 6 months in duration, should not be recorded by means of the codes in this book but by a code from Chapter XXI of ICD-10, such as Z63.4 (disappearance or death of family member) plus, for example, Z71.9 (counselling) or Z73.3 (stress not elsewhere classified). Grief reactions of any duration, considered to be abnormal because of their form or content, should be coded by means of one of the codes below (F43.22, F43.23, F43.24 or F43.25), and those of comparatively normal form and content but of duration more than 6 months by means of F43.21 (prolonged depressive reaction).

DCR-10

A. Onset of symptoms must occur within 1 month of exposure to an identifiable psy-

⇒

chosocial stressor, not of an unusual or catastrophic type.

B. The individual manifests symptoms or behaviour disturbance of the types found in any of the affective disorders (F30–F39) (except for delusions and hallucinations), any disorders in F40–F48 (neurotic, stress-related and somatoform disorders) and conduct disorders. Symptoms may be variable in both form and severity.

The predominant feature of the symptoms may be further specified by the use of a fifth character:

F43.20   Brief depressive reaction. A transient mild depressive state of a duration not exceeding 1 month.

F43.21   Prolonged depressive reaction. A mild depressive state occurring in response to a prolonged exposure to a stressful situation but of a duration not exceeding 2 years.

F43.22   Mixed anxiety and depressive reaction. Both anxiety and depressive symptoms are prominent, but at levels no greater than those specified for mixed anxiety and depressive disorder (F41.2) or other mixed anxiety disorders (F41.3).

F43.23   With predominant disturbance of other emotions. The symptoms are usually of several types of emotion, such as anxiety, depression, worry, tensions and anger. Symptoms of anxiety and depression may meet the criteria for mixed anxiety and depressive disorder (F41.2) or for other mixed anxiety disorders (F41.3), but they are not so predominant that other more specific

$\Rightarrow$

depressive or anxiety disorders can be diagnosed. This category should also be used for reactions in children in whom regressive behaviour such as bed-wetting or thumb-sucking are also present.

F43.24 **With predominant disturbance of conduct.** The main disturbance is one involving conduct, e.g. an adolescent grief reaction resulting in aggressive or dissocial behaviour.

F43.25 **With mixed disturbance of emotions and conduct.** Both emotional symptoms and disturbances of conduct are prominent features.

F43.28 **With other specified predominant symptoms.**

C. Except in prolonged depressive reaction (F43.21) the symptoms do not persist for more than 6 months after the cessation of the stress or its consequences. (However, this should not prevent a provisional diagnosis being made if this criterion is not yet fulfilled).

| F43.8 | Other reactions to severe stress |

| F43.9 | Reaction to severe stress, unspecified |

| **F44** | **Dissociative (conversion) disorders** |

The common themes that are shared by dissociative or conversion disorders are a partial or complete loss of the normal integration between memories of the past, awareness of identity and immediate sensations, and control of bodily movements. All types of dissociative disorders tend to remit after a few weeks or months, particularly if their onset is associated with a traumatic life event. More chronic disorders, particularly paralyses and anaesthesias, may develop if the onset is associated with insoluble problems or interpersonal difficulties. These disorders have previously been classified as various types of 'conversion hysteria'. They are presumed to be psychogenic in origin, being associated closely in time with traumatic events, insoluble and intolerable problems or disturbed relationships. The symptoms often represent the patient's concept of how a physical illness would be manifest. Medical examination and investigation do not reveal the presence of any known physical or neurological disorder. In addition, there is evidence that the loss of function is an expression of emotional conflicts or needs. The symptoms may develop in close relationship to psychological stress, and often appear suddenly. Only disorders of physical functions normally under voluntary control and loss of sensations are included here. Disorders involving pain and other complex physical sensations mediated by the autonomic nervous system are classified under somatization disorder (F45.0). The possibility of the later appearance of serious physical or psychiatric disorders should always be kept in mind.

Includes: conversion:

- hysteria
- reaction

  hysterical psychosis

Excludes: malingering (conscious simulation) (Z76.5)

Diagnostic notes

Depersonalisation and derealization are not included here, since in those syndromes only limited aspects of personal feelings and identify are usually affected, and there is no associated loss of performance in terms of sensations, memories or movements.

DCR-10

G1. There must be no evidence of a physical disorder that can explain the characteristic symptoms of this disorder (although physical disorders may be present that give rise to other symptoms).

G2. There are convincing associations in time between the onset of symptoms of the disorder and stressful events, problems or needs.

F44.0 Dissociative amnesia

The main feature is loss of memory, usually of important recent events, that is not due to organic mental disorder and is too great to be explained by ordinary forgetfulness or fatigue. The amnesia is usually centred on traumatic events, such as accidents, or unexpected bereavements, and is usually partial and selective. Complete and generalized amnesia is rare, and is usually part of a fugue (F44.1). If this is the case, the disorder should be classified as such. The diagnosis should not be made in the presence of organic brain disorders, intoxication or excessive fatigue.

> *Excludes*: alcohol- or other psychoactive substance-induced amnesic disorder (F10–F19 with common fourth character .6).
>
> amnesia:
>
> • NOS (R41.1)
>
> • anterograde (R41.1)
>
> • retrograde (R41.2)
>
> non-alcoholic organic amnesic syndrome (F04)
>
> postictal amnesia in epilepsy (G40.–)

DCR-10

A. The general criteria for dissociative disorder (F44) must be met.

B. There must be amnesia, either partial or complete, for recent events or problems that were or still are traumatic or stressful.

C. The amnesia is too extensive and persistent to be explained by ordinary forgetfulness (although its depth and extent may vary from one assessment to the next) or by intentional simulation.

F44.1 Dissociative fugue

Dissociative fugue has all the features of dissociative amnesia plus purposeful travel beyond the usual everyday range. Although there is amnesia for the period of the fugue, the patient's behaviour during this time may appear completely normal to independent observers.

Excludes: postictal fugue in epilepsy (G40.–)

DCR-10

A. The general criteria for dissociative disorder (GF44) must be met.

B. The individual undertakes an unexpected yet organized journey away from home or from the ordinary places of work and social activities, during which self-care is largely maintained.

C. There is amnesia, either partial or complete, for the journey, which also meets criterion C for dissociative amnesia (F44.0).

F44.2 Dissociative stupor

Dissociative stupor is diagnosed on the basis of a profound diminution or absence of voluntary movement and normal responsiveness to external stimuli such as light, noise and touch, but examination and investigation reveal no evidence of a physical cause. In addition, there is positive evidence of psychogenic causation in the form of recent stressful events or problems.

Excludes: organic catatonic disorder (F06.1)

stupor:

- NOS (R40.1)
- catatonic (F20.2)
- depressive (F31–F33)
- manic (F30.2)

DCR-10

A. The general criteria for dissociative disorder (F44) must be met.

B. There is profound diminution or absence of voluntary movements and speech and of normal responsiveness to light, noise and touch.

C. Normal muscle tone, static posture and breathing (and often limited coordinated eye movements) are maintained.

F44.3 Trance and possession disorders

Disorders in which there is a temporary loss of the sense of personal identity and full awareness of the surroundings. Include here only trance states that are involuntary or unwanted, occurring outside religious or culturally accepted situations.

Excludes: states associated with:

- acute and transient psychotic disorders (F23.–)
- organic personality disorder (F07.0)
- postconcussional syndrome (F07.2)
- psychoactive substance intoxication (F10–F19 with common fourth character .0)
- schizophrenia (F20.–)

DCR-10

A. The general criteria for dissociative disorder (F44) must be met.

B. Either of the following must be present:

(1) **Trance.** There is temporary alteration of the state of consciousness, shown by any two of:

   (a) loss of the usual sense of personal identity;

   (b) narrowing of awareness of immediate surroundings, or unusually narrow and selective focusing on environmental stimuli;

   (c) limitation of movements, postures and speech to repetition of a small repertoire.

(2) **Possession disorder.** The individual is convinced that he or she has been taken over by a spirit, power, deity or other person.

C. Both (1) and (2) of criterion B must be unwanted and troublesome, occurring outside, or being a prolongation of, similar states in religious or other culturally accepted situations.

⇒

D. *Most commonly used exclusion clause.* The dis-order does not occur at the same time as schizophrenia or related disorders (F20–F29), or mood [affective] disorders (F30–F39) with hallucinations or delusions.

F44.4 – F44.7	Dissociative disorders of movement and sensation

Diagnostic notes

Criterion G2 above is particularly important for this subgroup of disorders. The symptoms can often be seen to represent the patient's concept of physical disorder, which may be at variance with physiological or ana-tomical principles.

Disorders involving only loss of sensations are included here; disorders involving additional sensations such as pain and other complex sensations mediated by the autonomic nervous system are included in somatoform disorders (F45.–).

The diagnosis of one of these disorders should be made with great caution in the presence of physical disorders of the nervous system, or in a previously well-adjusted individual with normal family and social relationships.

F44.4	Dissociative motor disorders

In the commonest varieties there is loss of ability to move the whole or a part of a limb or limbs. There may be close resemblance to almost any variety of ataxia, apraxia, akinesia, aphonia, dysarthria, dyskinesia, seiz-ures or paralysis.

Psychogenic:

• aphonia

• dysphonia

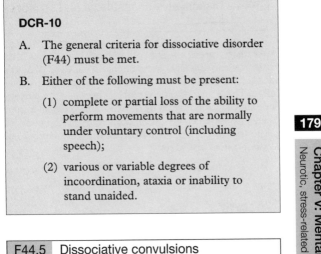

DCR-10

A. The general criteria for dissociative disorder (F44) must be met.

B. Either of the following must be present:

(1) complete or partial loss of the ability to perform movements that are normally under voluntary control (including speech);

(2) various or variable degrees of incoordination, ataxia or inability to stand unaided.

F44.5 Dissociative convulsions

Dissociative convulsions may mimic epileptic seizures very closely in terms of movements, but tongue-biting, bruising due to falling, and incontinence of urine are rare, and consciousness is maintained or replaced by a state of stupor or trance.

DCR-10

A. The general criteria for dissociative disorder (F44) must be met.

B. The individual exhibits sudden and unexpected spasmodic movements, closely resembling any of the varieties of epileptic seizure but not followed by loss of consciousness.

C. The symptoms in criterion B are not accompanied by tongue-biting, serious bruising or laceration due to falling, or urinary incontinence.

F44.6	Dissociative anaesthesia and sensory loss

Anaesthetic areas of skin often have boundaries that make it clear that they are associated with the patient's ideas about bodily functions, rather than medical knowledge. There may be differential loss between the sensory modalities which cannot be due to a neurological lesion. Sensory loss may be accompanied by complaints of paraesthesia. Loss of vision and hearing are rarely total in dissociative disorders.

Psychogenic deafness

DCR-10

A. The general criteria for dissociative disorder (F44) must be met.

B. Either of the following must be present:

   (1) partial or complete loss of any or all of the normal cutaneous sensations over part or all of the body (specify: touch, pinprick, vibration, heat, cold);

   (2) partial or complete loss of vision, hearing, or smell (specify).

F44.7	Mixed dissociative (conversion) disorders

Combination of disorders specified in F44.0–F44.6.

F44.8	Other dissociative (conversion) disorders

This residual code may be used to indicate other dissociative and conversion states that meet criteria A and B for F44, but do not meet the criteria for F44.0–F44.7 listed above.

Included here are: Psychogenic

- confusion
- twilight state.

F44.80 Ganser's syndrome (approximate answers)

F44.81 Multiple personality disorder

DCR-10

A. Two or more distinct personalities exist within the individual, only one being evident at a time.

B. Each personality has its own memories, preferences and behaviour patterns, and at some time (and recurrently) takes full control of the individual's behaviour.

C. There is inability to recall important personal information which is too extensive to be explained by ordinary forgetfulness.

D. The symptoms are not due to organic mental disorders (F00–F09) (e.g. epileptic disorders) or to psychoactive substance-related disorders (F10–F19) (e.g. intoxication or withdrawal).

F44.82 Transient dissociative [conversion] disorders occurring in childhood and adolescence

F44.88 Other specified dissociative [conversion] disorders.

Diagnostic notes

Specific research criteria are not given for all disorders mentioned above, since these other dissociative states are rare and not well described. Research workers studying these conditions in detail should specify their own criteria according to the purposes of their studies.

F44.9	Dissociative [conversion] disorder, unspecified

F45	Somatoform disorders

The main feature is repeated presentation of physical symptoms together with persistent requests for medical investigations, in spite of repeated negative findings and reassurances by doctors that the symptoms have no physical basis. If any physical disorders are present, they do not explain the nature and extent of the symptoms or the distress and preoccupation of the patient.

Excludes: dissociative disorders (F44.–)

hair-plucking (F98.4)

lalling (F80.0)

lisping (F80.8)

nail-biting (F98.9)

psychological or behavioural factors associated with disorders or diseases classified elsewhere (F54)

sexual dysfunction, not caused by organic disorder or disease (F52.–)

thumb-sucking (F98.8)

tic disorders (in childhood and adolescence) (F95.–)

Tourette's syndrome (F95.2)

trichotillomania (F63.3)

Diagnostic notes

Persons with these disorders may also show a degree of attention-seeking (histrionic) behaviour, particularly if they are frustrated by their failure to persuade doctors of the essentially physical nature of their illness and of the need for further investigations or examinations.

F45.0   Somatization disorder

The main features are multiple, recurrent and frequently changing physical symptoms of at least 2 years' duration. Most patients have a long and complicated history of contact with both primary and specialist medical care services, during which many negative investigations or fruitless exploratory operations may have been carried out. Symptoms may be referred to any part or system of the body. The course of the disorder is chronic and fluctuating, and is often associated with disruption of social, interpersonal and family behaviour. Short-lived (less than 2 years) and less striking symptom patterns should be classified under undifferentiated somatoform disorder (F45.1).

Multiple psychosomatic disorder

Excludes: malingering   (conscious   simulation) (Z76.5)

DCR-10

A. There must be a history of at least 2 years' complaints of multiple and variable physical symptoms that cannot be explained by any detectable physical disorders. (Any physical disorders that are known to be present do not explain the severity, extent, variety and persistence of the physical complaints, or the associated social disability.) If some symptoms clearly due to autonomic arousal are present, they are not a major feature of the disorder in that they are not particularly persistent or distressing.

B. Preoccupation with the symptoms causes persistent distress and leads the patient to seek repeated (three or more) consultations or sets of investigations with either primary

$\Rightarrow$

care or specialist doctors. In the absence of medical services within either the financial or physical reach of the patient there must be persistent self-medication or multiple consultations with local healers.

C. There is persistent refusal to accept medical reassurance that there is no adequate physical cause for the physical symptoms. (Short-term acceptance of such reassurance, i.e. for a few weeks during or immediately after investigations, does not exclude this diagnosis.)

D. There must be a total of six or more symptoms from the following list, with symptoms occurring in at least two separate groups:

Gastrointestinal symptoms

(1) abdominal pain

(2) nausea

(3) feeling bloated or full of gas

(4) bad taste in mouth, or excessively coated tongue

(5) complaints of vomiting or regurgitation of food

(6) complaints of frequent and loose bowel motions or discharge of fluids from anus.

Cardiovascular symptoms

(7) breathlessness without exertion

(8) chest pains.

Genitourinary symptoms

(9) dysuria or complaints of frequency of micturition

(10) unpleasant sensations in or around the genitals

(11) complaints of unusual or copious vaginal discharge.

Skin and pain symptoms

(12) blotchiness or discoloration of the skin

(13) pain in the limbs, extremities or joints

(14) unpleasant numbness or tingling sensations.

E. *Most commonly used exclusion clause.* Symptoms do not occur only during any of the schizophrenic or related disorders (F20–F29), any of the mood [affective] disorders (F30–F39), or panic disorder (F41.0).

F45.1   Undifferentiated somatoform disorder

When somatoform complaints are multiple, varying and persistent, but the complete and typical picture of somatization disorder is not fulfilled, the diagnosis of undifferentiated somatoform disorder should be considered.

Undifferentiated psychosomatic disorder

DCR-10

A. Criteria A, C and E for somatization disorder (F45.0) are met, except that the duration of the disorder is at least 6 months.

B. One or both of criteria B and D for somatization disorder (F45.0) are incompletely fulfilled.

F45.2   Hypochondriacal disorder

The essential feature is a persistent preoccupation with the possibility of having one or more serious and progressive physical disorders. Patients manifest persistent somatic complaints or a persistent preoccupation with their physical appearance. Normal or commonplace sensations and appearances are often interpreted by patients as abnormal and distressing, and attention is usually focused upon only one or two organs or systems of the body. Marked depression and anxiety are often present, and may justify additional diagnoses.

Body dysmorphic disorder

Dysmorphophobia (non-delusional)

Hypochondriacal neurosis

Hypochondriasis

Nosophobia

Excludes: delusional dysmorphophobia (F22.8)

fixed delusions about bodily functions or shape (F22.–)

DCR-10

A. Either of the following must be present:

(1) persistent belief, of at least 6 months' duration, of the presence of a maximum of two serious physical diseases (of which at least one must be specifically named by the patient);

(2) persistent preoccupation with a presumed deformity or disfigurement (body dysmorphic disorder).

B. Preoccupation with the belief and the symptoms causes persistent distress or interference with personal functioning in daily living, and leads the patient to seek medical treatment or investigations (or equivalent help from local healers).

C. There is persistent refusal to accept medical reassurance that there is no physical cause for the symptoms or physical abnormality.

⇒

(Short-term acceptance of such reassurance, i.e. for a few weeks during or immediately after investigations, does not exclude this diagnosis.)

D. *Most commonly used exclusion clause*. The symptoms do not occur only during any of the schizophrenic and related disorders (F20–F29, particularly F22) or any of the mood [affective] disorders (F30–F39).

| F45.3 | Somatoform autonomic dysfunction |

Symptoms are presented by the patient as if they were due to a physical disorder of a system or organ that is largely or completely under autonomic innervation and control, i.e. the cardiovascular, gastrointestinal, respiratory and urogenital systems. The symptoms are usually of two types, neither of which indicates a physical disorder of the organ or system concerned. First, there are complaints based upon objective signs of autonomic arousal, such as palpitations, sweating, flushing, tremor and expression of fear and distress about the possibility of a physical disorder. Secondly, there are subjective complaints of a non-specific or changing nature, such as fleeting aches and pains, sensations of burning, heaviness, tightness, and feelings of being bloated or distended, which are referred by the patient to a specific organ or system.

Cardiac neurosis

Da Costa's syndrome

Gastric neurosis

Effort syndrome

Neurocirculatory asthenia

Psychogenic forms of:

• aerophagy

• cough

• diarrhoea

- dyspepsia
- dysuria
- flatulence
- hiccough
- hyperventilation
- increased frequency of micturition
- irritable bowel syndrome
- pylorospasm

Excludes: psychological and behavioural factors associated with disorders or diseases classified elsewhere (F54)

DCR-10

A. There must be symptoms of autonomic arousal that are attributed by the patient to a physical disorder of one or more of the following systems or organs:

(1) heart and cardiovascular system

(2) upper gastrointestinal tract (oesophagus and stomach)

(3) lower gastrointestinal tract

(4) respiratory system

(5) genitourinary system

B. Two or more of the following autonomic symptoms must be present:

(1) palpitations

(2) sweating (hot and cold)

(3) dry mouth

(4) flushing or blushing

(5) epigastric discomfort, 'butterflies' or churning in the stomach.

⇒

C. One or more of the following symptoms must be present:

 (1) chest pains or discomfort in and around the precordium

 (2) dyspnoea or hyperventilation

 (3) excessive tiredness on mild exertion

 (4) aerophagy, hiccough or burning sensations in chest or epigastrium

 (5) reported frequent bowel movements

 (6) increased frequency of micturition or dysuria

 (7) feeling of being bloated, distended or heavy.

D. There is no evidence of a disturbance of structure or function in the organs or systems about which patient is concerned.

E. *Most commonly used exclusion clause.* These symptoms do not occur only in the presence of phobic disorders (F40.0–F40.3) or panic disorder (F41.0).

A fifth character may be used to classify the individual disorders in this group, indicating the organ or system regarded by the patient as the origin of the symptoms:

 F45.30 Heart and cardiovascular system, includes cardiac neurosis, neurocirculatory asthenia, Da Costa's syndrome

 F45.31 Upper gastrointestinal tract. *Includes:* psychogenic aerophagy, hiccough, gastric neurosis

 F45.32 Lower gastrointestinal tract. *Includes:* psychogenic irritable bowel syndrome, psychogenic diarrhoea, gas syndrome

⇒

> F45.33   Respiratory system. *Includes:* hyperventilation
>
> F45.34   Genitourinary system. *Includes:* psychogenic increase of frequency of micturition and dysuria
>
> F45.38   Other organ or system.

F45.4   Persistent somatoform pain disorder

The predominant complaint is of persistent, severe and distressing pain, which cannot be explained fully by a physiological process or a physical disorder, and which occurs in association with emotional conflict or psychosocial problems that are sufficient to allow the conclusion that they are the main causative influences. The result is usually a marked increase in support and attention, either personal or medical. Pain presumed to be of psychogenic origin occurring during the course of depressive disorders or schizophrenia should not be included here.

Psychalgia

Psychogenic:

• backache

• headache

Somatoform pain disorder

Excludes: backache NOS (M54.9) tension headache (G44.2)

pain:

• NOS (R52.9)

• acute (R52.0)

• chronic (R52.2)

• intractable (R52.1)

Diagnostic notes

Pain due to known or inferred psychophysiological

mechanisms such as muscle tension pain or migraine, but still believed to have a psychological cause, should be coded by the use of F54 (psychological or behavioural factors associated with disorders or diseases classified elsewhere) plus an additional code from elsewhere in ICD-10 (e.g. migraine, G43–).

DCR-10

A. There is persistent severe and distressing pain (for at least 6 months and continuously on most days), in any part of the body, which cannot be explained adequately by evidence of a physiological process or a physical disorder, and which is consistently the main focus of the patient's attention.

B. *Most commonly used exclusion clause.* This disorder does not occur in the presence of schizophrenia or related disorders (F20–F29), or only during any of the mood [affective] disorders (F30–F39), somatization disorder (F45.0), undifferentiated somatoform disorder (F45.1) or hypochondriacal disorder (F45.2).

F45.8   Other somatoform disorders

Any other disorders of sensation, function and behaviour, not due to physical disorders, which are not mediated through the autonomic nervous system, which are limited to specific systems or parts of the body, and which are closely associated in time with stressful events or problems.

Psychogenic:

- dysmenorrhoea
- dysphagia, including 'globus hystericus'
- pruritus
- torticollis

Teeth-grinding

Diagnostic notes

In these disorders the presenting complaints are not mediated through the autonomic nervous system, and are limited to specific systems or parts of the body, such as the skin. This is in contrast to the multiple and often changing complaints of the origin of symptoms and distress found in somatization disorder (F45.0) and undifferentiated somatoform disorder (F45.1). Tissue damage is not involved.

Any other disorders of sensation not due to physical disorders, which are closely associated in time with stressful events or problems, or which result in significantly increased attention for the patient, either personal or medical, should also be classified here.

F45.9   Somatoform disorder, unspecified

Psychomatic disorder NOS

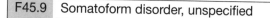

F48   **Other neurotic disorders**

F48.0   Neurasthenia

Considerable cultural variations occur in the presentation of this disorder, and two main types occur, with substantial overlap. In one type the main feature is a complaint of increased fatigue after mental effort, often associated with some decrease in occupational performance or coping efficiency in daily tasks. The mental fatiguability is typically described as an unpleasant intrusion of distracting associations or recollections, difficulty in concentrating and generally inefficient thinking. In the other type, the emphasis is on feelings of bodily or physical weakness and exhaustion after only minimal effort, accompanied by a feeling of muscular aches and pains and inability to relax. In both types a variety of other unpleasant physical feelings is common, such as dizziness, tension headaches and feelings of general instability. Worry about decreasing mental and bodily wellbeing, irritability, anhedonia and varying minor degrees of both depression and anxiety are all common. Sleep is often disturbed in its initial and middle phases but hypersomnia may also be prominent.

Fatigue syndrome

Use additional code, if desired, to identify previous physical illness.

Excludes: asthenia NOS (R53)

burnout (Z73.0)

malaise and fatigue (R53)

postviral fatigue syndrome (G93.3)

psychasthenia (F48.8)

Diagnostic notes

In many countries neurasthenia is not generally used as a diagnostic category. Many of the cases so diagnosed in countries where this diagnosis is in use would probably meet the current criteria for depressive disorder or anxiety disorder. There are, however, patients whose symptoms fit the description of neurasthenia better than that of any other syndrome, and such cases seem to be more frequent in some cultures than in others.

DCR-10

A. Either of the following must be present:

(1) persistent and distressing complaints of feelings of exhaustion after minor mental effort (such as performing or attempting to perform everyday tasks that do not require unusual mental effort);

(2) Persistent and distressing complaints of feelings of fatigue and bodily weakness after minor physical effort.

B. At least one of the following symptoms must be present:

(1) feelings of muscular aches and pains

    (2) dizziness

    (3) tension headaches

    (4) sleep disturbance

    (5) inability to relax

    (6) irritability.

C. The patient is unable to recover from the symptoms in criterion A(1) or (2) by means of rest, relaxation or entertainment.

D. The duration of the disorder is at least 3 months.

E. *Most commonly used exclusion clause.* The disorder does not occur in the presence of organic emotionally labile disorder (F06.6), postencephalitic syndrome (F07.1), postconcussional syndrome (F07.2), mood [affective] disorders (F30–F39), panic disorder (F41.0) or generalized anxiety disorder (F41.1).

F48.1   Depersonalization–derealization syndrome

A rare disorder in which the patient complains spontaneously that his or her mental activity, body and surroundings are changed in their quality, so as to be unreal, remote or automatized. Among the varied phenomena of the syndrome, patients complain most frequently of loss of emotions and feelings of estrangement or detachment from their thinking, their body or the real world. In spite of the dramatic nature of the experience, the patient is aware of the unreality of the change. The sensorium is normal and the capacity for emotional expression intact.

Diagnostic notes

This disorder must be distinguished from other disorders in which 'change of personality' or 'splitting of self' are experienced or referred to, such as schizophrenia, dissociative disorders and some instances of early dementia. This diagnosis should not be used as a main or single diagnosis when the syndrome arises in the presence of other mental disorders, such as organic confusional or delusional states (F05.–, F06.–), intoxication by alcohol or drugs (F1x.0), schizophrenia and related disorders (F20–F29), mood [affective] disorders (F30–F39), anxiety disorders (F40.–, F41.–) or other conditions (such as marked fatigue, hypoglycaemia, or immediately preceding or following epileptic seizures). However, these syndromes often occur during the course of many other psychiatric disorders, and are appropriately recorded as a secondary or additional diagnosis to a different main diagnosis. Their occurrence as an isolated syndrome is much less common.

DCR-10

A. Either of the following must be present:

(1) **Depersonalization** The patient complains of a feeling of being distant or 'not really here'. For example, individuals may complain that their emotions, feelings or experience of the inner self are detached, strange, not their own or unpleasantly lost, or that their emotions or movements seem as if they belong to someone else, or that they feel as if acting in a play;

(2) **Derealization** The patient complains of a feeling of unreality. For example, there may be complaints that the surroundings or specific objects look strange, distorted, flat, colourless, lifeless, dreary, uninteresting, or like a stage upon which everyone is acting.

B. There is retention of insight, in that the patient realizes that the change is not imposed from outside by other persons or forces.

F48.8 Other specified neurotic disorders

Briquet's disorder

Dhat syndrome

Occupational neurosis, including writer's cramp

Psychasthenia

Psychasthenic neurosis

Psychogenic syncope.

This category includes mixed disorders of behaviour, beliefs and emotions, which are of uncertain aetiology and nosological status and which occur with particular frequency in certain cultures (see also Annex 2); examples include Dhat syndrome (undue concern about the debilitating effects of the passage of semen), koro (anxiety and fear that the penis will retract into the abdomen and cause death), and latah (imitative and automatic response behaviour). The strong association of these syndromes with locally accepted cultural beliefs and patterns of behaviour indicates that they are probably best regarded as not delusional.

F48.9 Neurotic disorder, unspecified

Neurosis NOS

Behavioural syndromes associated with physiological disturbances and physical factors (F50–F59)

F50   Eating disorders

Excludes: anorexia NOS (R63.0)

feeding

- difficulties and mismanagement (R63.3)
- disorder of infancy or childhood (F98.2)

polyphagia (R63.2)

F50.0   Anorexia nervosa

A disorder characterized by deliberate weight loss, induced and sustained by the patient. It occurs most commonly in adolescent girls and young women, but adolescent boys and young men may also be affected, as may children approaching puberty and older women up to the menopause. The disorder is associated with a specific psychopathology whereby a dread of fatness and flabbiness of body contour persists as an intrusive overvalued idea, and the patients impose a low weight threshold on themselves. There is usually undernutrition of varying severity, with secondary endocrine and metabolic changes and disturbances of bodily function. The symptoms include restricted dietary choice, excessive exercise, induced vomiting and purgation, and use of appetite suppressants and diuretics.

Excludes: loss of appetite (R63.0)

- psychogenic (F50.8)

DCR-10

A. There is weight loss or, in children, a lack of weight gain, leading to a body weight at least 15% below the normal or expected weight for age and height.

B. The weight loss is self-induced by avoidance of 'fattening foods'.

C. There is self-perception of being too fat, with an intrusive dread of fatness, which leads to a self-imposed low weight threshold.

D. A widespread endocrine disorder involving the hypothalamic–pituitary–gonadal axis is manifest in women as amenorrhoea and in men as a loss of sexual interest and potency. (An apparent exception is the persistence of vaginal bleeds in anorexic women who are on replacement hormonal therapy, most commonly taken as a contraceptive pill.)

E. The disorder does not meet criteria A and B for bulimia nervosa (F50.2).

Diagnostic notes

The following features support the diagnosis, but are not essential elements: self-induced vomiting, self-induced purging, excessive exercise and use of appetite suppressants and/or diuretics. If onset is prepubertal, the sequence of pubertal events is delayed or even arrested (growth ceases; in girls the breasts do not develop and there is a primary amenorrhoea; in boys the genitals remain juvenile). With recovery puberty is often completed normally, but the menarche is late.

F50.1 Atypical anorexia nervosa

Disorders that fulfil some of the features of anorexia nervosa but in which the overall clinical picture does not justify that diagnosis. For instance, one of the key symptoms, such as amenorrhoea or marked dread of being fat, may be absent in the presence of marked weight loss and weight-reducing behaviour. This diagnosis should not be made in the presence of known physical disorders associated with weight loss.

Diagnostic notes

Researchers studying atypical forms of anorexia nervosa are recommended to make their own decisions about the number and type of criteria to be fulfilled.

F50.2	Bulimia nervosa

A syndrome characterized by repeated bouts of overeating and an excessive preoccupation with the control of body weight, leading to a pattern of overeating followed by vomiting or use of purgatives. This disorder shares many psychological features with anorexia nervosa, including an overconcern with body shape and weight. Repeated vomiting is likely to give rise to disturbances of body electrolytes and physical complications. There is often, but not always, a history of an earlier episode of anorexia nervosa, the interval ranging from a few months to several years.

Bulimia NOS

Hyperorexia nervosa

DCR-10

A. There are recurrent episodes of overeating (at least twice a week over a period of 3 months) in which large amounts of food are consumed in short periods of time.

B. There is persistent preoccupation with eating, and a strong desire or a sense of compulsion to eat (craving).

C. The patient attempts to counteract the 'fattening' effects of food by one or more of the following:

(1) self-induced vomiting

⇒

(2) self-induced purging

(3) alternating periods of starvation

(4) use of drugs such as appetite suppressants, thyroid preparations or diuretics; when bulimia occurs in diabetic patients they may choose to neglect their insulin treatment.

D. There is self-perception of being too fat, with an intrusive dread of fatness (usually leading to underweight).

F50.3 Atypical bulimia nervosa

Disorders that fulfil some of the features of bulimia nervosa but in which the overall clinical picture does not justify that diagnosis. For instance, there may be recurrent bouts of overeating and overuse of purgatives without significant weight change, or the typical over-concern about body shape and weight may be absent.

Diagnostic notes

Researchers studying atypical forms of bulimia nervosa, such as those involving normal or excessive body weight, are recommended to make their own decisions about the number and type of criteria to be fulfilled.

F50.4 Overeating associated with other psychological disturbances

Overeating due to stressful events, such as bereavement, accident, childbirth, etc.

Psychogenic overeating

Excludes: obesity (E66.–)

Researchers wishing to use this category are recommended to design their own criteria.

F50.5 Vomiting associated with other psychological disturbances

Repeated vomiting that occurs in dissociative disorders (F44.–) and hypochondriacal disorder (F45.2), and which is not solely due to conditions classified outside this chapter. This subcategory may also be used in addition to 021.– (excessive vomiting in pregnancy) when emotional factors are predominant in the causation of recurrent nausea and vomiting in pregnancy.

Psychogenic vomiting

Excludes: nausea (R11)

vomiting NOS (R11)

Researchers wishing to use this category are recommended to design their own criteria.

F50.8 Other eating disorders

Pica in adults

Psychogenic loss of appetite

Excludes: pica of infancy and childhood (F98.3)

F50.9 Eating disorder, unspecified

F51 Non-organic sleep disorders

In many cases a disturbance of sleep is one of the symptoms of another disorder, either mental or physical. Whether a sleep disorder in a given patient is an independent condition or simply one of the features of another disorder classified elsewhere, either in this chapter or in others, should be determined on the basis of its clinical presentation and course as well as on the therapeutic considerations and priorities at the time of the consultation. Generally, if the sleep disorder is one of the major complaints and is perceived as a condition in itself, the present code should be used along with other pertinent diagnoses describing the psychopathology and pathophysiology involved in a given case. This category includes only those sleep disorders in which emotional causes are considered to be a primary factor, and which are not due to identifiable physical disorders classified elsewhere.

Excludes: sleep disorders (organic) (G47.–)

Diagnostic notes

A more comprehensive classification of sleep disorders is available (Diagnostic Classification Steering Committee 1990 International classification of sleep disorders: diagnostic and coding manual. Rochester, American Sleep Disorders Association), but it should be noted that this is organized differently from ICD-10.

For some research purposes, where particularly homogeneous groups of sleep disorders are required, four or more events occurring within a 1-year period may be considered as a criterion for the use of categories F51.3, F51.4 and F51.5

F51.0 Non-organic insomnia

A condition of unsatisfactory quantity and/or quality of sleep, which persists for a considerable period of time, including difficulty falling asleep, difficulty staying asleep or early final wakening. Insomnia is a common symptom of many mental and physical disorders, and should be classified here in addition to the basic disorder only if it dominates the clinical picture.

Excludes: insomnia (organic) (G47.0)

Diagnostic notes

Children are often said to have difficulty sleeping when in reality the problem is a difficulty in the management of bedtime routines (rather than of sleep per se). Bedtime difficulties should not be coded here but in Chapter XXI of ICD-10 (Z62.0, inadequate parental supervision and control).

203

Chapter V: Mental and behavioural disorders
Behavioural syndromes associated with physiological disturbances and physical factors

DCR-10

A. The individual complains of difficulty falling asleep, difficulty maintaining sleep or non-refreshing sleep.

B. The sleep disturbance occurs at least three times a week for at least 1 month.

C. The sleep disturbance results in marked personal distress or interferences with personal functioning in daily living.

D. There is no known causative organic factor, such as a neurological or other medical condition, psychoactive substance use disorder or a medication.

| F51.1 | Non-organic hypersomnia |

Hypersomnia is defined as a condition of either excessive daytime sleepiness and sleep attacks (not accounted for by an inadequate amount of sleep) or prolonged transition to the fully aroused state upon awakening. In the absence of an organic factor for the occurrence of hypersomnia, this condition is usually associated with mental disorders.

Excludes: hypersomnia (organic) (G47.1)

narcolepsy (G47.4)

DCR-10

A. The individual complains of excessive daytime sleepiness or sleep attacks, or of prolonged transition to the fully aroused state upon awakening (sleep drunkenness), which is not accounted for by an inadequate amount of sleep.

B. This sleep disturbance occurs nearly every

⇒

day for at least 1 month or recurrently for shorter periods of time, and causes either marked distress or interference with personal functioning in daily living.

C. There are no auxiliary symptoms of narcolepsy (cataplexy, sleep paralysis, hypnagogic hallucinations) and no clinical evidence for sleep apnoea (nocturnal breath cessation, typical intermittent snorting sounds etc.).

D. There is no known causative organic factor, such as a neurological or other medical condition, psychoactive substance use disorder or a medication.

Diagnostic notes

If hypersomnia occurs only as one of the symptoms of a mental disorder, such as an affective disorder, the main diagnosis should be that of the underlying mental disorder. The diagnosis of non-organic hypersomnia should be added, however, if hypersomnia is the predominant complaint. When another diagnosis cannot be made, the present code should be used alone. The most important differential diagnosis is from narcolepsy (G47.4).

F51.2 Non-organic disorder of the sleep–wake schedule

A lack of synchrony between the sleep–wake schedule and the desired sleep–wake schedule for the individual's environment, resulting in a complaint of either insomnia or hypersomnia.

Psychogenic inversion of:

- circadian
- nyctohemeral } rhythm
- sleep

Excludes: disorders of the sleep–wake schedule (organic) (G47.2)

DCR-10

A. The individual's sleep–wake pattern is out of synchrony with the desired sleep–wake schedule, as imposed by societal demands and shared by most people in the individual's environment.

B. As a result of disturbance of the sleep–wake schedule, the individual experiences insomnia during the major sleep period or hypersomnia during the waking period, nearly every day for at least 1 month or recurrently for shorter periods of time.

C. The unsatisfactory quantity, quality and timing of sleep causes either marked personal distress or interference with personal functioning in daily living.

D. There is no known causative organic factor, such as a neurological or other medical condition, psychoactive substance use disorder or a medication.

F51.3 Sleepwalking (somnambulism)

A state of altered consciousness in which phenomena of sleep and wakefulness are combined. During a sleepwalking episode the individual arises from bed, usually during the first third of nocturnal sleep, and walks about, exhibiting low levels of awareness, reactivity and motor skill. Upon awakening there is usually no recall of the event.

DCR-10

A. The predominant symptom is repeated (two or more) episodes of rising from bed, usually during the first third of nocturnal sleep, and walking about for between several minutes and half an hour.

B. During an episode the individual has a blank, staring face, is relatively unresponsive to the efforts of others to influence the event or to communicate with him or her, and can be awakened only with considerable difficulty.

C. Upon awakening (either from an episode or the next morning), the individual has amnesia for the episode.

D. Within several minutes of awakening from the episode there is no impairment of mental activity or behaviour, although there may initially be a short period of some confusion and disorientation.

E. There is no evidence of an organic mental disorder, such as dementia, or a physical disorder such as epilepsy.

F51.4 Sleep terrors (night terrors)

Nocturnal episodes of extreme terror and panic associated with intense vocalization, motility and high levels of autonomic discharge. The individual sits up or gets up, usually during the first third of nocturnal sleep, with a panicky scream. Quite often he or she rushes to the door as if trying to escape, although very seldom leaves the room. Recall of the event, if any, is very limited (usually to one or two fragmentary mental images).

DCR-10

A. Repeated (two or more) episodes in which the individual gets up from sleep with a panicky scream and intense anxiety, body motility and autonomic hyperactivity (such as tachycardia, heart pounding, rapid breathing and sweating).

B. The episodes occur mainly during the first third of sleep.

C. The duration of the episode is less than 10 minutes.

D. If others try to comfort the individual during the episode there is a lack of response followed by disorientation and perseverative movements.

E. The individual has limited recall for the event.

F. There is no known causative organic factor, such as a neurological or other medical condition, psychoactive use disorder or a medication.

| F51.5 | Nightmares |

Dream experiences loaded with anxiety or fear. There is very detailed recall of the dream content. The dream experience is very vivid and usually includes themes involving threats to survival, security or self-esteem. Quite often there is a recurrence of the same or similar frightening nightmare themes. During a typical episode there is a degree of autonomic discharge but no appreciable vocalization or body motility. Upon awakening the individual rapidly becomes alert and oriented.

Dream anxiety disorder

DCR-10

A. The individual wakes from nocturnal sleep or naps with detailed and vivid recall of intensely frightening dreams, usually involving threats to survival, security or self-esteem. The awakening may occur during any part of the sleep period, but typically during the second half. ⇒

B. Upon awakening from the frightening dreams, the individual rapidly becomes oriented and alert.

C. The dream experience itself and the disturbance of sleep resulting from the awakenings associated with the episodes cause marked distress to the individual.

D. There is no known causative organic factor, such as a neurological or other medical condition, psychoactive substance use disorder or a medication.

F51.8	Other non-organic sleep disorders

F51.9	Non-organic sleep disorder, unspecified

Emotional sleep disorder NOS

F52	Sexual dysfunction, not caused by organic disorder or disease

Sexual dysfunction covers the various ways in which an individual is unable to participate in a sexual relationship as he or she would wish. Sexual response is a psychosomatic process and both psychological and somatic processes are usually involved in the causation of sexual dysfunction.

Excludes: Dhat syndrome (F48.8)

DCR-10

G1. The subject is unable to participate in a sexual relationship as he or she would wish.

G2. The dysfunction occurs frequently, but may be absent on some occasions.

$\Rightarrow$

G3. The dysfunction has been present for at least 6 months.

G4. The dysfunction is not entirely attributable to any of the other mental and behavioural disorders in ICD-10, physical disorders (such as endocrine disorder) or drug treatment.

Diagnostic notes

Measurement of each form of dysfunction can be based on rating scales that assess severity as well as frequency of the problem. More than one type of dysfunction can coexist.

F52.0 Lack or loss of sexual desire

Loss of sexual desire is the principal problem and is not secondary to other sexual difficulties, such as erectile failure or dyspareunia.

Frigidity

Hypoactive sexual desire disorder

DCR-10

A. The general criteria for sexual dysfunction (F52) must be met.

B. Lack or loss of sexual desire, manifest by diminution of seeking out sexual cues, of thinking about sex with associated feelings of desire or appetite, or of sexual fantasies.

C. Lack of interest in initiating sexual activity either with partner or as solitary masturbation, resulting in a frequency of activity clearly lower than expected, taking into account age and context, or in a frequency very clearly reduced from previous much higher levels.

Either the prospect of sexual interaction produces sufficient fear or anxiety that sexual activity is avoided (sexual aversion) or sexual responses occur normally and orgasm is experienced but there is a lack of appropriate pleasure (lack of sexual enjoyment).

Anhedonia (sexual)

F52.10 Sexual aversion

DCR-10

A. The general criteria for sexual dysfunction (F52) must be met.

B. The prospect of sexual interaction with a partner produces sufficient aversion, fear or anxiety that sexual activity is avoided or, if it occurs, is associated with strong negative feelings and an inability to experience any pleasure.

C. The aversion is not a result of performance anxiety (reaction to previous failure of sexual response).

F52.11 Lack of sexual enjoyment

DCR-10

A. The general criteria for sexual dysfunction (F52) must be met.

B. Genital response (orgasm and/or ejaculation) occurs during sexual stimulation but is not accompanied by pleasurable sensations or feelings of pleasant excitement.

⇒

C. There is no manifest and persistent fear or anxiety during sexual activity (see F52.10, sexual aversion).

F52.2   Failure of genital response

The principal problem in men is erectile dysfunction (difficulty in developing or maintaining an erection suitable for satisfactory intercourse). In women the principal problem is vaginal dryness or failure of lubrication.

Female sexual arousal disorder

Male erectile disorder

Psychogenic impotence

Excludes: impotence of organic origin (N48.4)

DCR-10

A. The general criteria for sexual dysfunction (F52) must be met.
In addition, for men:

B. Erection sufficient for intercourse fails to occur when intercourse is attempted. The dysfunction takes one of the following forms:

   (1) full erection occurs during the early stages of lovemaking but disappears or declines when intercourse is attempted (before ejaculation if it occurs);

   (2) erection does occur, but only at times when intercourse is not being considered;

   (3) partial erection, insufficient for intercourse, occurs, but not full erection;

   (4) no penile tumescence occurs at all.

⇒

In addition, for women:

B. There is failure of genital response, experienced as failure of vaginal lubrication, together with inadequate tumescence of the labia. The dysfunction takes one of the following forms:

    (1) general: lubrication fails in all relevant circumstances;

    (2) lubrication may occur initially but fails to persist for long enough to allow comfortable penile entry;

    (3) situational: lubrication occurs only in some situations (e.g. with one partner but not another, or during masturbation, or when vaginal intercourse is not being contemplated).

F52.3 Orgasmic dysfunction

Orgasm either does not occur or is markedly delayed.

Inhibited orgasm (male) (female)

Psychogenic anorgasmy

DCR-10

A. The general criteria for sexual dysfunction (F52) must be met.

B. There is orgasmic dysfunction (either absence or marked delay of orgasm), which takes one of the following forms;

    (1) orgasm has never been experienced in any situation;

    (2) orgasmic dysfunction has developed after a period of relatively normal response:

(a) general: orgasmic dysfunction occurs in all situations and with any partner;

(b) situational:

for women: orgasm does occur in certain situations (e.g. when masturbating or with certain partners);

for men: one of the following can be applied:

> (i) orgasm only occurs during sleep, never during the waking state;
>
> (ii) orgasm never occurs in the presence of the partner;
>
> (iii) orgasm occurs in the presence of the partner but not during intercourse.

F52.4 Premature ejaculation

The inability to control ejaculation sufficiently for both partners to enjoy sexual interaction.

DCR-10

A. The general criteria for sexual dysfunction (F52) must be met.

B. There is an inability to delay ejaculation sufficiently to enjoy lovemaking, manifest as either of the following:

> (1) occurrence of ejaculation before or very soon after the beginning of intercourse (if a time limit is required: before or within 15 seconds of the beginning of intercourse):

$\Rightarrow$

213

Chapter V: Mental and behavioural disorders
Behavioural syndromes associated with physiological disturbances and physical factors

(2) ejaculation occurs in the absence of sufficient erection to make intercourse possible.

C. The problem is not the result of prolonged abstinence from sexual activity.

| F52.5 | Non-organic vaginismus |

Spasm of the pelvic floor muscles that surround the vagina, causing occlusion of the vaginal opening. Penile entry is either impossible or painful.

Psychogenic vaginismus

Excludes: vaginismus (organic) (N94.2)

DCR-10

A. The general criteria for sexual dysfunction (F52) must be met.

B. There is spasm of the perivaginal muscles, sufficient to prevent entry or make it uncomfortable. The dysfunction takes one of the following forms:

(1) normal response has never been experienced;

(2) vaginismus has developed after a period of relatively normal response:

(a) when vaginal entry is not attempted, a normal sexual response may occur;

(b) any attempt at sexual contact leads to generalized fear and efforts to avoid vaginal entry (e.g. spasm of the adductor muscles of the thighs).

F52.6 Non-organic dyspareunia

Dyspareunia (pain during sexual intercourse) occurs in both women and men. It can often be attributed to local pathology and should then properly be categorized under the pathological condition. This category is to be used only if there is no primary non-organic sexual dysfunction (e.g. vaginismus or vaginal dryness).

Psychogenic dyspareunia

Excludes: dyspareunia (organic) (N94.1)

DCR-10

A. The general criteria for sexual dysfunction (F52) must be met.

In addition, for women:

B. pain is experienced at the entry of the vagina, either throughout sexual intercourse or only when deep thrusting of the penis occurs.

C. The disorder is attributable to vaginismus or failure of lubrication; dyspareunia of organic origin should be classified according to the underlying disorder.

In addition, for men:

B. Pain or discomfort is experienced during sexual response. (The timing of pain and the exact localization should be carefully recorded.)

C. The discomfort is not the result of local physical factors. If physical factors are found, the dysfunction should be classified elsewhere.

F52.7 Excessive sexual drive

Nymphomania

Satyriasis

Diagnostic notes

No research criteria are attempted for this category. Researchers studying this category are recommended to design their own criteria.

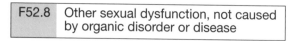

F52.8	Other sexual dysfunction, not caused by organic disorder or disease

F52.9	Unspecified sexual dysfunction, not caused by organic disorder or disease

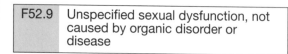

F53	Mental and behavioural disorders associated with the puerperium, not elsewhere classified

This category includes only mental disorders associated with the puerperium (commencing within 6 weeks of delivery) that do not meet the criteria for disorders classified elsewhere in this chapter, either because insufficient information is available, or because it is considered that special additional clinical features are present that make their classification elsewhere inappropriate.

Diagnostic notes

The inclusion of this category is a recognition of the severe practical problems in many developing countries that make the gathering of details about many cases of puerperal illness virtually impossible. However, even in the absence of sufficient information to allow a diagnosis (usually of an affective disorder, and more rarely of schizophrenia), there will usually be enough known to allow the diagnosis of a mild (F53.0) or severe (F53.1) disorder. This subdivision is useful for the estimation of workload and for decisions about the provision of services. Psychiatrists who are of the minority opinion that special postpartum psychoses exist that are clearly distinguishable from affective disorder or schizophrenia should use this category, but need to be aware of its real purpose.

After the code from this chapter indicating the type of mental disorder, a second code from Chapter XV of ICD-10 should be used (O99.3) to indicate association with the puerperium.

This category should be used in research work only in exceptional circumstances.

217

Chapter V: Mental and behavioural disorders
Behavioural syndromes associated with physiological disturbances and physical factors

F53.0 Mild mental and behavioural disorders associated with the puerperium, not elsewhere classified

Depression:

- postnatal NOS
- postpartum NOS

F53.1 Severe mental and behavioural disorders associated with the puerperium, not elsewhere classified

Puerperal psychosis NOS

F53.8 Other mental and behavioural disorders associated with the puerperium, not elsewhere classified

F53.9 Puerperal mental disorder, unspecified

F54 Psychological and behavioural factors associated with disorders or diseases classified elsewhere

This category should be used to record the presence of psychological or behavioural influences thought to have influenced the manifestation, or affected the course, of physical disorders that can be classified using other chapters of ICD-10. Any resulting mental disturbances are usually mild and often prolonged (such as worry, emotional conflict, apprehension), and do not of themselves justify the use of any of the categories in the rest of this book.

Psychological factors affecting physical conditions

Examples of the use of this category are:

asthma F54 and J45.–

dermatitis F54 and L23–L25

gastric ulcer F54 and K25.–

mucous colitis F54 and K58.–

ulcerative colitis F54 and K51.–

urticaria F54 and L50.–

Use additional code, if desired, to identify the associated physical disorder.

Excludes: tension-type headache (G44.2)

Diagnostic notes

In the rare instances where an overt psychiatric disorder is thought to have caused a physical disorder, a second additional code should be used to record the psychiatric disorder.

F55 Abuse of non-dependence-producing substances

A wide variety of medicaments and folk remedies may be involved, but the particularly important groups are (a) psychotropic drugs that do not produce dependence, such as antidepressants; (b) laxatives; and (c) analgesics that may be purchased without medical prescription, such as aspirin and paracetamol.

Persistent use of these substances often involves unnecessary contacts with medical professionals or supporting staff, and is sometimes accompanied by harmful physical effects of the substances. Attempts to dissuade or forbid the use of the substance are often met with resistance: for laxatives and analgesics this may be in spite of warnings about (or even the development of) physical harm such as renal dysfunction or electrolyte disturbances. Although it is usually clear that the patient has a strong motivation to take the substance, dependence or withdrawal symptoms do not develop as in the case of the psychoactive substances specified in F10–F19.

Abuse of:

- antacids

- herbal or folk remedies

- steroids or hormones

- vitamins

Laxative habit

Excludes: abuse of psychoactive substances (F10–F19)

A fourth character may be used to identify the type of substance involved:

F55.0   Antidepressants

(such as tetracyclic antidepressants and monoamine oxidase inhibitors)

F55.1   Analgesics

(such as aspirin, paracetamol, phenacetin, not specified as psychoactive in F10–F19)

F55.3   Antacids

F55.4   Vitamins

F55.5   Steroids or hormones

| F55.6 | Specific herbal or folk remedies |

| F55.8 | Other substances that do not produce dependence |

(such as diuretics)

| F55.9 | Unspecified |

| **F59** | **Unspecified behavioural syndromes associated with physiological disturbances and physical factors** |

Psychogenic physiological dysfunction NOS

Disorders of adult personality and behaviour (F60–F69)

This block includes a variety of conditions and behaviour patterns of clinical significance which tend to be persistent, and appear to be the expression of the individual's characteristic lifestyle and mode of relating to himself or herself and others. Some of these conditions and patterns of behaviour emerge early in the course of individual development, as a result of both constitutional factors and social experience, while others are acquired later in life. Specific personality disorders (F60.–), mixed and other personality disorders (F61.–) and enduring personality changes (F62.–) are deeply ingrained and enduring behaviour patterns, manifesting as inflexible responses to a broad range of personal and social situations. They represent extreme or significant deviations from the way in which the average individual in a given culture perceives, thinks, feels and, particularly, relates to others. Such behaviour patterns tend to be stable and to encompass multiple domains of behaviour and psychological functioning. They are frequently, but not always, associated with various degrees of subjective distress and problems of social performance.

Diagnostic notes

Personality disorders differ from personality change in their timing and the mode of their emergence; they are developmental conditions which appear in late childhood or adolescence and continue into adulthood. They are not secondary to another mental disorder or to brain disease, although they may precede and coexist with other disorders. In contrast, personality change is acquired, usually during adult life, following severe or prolonged stress, extreme environmental deprivation, serious psychiatric disorder or brain disease or injury (see F07.–).

Clyclothymia and schizotypal disorder were formerly classified with the personality disorders, but are now listed elsewhere (cyclothymia in F30–F39 and schizotypal disorder in F20–F29).

These are severe disturbances in the personality and behavioural tendencies of the individual not directly resulting from disease, damage or other insult to the brain, or from another psychiatric disorder. They usually involve several areas of the personality and are nearly always associated with considerable personal distress and social disruption. They are usually manifest since childhood or adolescence and continue throughout adulthood.

DCR-10

G1. There is evidence that the individual's characteristic and enduring patterns of inner experience and behaviour as a whole deviate markedly from the culturally expected and accepted range (or 'norm'). Such deviation must be manifest in more than one of the following areas:

(1) cognition (i.e. ways of perceiving and interpreting things, people and events; forming attitudes and images of self and others);

(2) affectivity (range, intensity and appropriateness of emotional arousal and response);

(3) control over impulses and gratification of needs;

(4) manner of relating to others and of handling interpersonal situations.

G2. The deviation must manifest itself pervasively as behaviour that is inflexible, maladaptive or otherwise dysfunctional across a broad range of personal and social situations (i.e. not being limited to one specific 'triggering' stimulus or situation).

⇒

G3.   There is personal distress, or adverse impact on the social environment, or both, clearly attributable to the behaviour referred to in criterion G2.

G4.   There must be evidence that the deviation is stable and of long duration, having its onset in late childhood or adolescence.

G5.   The deviation cannot be explained as a manifestation or consequence of other adult mental disorders, although episodic or chronic conditions from sections F00–F59 or F70–F79 of this classification may coexist with or be superimposed upon the deviation.

G6.   Organic brain disease, injury or dysfunction must be excluded as the possible cause of the deviation. (If an organic causation is demonstrable, category F07.– should be used.)

Diagnostic notes

The assessment criteria G1–G6 above should be based on as many sources of information as possible. Although it is sometimes possible to obtain sufficient evidence from a single interview with the individual, as a general rule it is recommended that more than one interview should take place and history be collected from informants or past records.

For further research, it is suggested that subcriteria should be developed to define behaviour patterns specific to different cultural settings concerning social norms, rules and obligations where needed (such as examples of irresponsibility and disregard of social norms in dissocial personality disorder).

For research purposes the diagnosis of personality disorder requires the identification of a subtype. (More than one subtype can be coded if there is compelling evidence that the individual meets multiple sets of criteria.)

F60.0 Paranoid personality disorder

Personality disorder characterized by excessive sensitivity to setbacks; unforgiveness of insults; suspiciousness and a tendency to distort experience by misconstruing the neutral or friendly actions of others as hostile or contemptuous; recurrent suspicions, without justification, regarding the sexual fidelity of the spouse or sexual partner; and a combative and tenacious sense of personal rights. There may be excessive self-importance and there is often excessive self-reference.

Personality (disorder):

- expansive paranoid
- fanatic
- querulant
- paranoid
- sensitive paranoid

Excludes: paranoia (F22.0):

  • querulans (F22.8)

  paranoid:

  • psychosis (F22.0)

  • schizophrenia (F20.0)

  • state (F22.0)

DCR-10

A. The general criteria for personality disorder (F60) must be met.

B. At least four of the following must be present:

  (1) excessive sensitivity to setbacks and rebuffs;

  (2) tendency to bear grudges persistently, e.g. refusal to forgive insults, injuries or slights;

  (3) suspiciousness and a pervasive tendency

⇒

to distort experience by misconstruing the neutral or friendly actions of others as hostile or contemptuous;

(4) a combative and tenacious sense of personal rights out of keeping with the actual situation;

(5) recurrent suspicions, without justification, regarding sexual fidelity of spouse or sexual partner;

(6) persistent self-referential attitude, associated particularly with excessive self-importance;

(7) preoccupation with ubsubstantiated 'conspiratorial' explanations of events either immediate to the patient or in the world at large.

F60.1 Schizoid personality disorder

Personality disorder characterized by withdrawal from affectional, social and other contacts, with a preference for fantasy, solitary activities and introspection. There is a limited capacity to express feelings and to experience pleasure.

Excludes: Asperger's syndrome (F84.5)

delusional disorder (F22.0)

schizoid disorder of childhood (F84.5)

schizophrenia (F20.–)

schizotypal disorder (F21)

DCR-10

A. The general criteria for personality disorder (F60) must be met.

⇒

B. At least four of the following must be present:

(1) few, if any, activities provide pleasure;

(2) display of emotional coldness, detachment or flattened affectivity;

(3) a limited capacity to express either warm, tender feelings or anger towards others;

(4) an appearance of indifference to either praise or criticism;

(5) little interest in having sexual experiences with another person (taking into account age);

(6) consistent choice of solitary activities;

(7) excessive preoccupation with fantasy and introspection;

(8) no desire for, or possession of, any close friends or confiding relationships (or only one);

(9) marked insensitivity to prevailing social norms and conventions (disregard for such norms and conventions is unintentional).

F60.2 Dissocial personality disorder

Personality disorder characterized by disregard for social obligations and callous unconcern for the feelings of others. There is gross disparity between behaviour and the prevailing social norms. Behaviour is not readily modifiable by adverse experience, including punishment. There is a low tolerance to frustration and a low threshold for discharge of aggression, including violence; there is a tendency to blame others, or to offer plausible rationalizations for the behaviour bringing the patient into conflict with society.

Personality (disorder):

- amoral
- antisocial
- asocial
- psychopathic
- sociopathic

Excludes: conduct disorders (F91.–)

emotionally unstable personality disorder (F60.3)

DCR-10

A. The general criteria for personality disorder (F60) must be met.

B. At least three of the following must be present:

(1) callous unconcern for the feelings of others;

(2) gross and persistent attitude of irresponsibility and disregard for social norms, rules and obligations;

(3) incapacity to maintain enduring relationships, though with no difficulty in establishing them;

(4) very low tolerance to frustration and a low threshold for discharge of aggression, including violence;

(5) incapacity to experience guilt, or to profit from adverse experience, particularly punishment;

(6) marked proneness to blame others, or to offer plausible rationalizations for the behaviour that has brought the individual into conflict with society.

Diagnostic notes

Persistent irritability and the presence of conduct disorder during childhood and adolescence complete the clinical picture but are not required for the diagnosis. It is suggested that subcriteria should be developed to define behaviour patterns specific to different cultural settings concerning social norms, rules and obligations where needed (such as examples of irresponsibility and disregard of social norms).

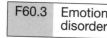

F60.3 Emotionally unstable personality disorder

Personality disorder characterized by a definite tendency to act impulsively and without consideration of the consequences; the mood is unpredictable and capricious. There is a tendency towards outbursts of emotion and an inability to control the behavioural explosions. There is a tendency to quarrelsome behaviour and to conflicts with others, especially when impulsive acts are thwarted or censored. Two types may be distinguished: the impulsive type, characterized predominantly by emotional instability and lack of impulsive control, and the borderline type, characterized in addition by disturbances in self-image, aims and internal preferences, by chronic feelings of emptiness, by intense and unstable interpersonal relationships, and by a tendency to self-destructive behaviour, including suicide gestures and attempts.

Personality (disorder):

- aggressive
- borderline
- explosive

Excludes: dissocial personality disorder (F60.2)

F60.30 Impulsive type

DCR-10

A. The general criteria for personality disorder (F60) must be met.

⇒

B. At least three of the following must be present, one of which must be (2):

   (1) marked tendency to act unexpectedly and without consideration of the consequences;

   (2) marked tendency to quarrelsome behaviour and to conflicts with others, especially when impulsive acts are thwarted or criticized;

   (3) liability to outbursts of anger or violence, with inability to control the resulting behavioural explosions;

   (4) difficulty in maintaining any course of action that offers no immediate reward;

   (5) unstable and capricious mood.

F60.31 Borderline type

DCR-10

A. The general criteria for personality disorder (F60) must be met.

B. At least three of the symptoms mentioned in criterion B for F60.30 must be present, with at least two of the following in addition:

   (1) disturbances in and uncertainty about self-image, aims and internal preferences (including sexual);

   (2) liability to become involved in intense and unstable relationships, often leading to emotional crises;

   (3) excessive efforts to avoid abandonment;

   (4) recurrent threats or acts of self-harm;

   (5) chronic feelings of emptiness.

F60.4   Histrionic personality disorder

Personality disorder characterized by shallow and labile affectivity, self-dramatization, theatricality, exaggerated expression of emotions, suggestibility, egocentricity, self-indulgence, lack of consideration for others, easily hurt feelings and continuous seeking for appreciation, excitement and attention.

Personality (disorder):

- hysterical
- psychoinfantile

DCR-10

A. The general criteria for personality disorder (F60) must be met.

B. At least four of the following must be present:

  (1) self-dramatization, theatricality or exaggerated expression of emotions;

  (2) suggestibility (the individual is easily influenced by others or by circumstances);

  (3) shallow and labile affectivity;

  (4) continual seeking for excitement and activities in which the individual is the centre of attention;

  (5) inappropriate seductiveness in appearance or behaviour;

  (6) overconcern with physical attractiveness.

Diagnostic notes

Egocentricity, self-indulgence, continuous longing for appreciation, lack of consideration for others, feelings that are easily hurt and persistent manipulative behaviour complete the clinical picture, but are not required for the diagnosis.

F60.5 Anankastic personality disorder

Personality disorder characterized by feelings of doubt, perfectionism, excessive conscientiousness, checking and preoccupation with details, stubbornness, caution and rigidity. There may be insistent and unwelcome thoughts or impulses that do not attain the severity of an obsessive–compulsive disorder.

Personality (disorder):

- compulsive

- obsessive

- obsessive–compulsive

Excludes
obsessive–compulsive disorder (F42.–)

DCR-10

A. The general criteria for personality disorder (F60) must be met.

B. At least four of the following must be present:

(1) feelings of excessive doubt and caution;

(2) preoccupation with details, rules, lists, order, organization or schedule;

(3) perfectionism that interferes with task completion;

(4) excessive conscientiousness and scrupulousness;

(5) undue preoccupation with productivity to the exclusion of pleasure and interpersonal relationships;

(6) excessive pedantry and adherence to social conventions;

(7) rigidity and stubbornness;

⇒

(8) unreasonable insistence by the individual that others submit to exactly his or her way of doing things, or unreasonable reluctance to allow others to do things.

F60.6 Anxious (avoidant) personality disorder

Personality disorder characterized by feelings of tension and apprehension, insecurity and inferiority. There is a continuous yearning to be liked and accepted, a hypersensitivity to rejection and criticism, with restricted personal attachments and a tendency to avoid certain activities by habitual exaggeration of the potential dangers or risks in everyday situations.

DCR-10

A. The general criteria for personality disorder (F60) must be met.

B. At least four of the following must be present:

(1) persistent and pervasive feelings of tension and apprehension;

(2) belief that one is socially inept, personally unappealing or inferior to others;

(3) excessive preoccupation with being critized or rejected in social situations;

(4) unwillingness to become involved with people unless certain of being liked;

(5) restrictions in lifestyle because of need for physical security;

(6) avoidance of social or occupational activities that involve significant interpersonal contact, because of fear of criticism, disapproval or rejection.

F60.7 Dependent personality disorder

Personality disorder characterized by pervasive reliance on other people to make one's major and minor life decisions, great fear of abandonment, feelings of help-lessness and incompetence, passive compliance with the wishes of elders and others, and a weak response to the demands of daily life. Lack of vigour may show itself in the intellectual or emotional spheres; there is often a tendency to transfer responsibility to others.

Personality (disorder):

- asthenic
- inadequate
- passive
- self-defeating

DCR-10

A. The general criteria for personality disorder (F60) must be met.

B. At least four of the following must be present:

(1) encouraging or allowing others to make most of one's important life decisions;

(2) subordination of one's own needs to those of others on whom one is dependent, and undue compliance with their wishes;

(3) unwillingness to make even reasonable demands on the people one depends on;

(4) feeling uncomfortable or helpless when alone, because of exaggerated fears of inability to care for oneself;

(5) preoccupation with fears of being left to care for oneself;

(6) limited capacity to take everyday decisions without an excessive amount of advice and reassurance from others.

Personality (disorder):

- eccentric
- 'haltlose' type
- immature
- narcissistic
- passive–aggressive
- psychoneurotic

Diagnostic notes

If none of the preceding rubrics is fitting, but a condition meeting the general criteria for personality disorder listed under F60 is nevertheless present, this code should be used (see also Annex 1). For research purposes an extra character may be added for identifying specific personality disorders not currently in ICD-10. In using code F60.8, it is recommended always to record a vignette description of the specific disorder.

F60.9 Personality disorder, unspecified

Character neurosis NOS

Pathological personality NOS

F61 Mixed and other personality disorders

This category is intended for personality disorders that are often troublesome but do not demonstrate the specific pattern of symptoms that characterize the disorders described in F60.–. As a result they are often more difficult to diagnose than the disorders in F60.–. Examples include – mixed personality disorders with features of several of the disorders in F60.– but without a predominant set of symptoms that would allow a more specific diagnosis; and troublesome personality changes not classifiable to F60.– or F62.–, and regarded as secondary to a main diagnosis of a coexisting affective or anxiety disorder.

Excludes: accentuated personality traits (Z73.1)

DCR-10

No attempt has been made to provide standard sets of criteria in detail for these mixed disorders, since those doing research in this field will prefer to state their own criteria depending upon the purpose of their studies. For such work, the following codes are suggested:

F61.0   Mixed personality disorders*

Features of several of the disorders in F60.– are present, but not to the extent that the criteria for any of the specified personality disorders in that category are met.

F61.1   Troublesome personality changes*

F60.9   Personality disorder, unspecified

F62   Enduring personality changes, not attributable to brain damage and disease

Disorders of adult personality and behaviour that have developed in persons with no previous personality disorder following exposure to catastrophic or excessive

*This four-character code is not included in Chapter V(F) of ICD-10.

prolonged stress, or following a severe psychiatric illness. These diagnoses should be made only when there is evidence of a definite and enduring change in a person's pattern of perceiving, relating to or thinking about the environment and him- or herself. The personality change should be significant and be associated with inflexible and maladaptive behaviour not present before the pathological experience. The change should not be a direct manifestation of another mental disorder or a residual symptom of any antecedent mental disorder.

Excludes: personality and behavioral disorder due to brain disease, damage and dysfunction (F07.–)

F62.0	Enduring personality change after catastrophic experience

Enduring personality change, present for at least 2 years, following exposure to catastrophic stress. The stress must be so extreme that it is not necessary to consider personal vulnerability in order to explain its profound effect on the personality. The disorder is characterized by a hostile or distrustful attitude towards the world, social withdrawal, feelings of emptiness or hopelessness, a chronic feeling of 'being on edge' as if constantly threatened, and estrangement. Post-traumatic stress disorder (F43.1) may precede this type of personality change.

Personality change after:

- concentration camp experiences

- disasters

- prolonged:

  - captivity with an imminent possibility of being killed

  - exposure to life-threatening situations such as being a victim of terrorism

- torture

Excludes: post-traumatic stress disorder (F43.1)

DCR-10

A. There must be evidence (from the personal history or from key informants) of a definite and persistent change in the individual's patter of perceiving, relating to and thinking about the environment and the self, following exposure to catastrophic stress (e.g. concentration camp experience; torture; disaster; prolonged exposure to life-threatening situations).

B. The personality change should be significant and represent inflexible and maladaptive features, as indicated by the presence of at least two of the following:

   (1) a permanent hostile or distrustful attitude toward the world in a person who previously showed no such traits;

   (2) social withdrawal (avoidance of contacts with people other than a few close relatives with whom the individual lives) which is not due to another current mental disorder (such as a mood disorder);

   (3) a constant feeling of emptiness or hopelessness, not limited to a discrete episode of mood disorder, which was not present before the catastrophic stress experience; this may be associated with increased dependency on others, inability to express negative or aggressive feelings, and prolonged depressive mood without any evidence of depressive disorder before exposure to the catastrophic stress;

   (4) an enduring feeling of being 'on edge' or of being threatened without any external cause, as evidenced by an increased vigilance and irritability in a person who

⇒

previously showed no such traits or hyperalertness; this chronic state of inner tension and feeling threatened may be associated with a tendency to excessive drinking or use of drugs;

(5) a permanent feeling of being changed or of being different from others (estrangement); this feeling may be associated with an experience of emotional numbness.

C. The change should cause significant interference with personal functioning in daily living, personal distress or adverse impact on the social environment.

D. The personality change should have developed after the catastrophic experience, and there should be no history of a pre-existing adult personality disorder or trait accentuation, or of personality or developmental disorders during childhood or adolescence that could explain the current personality traits.

E. The personality change must have been present for at least 2 years. It is not related to episodes of any other mental disorder (except post-traumatic stress disorder) and cannot be explained by brain damage or disease.

F. The personality change meeting the above criteria is often preceded by a post-traumatic stress disorder (F43.1). The symptoms of the two conditions can overlap and the personality change may be a chronic outcome of a post-traumatic stress disorder. However, an enduring personality change should not be assumed in such cases unless, in addition to at least 2 years of post-traumatic stress disorder, there has been a further period of no less than 2 years during which the above criteria have been met.

F62.1 Enduring personality change after psychiatric illness

Personality change, persisting for at least 2 years, attributable to the traumatic experience of suffering from a severe psychiatric illness. The change cannot be explained by a previous personality disorder and should be differentiated from residual schizophrenia and other states of incomplete recovery from an antecedent mental disorder. This disorder is characterized by an excessive dependence on and a demanding attitude towards others; conviction of being changed or stigmatized by the illness, leading to an inability to form and maintain close and confiding personal relationships and to social isolation; passivity, reduced interests and diminished involvement in leisure activities; persistent complaints of being ill, which may be associated with hypochondriacal claims and illness behaviour; dysphoric or labile mood, not due to the presence of a current mental disorder or antecedent mental disorder with residual affective symptoms; and long-standing problems in social and occupational functioning.

DCR-10

A. There must be evidence of a definite and enduring change in the individual's pattern of perceiving, relating to and thinking about the environment and the self, following the experience of suffering from one or several episodes of psychiatric illness from which he or she has recovered clinically without residual symptoms.

B. The personality change should be significant and represent inflexible and maladaptive features, as indicated by the presence of at least two of the following:

   (1) dependence on others (the individual passively assumes, or demands, that others take responsibility for his or her own life, and is unwilling to decide on

important issues related to his or her actions or future);

(2) social withdrawal or isolation, which is secondary to a conviction (not delusional) or feeling of being 'changed' or stigmatized as a result of the illness; this conviction or feeling may be strengthened by societal attitudes but cannot be completely explained by the objective social circumstances; feeling vulnerable to others' moral opprobrium (narcissistic injury) may also be a factor but such feeling should be egosyntonic if it is to be considered an enduring personality trait;

(3) passivity, reduced interests and diminished involvement in previously entertained leisure activities (which may reinforce the social isolation);

(4) a change in self-perception, leading to a frequent or constant claim of being ill; this may be associated with hypochondriacal behaviour and an increased utilization of psychiatric or other medical services;

(5) a demanding attitude toward other people in which the individual expects special favour or considers himself or herself deserving of special attention or treatment;

(6) dysphoric or labile mood, not due to a current mental disorder or antecedent mental disorder with residual affective symptoms.

C. The personality change following the psychiatric illness must be understandable in terms of the individual's subjective emotional experience of the situation, his or her previous adjustment, vulnerabilities and

⇒

life situation, including the attitudes or
reactions of significant others following the
illness.

D. The personality change should cause
significant interference with personal
functioning in daily living, personal distress
or adverse impact on the social
environment.

E. There should be no history of a pre-existing
adult personality disorder or trait
accentuation, or of personality or
developmental disorders during childhood
or adolescence that could explain the current
personality traits.

F. The personality change has been present for
at least 2 years and is not a manifestation of
another mental disorder or secondary to
brain damage or disease.

| F62.8 | Other enduring personality changes |

Chronic pain personality syndrome

| F62.9 | Enduring personality change, unspecified |

| F63 | Habit and impulse disorders |

This category includes certain disorders of behaviour
that are not classifiable under other categories. They are
characterized by repeated acts that have no clear rational
motivation, cannot be controlled and generally harm the
patient's own interests and those of other people. The
patient reports that the behaviour is associated with
impulses to action. The cause of these disorders is not
understood and they are grouped together because of

broad descriptive similarities, not because they are known to share any other important features.

Excludes: habitual excessive use of alcohol or psychoactive substances (F10–F19)

impulse and habit disorders involving sexual behaviour (F65.–)

| F63.0 | Pathological gambling |

The disorder consists of frequent, repeated episodes of gambling that dominate the patient's life to the detriment of social, occupational, material and family values and commitments.

Compulsive gambling

Excludes: excessive gambling by manic patients (F30.–)

gambling and betting NOS (Z72.6)

gambling in dissocial personality disorder (F60.2)

DCR-10

A. Two episodes of gambling occur over a period of at least 1 year.

B. These episodes do not have a profitable outcome for the individual but are continued despite personal distress and interference with personal functioning in daily living.

C. The individual describes an intense urge to gamble which is difficult to control, and reports that he or she is unable to stop gambling by an effort of will.

D. The individual is preoccupied with thoughts or mental images of the act of gambling or the circumstances surrounding the act.

F63.1 Pathological fire-setting (pyromania)

Disorder characterized by multiple acts of, or attempts at, setting fire to property or other objects, without apparent motive, and by a persistent preoccupation with subjects related to fire and burning. This behaviour is often associated with feelings of increasing tension before the act and intense excitement immediately after-wards.

Excludes: fire-setting (by) (in):

- adult with dissocial personality disorder (F60.2)
- alcohol or psychoactive substance intoxication (F10–F19, with common fourth character .0)
- as the reason for observation for suspected mental disorder (Z03.2)
- conduct disorders (F91.–)
- organic mental disorders (F00–F09)
- schizophrenia (F20.–)

DCR-10

A. There are two or more acts of fire-setting without apparent motive.

B. The individual describes an intense urge to set fire to objects, with a feeling of tension before the act and relief afterwards.

C. The individual is preoccupied with thoughts or mental images of fire-setting or of the circumstances surrounding the act (e.g. abnormal interest in fire-engines, or in calling out the fire service).

F63.2 Pathological stealing (kleptomania)

Disorder characterized by repeated failure to resist impulses to steal objects that are not acquired for personal use or monetary gain. The objects may instead be discarded, given away or hoarded. This behaviour is usually accompanied by an increasing sense of tension before, and a sense of gratification during and immediately after, the act.

Excludes: depressive disorder with stealing (F31–F33)

organic mental disorders (F00–F09)

shoplifting as the reason for observation for suspected mental disorder (Z03.2)

DCR-10

A. There are two or more thefts in which the individual steals without any apparent motive of personal gain or gain for another person.

B. The individual describes an intense urge to steal, with a feeling of tension before the act and relief afterwards.

F63.3 Trichotillomania

A disorder characterized by noticeable hair-loss due to a recurrent failure to resist impulses to pull out hairs. The hair-pulling is usually preceded by mounting tension and is followed by a sense of relief or gratification. This diagnosis should not be made if there is a pre-existing inflammation of the skin, or if the hair-pulling is in response to a delusion or a hallucination.

Excludes: stereotyped movement disorder with hair-plucking (F98.4)

DCR-10

A. Noticeable hair-loss is caused by the individual's persistent and recurrent failure to resist impulses to pull out hairs.

B. The individual describes an intense urge to pull out hairs, with mounting tension before the act and a sense of relief afterwards.

C. There is no pre-existing inflammation of the skin, and the hairpulling is not in response to a delusion or hallucination.

| F63.8 | Other habit and impulse disorders |

Other kinds of persistently repeated maladaptive behaviour that are not secondary to a recognized psychiatric syndrome, and in which it appears that the patient is repeatedly failing to resist impulses to carry out the behaviour. There is a prodromal period of tension with a feeling of release at the time of the act.

Intermittent explosive disorder

| F63.9 | Habit and impulse disorder, unspecified |

| F64 | Gender identity disorders |

| F64.0 | Transsexualism |

A desire to live and be accepted as a member of the opposite sex, usually accompanied by a sense of discomfort with, or inappropriateness of, one's anatomic sex, and a wish to have surgery and hormonal treatment to make one's body as congruent as possible with one's preferred sex.

DCR-10

A. The individual desires to live and be accepted as a member of the opposite sex, usually accompanied by the wish to make his or her body as congruent as possible with the preferred sex through surgery and hormonal treatment.

B. The transsexual identity has been present persistently for at least 2 years.

C. The disorder is not a symptom of another mental disorder, such as schizophrenia, nor is it associated with chromosome abnormality.

F64.1	Dual-role transvestism

The wearing of clothes of the opposite sex for part of the individual's existence in order to enjoy the temporary experience of membership of the opposite sex, but without any desire for a more permanent sex change or associated surgical reassignment, and without sexual excitement accompanying the cross-dressing.

Gender identity disorder of adolescence or adulthood, non-transsexual type

Excludes: fetishistic transvestism (F65.1)

DCR-10

A. The individual wears clothes of the opposite sex in order to experience temporarily membership of the opposite sex.

B. There is no sexual motivation for the cross-dressing.

C. The individual has no desire for a permanent change to the opposite sex.

F64.2 Gender identity disorder of childhood

A disorder, usually first manifest during early childhood (and always well before puberty), characterized by a persistent and intense distress about assigned sex, together with a desire to be (or insistence that one is) of the other sex. There is a persistent preoccupation with the dress and activities of the opposite sex and repudiation of the individual's own sex. The diagnosis requires a profound disturbance of the normal gender identity; mere tomboysihness in girls or girlish behaviour in boys is not sufficient. Gender identity disorders in individuals who have reached or are entering puberty should not be classified here but in F66.–.

Excludes: egodystonic sexual orientation (F66.1)

sexual maturation disorder (F66.0)

DCR-10

For girls:

A. The individual shows persistent and intense distress about being a girl, and has a stated desire to be a boy (not merely a desire for any perceived cultural advantages to being a boy), or insists that she is a boy.

B. Either of the following must be present:

(1) persistent marked aversion to normative feminine clothing and insistence on wearing stereotypical masculine clothing, e.g. boys' underwear and other accessories;

(2) persistent repudiation of female anatomical structures, as evidenced by at least one of the following:

   (a) an assertion that she has, or will grow, a penis;

   (b) rejection of urinating in a sitting position;

⇒

      (c) assertion that she does not want to grow breasts or menstruate.

C. The girl has not yet reached puberty.

D. The disorder must have been present for at least 6 months.

For boys:

A. The individual shows persistent and intense distress about being a boy, and has a desire to be a girl or, more rarely, insists that he is a girl.

B. Either of the following must be present:

    (1) preoccupation with stereotypic female activities, as shown by a preference for either cross-dressing or simulating female attire, or by an intense desire to participate in the games and pastimes of girls and rejection of stereotypical male toys, games and activities;

    (2) persistent repudiation of male anatomical structures, as indicated by at least one of the following repeated assertions:

      (a) that he will grow up to become a woman (not merely in role);

      (b) that his penis or testes are disgusting or will disappear;

      (c) that it would be better not to have a penis or testes.

C. The boy has not yet reached puberty.

D. The disorder must have been present for at least 6 months.

| F64.8 | Other gender identity disorders |

| F64.9 | Gender identity disorder, unspecified |

Gender-role disorder NOS

| F65 | Disorders of sexual preference |

Includes: paraphilias

DCR-10

General criteria for all of F65.0–F65.8

G1. The individual experiences recurrent intense sexual urges and fantasies involving unusual objects or activities.

G2. The individual either acts on the urges or is markedly distressed by them.

G3. The preference has been present for at least 6 months.

| F65.0 | Fetishism |

Reliance on some non-living object as a stimulus for sexual arousal and sexual gratification. Many fetishes are extensions of the human body, such as articles of clothing or footwear. Other common examples are characterized by some particular texture such as rubber, plastic or leather. Fetish objects vary in their importance to the individual. In some cases they simply serve to enhance sexual excitement achieved in ordinary ways (e.g. having the partner wear a particular garment).

DCR-10

A. The general criteria for disorders of sexual preference (F65) must be met.

B. The fetish (a non-living object) is the most important source of sexual stimulation or is essential for satisfactory sexual response.

Diagnostic notes

Fetishism is limited almost exclusively to males.

F65.1	Fetishistic transvestism

The wearing of clothes of the opposite sex principally to obtain sexual excitement and to create the appearance of a person of the opposite sex. Fetishistic transvestism is distinguished from transsexual transvestism by its clear association with sexual arousal and the strong desire to remove the clothing once orgasm occurs and sexual arousal declines. It can occur as an earlier phase in the development of transsexualism.

Transvestic fetishism

DCR-10

A. The general criteria for disorders of sexual preference (F65) must be met.

B. The individual wears articles of clothing of the opposite sex in order to create the appearance and feeling of being a member of the opposite sex.

C. The cross-dressing is closely associated with sexual arousal. Once orgasm occurs and sexual arousal declines, there is a strong desire to remove the clothing.

F65.2 Exhibitionism

A recurrent or persistent tendency to expose the genitalia to strangers (usually of the opposite sex) or to people in public places, without inviting or intending closer contact. There is usually, but not invariably, sexual excitement at the time of exposure and the act is commonly followed by masturbation.

DCR-10

A. The general criteria for disorders of sexual preference (F65) must be met.

B. There is a recurrent or a persistent tendency to expose the genitalia to unsuspecting strangers (usually of the opposite sex), which is invariably associated with sexual arousal and masturbation.

C. There is no intention to have sexual intercourse with the 'witness(es)'.

F65.3 Voyeurism

A recurrent or persistent tendency to look at people engaging in sexual or intimate behaviour such as undressing. This is carried out without the observed people being aware, and usually leads to sexual excitement and masturbation.

DCR-10

A. The general criteria for disorders of sexual preference (F65) must be met.

B. There is a recurrent or a persistent tendency to look at people engaging in sexual or intimate behaviour such as undressing, which is associated with sexual excitement and masturbation.

⇒

> C. There is no intention of sexual involvement
>   with the person(s) observed.

F65.4 Paedophilia

A sexual preference for children, boys and girls or both, usually of prepubertal or early pubertal age.

> **DCR-10**
>
> A. The general criteria for disorders of sexual
>   preference (F65) must be met.
>
> B. There is a persistent or predominant pref-
>   erence for sexual activity with a prepubescent
>   child or children.
>
> C. The individual is at least 16 years old and at
>   least 5 years older than the child or children
>   in criterion B.

F65.5 Sadomasochism

A preference for sexual activity which involves the infliction of pain or humiliation, or bondage. If the subject
prefers to be the recipient of such stimulation this is
called masochism; if the provider, sadism. Often an
individual obtains sexual excitement from both sadistic
and masochistic activities.

Masochism

Sadism

> **DCR-10**
>
> A. The general criteria for disorders of sexual
>   preference (F65) must be met.

⇒

B. There is a preference for sexual activity, as recipient (masochism) or provider (sadism), or both, which involves at least one of the following:

(1) pain

(2) humiliation

(3) bondage

C. The sadomasochistic activity is the most important source of stimulation or is necessary for sexual gratification.

F65.6 Multiple disorders of sexual preference

Sometimes more than one abnormal sexual preference occurs in one person and there is none of first rank. The most common combination is fetishism, transvestism and sadomasochism.

F65.8 Other disorders of sexual preference

A variety of other patterns of sexual preference and activity, including making obscene telephone calls, rubbing up against people for sexual stimulation in crowded public places, sexual activity with animals, use of strangulation or anoxia for intensifying sexual excitement and a preference for partners with some particular anatomical abnormality such as an amputated limb.

Frotteurism

Necrophilia

Diagnostic notes

Erotic practices are too diverse and many too rare or idiosyncratic to justify a separate term for each. Swallowing urine, smearing faeces or piercing foreskin or nipples may be part of the behavioural repertoire in sadomasochism. Masturbatory rituals of various kinds are common, but the more extreme practices, such as the insertion of objects into the rectum or penile urethra, or partial self-strangulation, when they take the place of ordinary sexual contacts, amount to abnormalities. Necrophilia should also be coded here.

| F65.9 | Disorder of sexual preference, unspecified |

Sexual deviation NOS

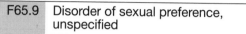

| F66 | Psychological and behavioural disorders associated with sexual development and orientation |

This section is intended to cover those types of problems that derive from variations of sexual development or orientation, when the sexual preference *per se* is not necessarily problematic or abnormal.

Sexual orientation by itself is not to be regarded as a disorder.

| F66.0 | Sexual maturation disorder |

The patient suffers from uncertainty about his or her gender identity or sexual orientation, which causes anxiety or depression. Most commonly this occurs in adolescents who are not certain whether they are homosexual, heterosexual or bisexual in orientation, or in individuals who, after a period of apparently stable sexual orientation (often within a long-standing relationship), find that their sexual orientation is changing.

| F66.1 | Egodystonic sexual orientation |

The gender identity or sexual preference (heterosexual, homosexual, bisexual or prepubertal) is not in doubt, but the individual wishes it were different because of associated psychological and behavioural disorders, and may seek treatment in order to change it.

| F66.2 | Sexual relationship disorder |

The gender identity or sexual orientation (heterosexual, homosexual or bisexual) is responsible for difficulties in forming or maintaining a relationship with a sexual partner.

| F66.8 | Other psychosexual development disorders |

| F66.9 | Psychosexual development disorder, unspecified |

| **F68** | **Other disorders of adult personality and behaviour** |

| F68.0 | Elaboration of physical symptoms for psychological reasons |

Physical symptoms compatible with and originally due to a confirmed physical disorder, disease or disability become exaggerated or prolonged due to the psychological state of the patient. The patient is commonly distressed by this pain or disability, and is often preoccupied with worries, which may be justified, of the possibility of prolonged or progressive disability or pain.

Compensation neurosis

Diagnostic notes

Dissatisfaction with the result of treatment or investigations, or disappointment with the amount of personal attention received in wards and clinics, may be a motivating factor. Some cases appear to be clearly motivated by the possibility of financial compensation following accidents or injuries, but the syndrome does not necessarily resolve rapidly even after successful litigation.

DCR-10

A. Physical symptoms originally due to a confirmed physical disorder, disease or disability become exaggerated or prolonged in excess of what can be explained by the physical disorder itself.

B. There is evidence for a psychological causation for the excess symptoms (such as evident fear of disability or death, possible financial compensation, disappointment at the standard of care experienced).

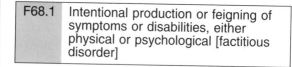

F68.1 Intentional production or feigning of symptoms or disabilities, either physical or psychological [factitious disorder]

The patient feigns symptoms repeatedly for no obvious reason and may even inflict self-harm in order to produce symptoms or signs. The motivation is obscure and presumably internal, with the aim of adopting the sick role. The disorder is often combined with marked disorders of personality and relationships.

Hospital hopper syndrome.

Münchhausen's syndrome

Peregrinating patient

Excludes: factitial dermatitis (L98.1)

person feigning illness (with obvious motivation) (Z76.5)

Münchhausen by proxy (child abuse) (T74.8)

Diagnostic notes

Malingering (Z76.5) is distinguished from this disorder by the clarity of the motivation. The commonest external motives for malingering include evading criminal prosecution, obtaining illicit drugs, avoiding military conscription or dangerous military duty, and attempts to obtain sickness benefits or improvements in housing conditions. Malingering is comparatively common in legal and military circles, and comparatively uncommon in ordinary civilian life.

DCR-10

A. The individual exhibits a persistent pattern of intentional production or feigning of symptoms and/or self-infliction of wounds in order to produce symptoms.

B. No evidence can be found for an external motivation, such as financial compensation, escape from danger or more medical care. (If such evidence can be found, category Z76.5, malingering should be used.)

C. *Most commonly used exclusion clause.* There is no confirmed physical or mental disorder that could explain the symptoms.

F68.8 Other specified disorders of adult personality and behaviour

Character disorder NOS

Relationship disorder NOS

Diagnostic notes

This category should be used for coding any specified disorder of adult personality and behaviour that cannot be classified under any one of the preceding headings.

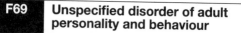

F69 Unspecified disorder of adult personality and behaviour

Diagnostic notes

This code should be used only as a last resort, if the presence of a disorder of adult personality and behaviour can be assumed but information to allow its diagnosis and allocation to a specific category is lacking.

Mental retardation (F70–F79)

A condition of arrested or incomplete development of the mind, which is especially characterized by impairment of skills manifested during the developmental period, skills which contribute to the overall level of intelligence, i.e. cognitive, language, motor and social abilities. Retardation can occur with or without any other mental or physical condition.

Degrees of mental retardation are conventionally estimated by standardized intelligence tests which can be supplemented by scales assessing social adaptation in a given environment. These measures provide an approximate indication of the degree of mental retardation. The diagnosis will also depend on the overall assessment of intellectual functioning by a skilled diagnostician.

Intellectual abilities and social adaptation may change over time and, however poor, may improve as a result of training and rehabilitation. Diagnosis should be based on the current levels of functioning.

The following fourth-character subdivisions are for use with categories F70–F79 to identify the extent of impairment of behaviour:

.0 With the statement of no, or minimal, impairment of behaviour

.1 significant impairment of behaviour requiring attention or treatment

.8 other impairments of behaviour

.9 without mention of impairment of behaviour.

Use additional code, if desired, to identify associated conditions such as autism, other developmental disorders, epilepsy, conduct disorders or severe physical handicap.

Diagnostic notes

A specially designed multiaxial system is required to do justice to the variety of personal, clinical and social statements needed for the assessment of the causes and consequences of mental retardation. One such system is now in preparation for this section of Chapter V (F) of ICD-10.

F70   Mild mental retardation

Approximate IQ range of 50–69 (in adults, mental age from 9 to under 12 years). Likely to result in some learning difficulties in school. Many adults will be able to work and maintain good social relationships and contribute to society.

Includes: feeble-mindedness

mild mental subnormality

F71   Moderate mental retardation

Approximate IQ range of 35–49 (in adults, mental age from 6 to under 9 years). Likely to result in marked developmental delays in childhood but most can learn to develop some degree of independence in self-care and acquire adequate communication and academic skills. Adults will need varying degrees of support to live and work in the community.

Includes: moderate mental subnormality

F72   Severe mental retardation

Approximate IQ range of 20–34 (in adults, mental age from 3 to under 6 years). Likely to result in continuous need of support.

Includes: severe mental subnormality

F73   Profound mental retardation

IQ under 20 (in adults, mental age below 3 years). Results in severe limitation in self-care, continence, communication and mobility.

Includes: profound mental subnormality

F78   Other mental retardation

F79   Unspecified mental retardation

Includes: mental:

- deficiency NOS
- subnormality NOS

DCR-10 for Mental retardation (F70–F79)

Detailed clinical diagnostic criteria that can be used internationally for research cannot be specified for mental retardation in the same way as they can for most of the other disorders in Chapter V (F). This is because the two main components of mental retardation, namely low cognitive ability and diminished social competence, are both profoundly affected by social and cultural influences in the way that they become manifest. Only general guidance can be given here about the most appropriate methods of assessment to use.

1. Level of cognitive abilities. Depending upon the cultural norms and expectations of the subjects, research workers must make their own judgements as to how best to estimate intelligence quotient or mental age according to the bands given in F7, as already given above.

2. Level of social competence. Within most European and American cultures the Vineland Social Maturity Scale[1] is recommended for use, if it is judged to be appropriate (modified versions or equivalent scales need to be developed for use in other cultures).

---

[1] Doll, E. A. *Vineland Social Maturity Scale, condensed manual of directions.* Circle Pines MN, American Guidance Service Inc., 1965.

Disorders of psychological development (F80–F89)

The disorders included in this block have in common (a) onset invariably during infancy or childhood; (b) impairment or delay in the development of functions that are strongly related to biological maturation of the central nervous system; and (c) a steady course without remissions and relapses. In most cases, the functions affected include language, visuospatial skills and motor coordination. Usually the delay or impairment has been present from as early as it could be detected reliably and will diminish progressively as the child grows older, although milder deficits often remain in adult life.

F80 Specific developmental disorders of speech and language

Disorders in which normal patterns of language acquisition are disturbed from the early stages of development. The conditions are not directly attributable to neurological or speech mechanism abnormalities, sensory impairments, mental retardation or environmental factors. Specific developmental disorders of speech and language are often followed by associated problems, such as difficulties in reading and spelling, abnormalities in interpersonal relationships and emotional and behavioural disorders.

F80.0 Specific speech articulation disorder

A specific developmental disorder in which the child's use of speech sounds is below the appropriate level for its mental age, but in which there is normal level of language skills.

Developmental:

- phonological disorder
- speech articulation disorder

dyslalia

functional speech articulation disorder

lalling

Excludes: speech articulation impairment (due to):

- aphrasia NOS (R47.0)
- apraxia (R48.2)
- hearing loss (H90–H91)
- mental retardation (F70–F79)
- with language developmental disorder:
- expressive (F80.1)
- receptive (F80.2)

Diagnostic notes

This disorder is also referred to as specific speech phonological disorder.

DCR-10

A. Articulation (phonological) skills, as assessed on standardized tests, are below the 2 standard deviations limit for the child's age.

B. Articulation (phonological) skills are at least 1 standard deviation below non-verbal IQ as assessed on standardized tests.

C. Language expression and comprehension, as assessed on standardized tests, are within the 2 standard deviations limit for the child's age.

D. There are no neurological, sensory or physical impairments that directly affect speech sound production, nor is there a pervasive developmental disorder (F84.–)

E. *Most commonly used exclusion clause.* Non-verbal IQ is below 70 on a standardized test.

F80.1   Expressive language disorder

A specific developmental disorder in which the child's ability to use expressive spoken language is markedly below the appropriate level for its mental age, but in which language comprehension is within normal limits. There may or may not be abnormalities in articulation.

Developmental dysphasia or aphasia, expressive type

Excludes: acquired aphasia with epilepsy [Landau–Kleffner] (F80.3)

developmental dysphasia or aphasia, receptive type (F80.2)

dysphasia and aphasia NOS (R47.0)

elective mutism (F94.0)

mental retardation (F70–F79)

pervasive developmental disorders (F84.–)

DCR-10

A. Expressive language skills, as assessed on standardized tests, are below the 2 standard deviations limit for the child's age.

B. Expressive language skills are at least 1 standard deviation below non-verbal IQ as assessed on standardized tests.

C. Receptive language skills, as assessed on standardized tests, are within the 2 standard deviations limit for the child's age.

D. Use and understanding of non-verbal communication and imaginative language functions are within the normal range.

E. There are no neurological, sensory or physical impairments that directly affect the use of spoken language, nor is there a pervasive developmental disorder (F84.–).

⇒

F. *Most commonly used exclusion clause.* Non-verbal IQ is below 70 on a standardized test.

F80.2 Receptive language disorder

A specific developmental disorder in which the child's understanding of language is below the appropriate level for its mental age. In virtually all cases expressive language will also be markedly affected and abnormalities in word-sound production are common.

Congenital auditory imperception

Developmental:

- dysphasia or aphasia, receptive type
- Wernicke's aphasia

Word deafness

Excludes: acquired aphasia with epilepsy [Landau–Kleffner] (F80.3)

autism (F84.0, F84.1)

dysphasia and aphasia:

- NOS (R47.0)
- expressive type (F80.1)

elective mutism (F94.0)

language delay due to deafness (H90–H91)

mental retardation (F70–F79)

Diagnostic note

This disorder is also referred to as mixed receptive/expressive disorder.

DCR-10

A. Language comprehension, as assessed on standardized tests, is below the 2 standard deviations limit for the child's age.

⇒

B. Receptive language skills are at least 1 standard deviation below non-verbal IQ as assessed on standardized tests.

C. There are no neurological, sensory or physical impairments that directly affect receptive language, nor is there a pervasive developmental disorder (F84.–).

D. *Most commonly used exclusion clause.* Non-verbal IQ is below 70 on a standardized test.

F80.3 Acquired aphasia with epilepsy [Landau–Kleffner syndrome]

A disorder in which the child, having previously made normal progress in language development, loses both receptive and expressive language skills but retains general intelligence; the onset of the disorder is accompanied by paroxysmal abnormalities on EEG, and in the majority of cases also by epileptic seizures. Usually the onset is between the ages of 3 and 7 years, with skills being lost over days or weeks. The temporal association between the onset of seizures and loss of language is variable, with one preceding the other (either way round) by a few months to two years. An inflammatory encephalitic process has been suggested as a possible cause of this disorder. About two-thirds of patients are left with a more or less severe receptive language deficit.

Excludes: aphasia (due to):

- NOS (R47.0)
- autism (F84.0, F84.1)
- disintegrative disorders of childhood (F84.2, F84.3)

DCR-10

A. Severe loss of expressive and receptive language skills occurs over a period of time not exceeding 6 months.

⇒

B. Language development was normal before the loss.

C. Paroxysmal EEG abnormalities affecting one or both temporal lobes becomes apparent within a time span extending from 2 years before to 2 years after the initial loss of language.

D. Hearing is within the normal range.

E. A level of non-verbal intelligence within the normal range is retained.

F. There is no diagnosable neurological condition other than that implicit in the abnormal EEG and the presence of epileptic seizures (when they occur).

G. The disorder does not meet the criteria for a pervasive developmental disorder (F84.–).

| F80.8 | Other developmental disorders of speech and language |

Lisping

| F80.9 | Developmental disorder of speech and language, unspecified |

Language disorder NOS

This category should be avoided as far as possible and should be used only for unspecified disorders in which there is significant impairment in the development of speech or language that cannot be accounted for by mental retardation, or by neurological, sensory or physical impairments that directly affect speech or language.

F81 Specific developmental disorders of scholastic skills

Disorders in which the normal patterns of skill acquisition are disturbed from the early stages of development. This is not simply a consequence of a lack of opportunity to learn, it is not solely a result of mental retardation, and it is not due to any form of acquired brain trauma or disease

F81.0 Specific reading disorder

The main feature is a specific and significant impairment in the development of reading skills that is not solely accounted for by mental age, visual acuity problems or inadequate schooling. Reading comprehension skill, reading word recognition, oral reading skill and the performance of tasks requiring reading may all be affected. Spelling difficulties are frequently associated with specific reading disorder and often remain into adolescence, even after some progress in reading has been made. Specific developmental disorders of reading are commonly preceded by a history of disorders in speech or language development. Associated emotional and behavioural disturbances are common during the school-age period.

'Backward reading'

Developmental dyslexia

Specific reading retardation

Excludes: alexia NOS (R48)

dyslexia NOS (R48.0)

reading difficulties secondary to emotional disorders (F93.–)

DCR-10

A. Either of the following must be present:

   (1) a score on reading accuracy and/or comprehension that is at least 2

⇒

standard errors of prediction below the level expected on the basis of the child's chronological age and general intelligence, with both reading skills and IQ assessment on an individually administered test standardized for the child's culture and educational system;

(2) a history of serious reading difficulties, or test scores that met criterion A(1) at an earlier age, plus a score on a spelling test that is at least 2 standard errors of prediction below the level expected on the basis of the child's chronological age and IQ.

B. The disturbance described in criterion A significantly interferes with academic achievement or with activities of daily living that require reading skills.

C. The disorder is not the direct result of a defect in visual or hearing acuity, or of a neurological disorder.

D. School experiences are within the average expectable range (i.e. there have been no extreme inadequacies in educational experiences).

E. *Most commonly used exclusion clause.* IQ is below 70 on an individually administered standardized test.

Possible additional inclusion criterion

For some research purposes, investigators may wish to specify a history of some level of impairment during the preschool years in speech, language, sound categorization, motor coordination, visual processing, attention or control or modulation of activity.

Diagnostic notes

The above criteria would not include general reading backwardness of a type that would fall within the clinical guidelines. The research diagnostic criteria for general reading backwardness would be the same as for specific reading disorder, except that criterion A(1) would specify reading skills 2 standard errors of prediction below the level expected on the basis of chronological age (i.e. not taking IQ into account), and criterion A(2) would follow the same principal for spelling. The validity of the differentiation between these two varieties of reading problem is not unequivocally established, but it seems that the specific type has a more specific association with language retardation (whereas general reading backwardness is associated with a wider range of developmental disabilities), and is more prevalent in boys than in girls.

There are further research differentiations that are based on analyses of the types of spelling error.

F81.1 Specific spelling disorder

The main feature is a specific and significant impairment in the development of spelling skills in the absence of a history of specific reading disorder, which is not solely accounted for by low mental age, visual acuity problems or inadequate schooling. The ability to spell orally and to write out words correctly are both affected.

Specific spelling retardation (without reading disorder)

Excludes: agraphia NOS (R48.8)

spelling difficulties:

- associated with a reading disorder (F81.0)

- due to inadequate teaching (Z55.8)

DCR-10

A. The score on a standardized spelling test is at least 2 standard errors of prediction below the level expected on the basis of the child's chronological age and general intelligence.

⇒

B. Scores on reading accuracy and comprehension and on arithmetic are within the normal range (± 2 standard deviations from the mean).

C. There is no history of significant reading difficulties.

D. School experience is within the average expectable range (i.e. there have been no extreme inadequacies in educational experiences).

E. Spelling difficulties have been present from the early stages of learning to spell.

F. The disturbance described in criterion A significantly interferes with academic achievement or with activities of daily living that require spelling skills.

G. *Most commonly used exclusion clause.* IQ is below 70 on an individually administered standardized test.

F81.2 Specific disorder of arithmetical skills

Involves a specific impairment in arithmetical skills that is not solely explicable on the basis of general mental retardation or of inadequate schooling. The deficit concerns mastery of basic computational skills of addition, subtraction, multiplication and division, rather than of the more abstract mathematical skills involved in algebra, trigonometry, geometry or calculus.

Developmental:

- acalculia
- arithmetical disorder
- Gerstmann's syndrome

Excludes:

acalculia NOS (R48.8)

arithmetical difficulties:

- association with a reading or spelling disorder (F81.3)
- due to inadequate teaching (Z55.8)

DCR-10

A. The score on a standardized arithmetic test is at least 2 standard errors of prediction below the level expected on the basis of the child's chronological age and general intelligence.

B. Scores on reading accuracy and comprehension and on spelling are within the normal range (± 2 standard deviations from the mean).

C. There is no history of significant reading or spelling difficulties.

D. School experience is within the average expectable range (i.e. there have been no extreme inadequacies in educational experiences).

E. Arithmetical difficulties have been present from the early stages of learning arithmetic.

F. The disturbance described in criterion A significantly interferes with academic achievement or with activities of daily living that require arithmetical skills.

G. *Most commonly used exclusion clause.* IQ is below 70 on an individually administered standardized test.

F81.3 Mixed disorder of scholastic skills

An ill-defined residual category of disorders in which both arithmetical and reading or spelling skills are significantly impaired, but in which the disorder is not solely explicable in terms of general mental retardation or of inadequate schooling. It should be used for disorders meeting the criteria for both F81.2 and either F81.0 or F81.1.

Excludes: specific:

- disorder of arithmetical skills (F81.2)
- reading disorder (F81.0)
- spelling disorder (F81.1)

F81.8 Other developmental disorders of scholastic skills

Developmental expressive writing disorder

F81.9 Developmental disorder of scholastic skills, unspecified

Knowledge acquisition disability NOS

Learning:

- disability NOS
- disorder NOS

This category should be avoided as far as possible and should be used only for unspecified disorders in which there is a significant disability of learning that cannot be solely accounted for by mental retardation, visual acuity problems or inadequate schooling.

F82 Specific developmental disorder of motor function

A disorder in which the main feature is a serious impairment in the development of motor coordination that is not solely explicable in terms of general intellectual retardation or of any specific congenital or acquired neurological disorder. Nevertheless, in most cases a careful clinical examination shows marked neurodevelopmental immaturities, such as choreiform movements of unsupported limbs or mirror movements and other associated motor features, as well as signs of impaired fine and gross motor coordination.

Clumsy child syndrome

Developmental:

- coordination disorder
- dyspraxia

Excludes: abnormalities of gait and mobility (R26.–)

lack of coordination (R27.–):

- secondary to mental retardation (F70–F79)

DCR-10

A. The score on a standardized test of fine or gross motor coordination is at least 2 standard deviations below the level expected for the child's chronological age.

B. The disturbance described in criterion A significantly interferes with academic achievement or with activities of daily living.

C. There is no diagnosable neurological disorder.

D. *Most commonly used exclusion clause.* IQ is below 70 on an individually administered standardized test.

F83 Mixed specific developmental disorders

A residual category for disorders in which there is some admixture of specific developmental disorders of speech and language, of scholastic skills and of motor function, but in which none predominates sufficiently to constitute the prime diagnosis. This mixed category should be used only when there is a major overlap between each of these specific developmental disorders. The disorders are usually, but not always, associated with some degree of general impairment of cognitive functions. Thus, the category should be used when there are dysfunctions meeting the criteria for two or more of F80.–, F81.– and F82.

F84 Pervasive developmental disorders

A group of disorders characterized by qualitative abnormalities in reciprocal social interactions and in patterns of communication, and by a restricted, stereotyped, repetitive repertoire of interests and activities. These qualitative abnormalities are a pervasive feature of the individual's functioning in all situations.

Use additional code, if desired, to identify any associated medical condition and mental retardation.

F84.0 Childhood autism

A type of pervasive developmental disorder that is defined by (a) the presence of abnormal or impaired development that is manifest before the age of 3 years, and (b) the characteristic type of abnormal functioning in all the three areas of psychopathology: reciprocal social interaction, communication and restricted, stereotyped, repetitive behaviour. In addition to these specific diagnostic features, a range of other non-specific problems are common, such as phobias, sleeping and eating disturbances, temper tantrums and (self-directed) aggression.

Autistic disorder

Infantile:

- autism
- psychosis

Kanner's syndrome

Excludes: autistic psychopathy (F84.5)

DCR-10

A. Abnormal or impaired development is evident before the age of 3 years in at least one of the following areas:

    (1) receptive or expressive language as used in social communication;

    (2) the development of selective social attachments or of reciprocal social interaction;

    (3) functional or symbolic play.

B. A total of at least six symptoms from (1), (2) and (3) must be present, with at least two from (1) and at least one from each of (2) and (3):

    (1) Qualitative abnormalities in reciprocal social interaction are manifest in at least two of the following areas:

        (a) failure adequately to use eye-to-eye gaze, facial expression, body posture and gesture to regulate social interaction;

        (b) failure to develop (in a manner appropriate to mental age, and despite ample opportunities) peer relationships that involve a mutual sharing of interests, activities, and emotions;

        (c) lack of socio-emotional reciprocity, as shown by an impaired or deviant response to other people's emotions; or lack of modulation of behaviour according to social context or a weak integration of social, emotional and communicative behaviours;

        (d) lack of spontaneous seeking to share enjoyment, interests or achievements with other people (e.g. a lack of showing, bringing or pointing out to other people objects of interest to the individual).

(2) Qualitative abnormalities in communication are manifest in at least one of the following areas:

(a) a delay in, a total lack of, development of spoken language that is not accompanied by an attempt to compensate through the use of gesture or mime as an alternative mode of communication (often preceded by a lack of communicative babbling);

(b) relative failure to initiate or sustain conversational interchange (at whatever level of language skills are present), in which there is reciprocal responsiveness to the communications of the other person;

(c) stereotyped and repetitive use of language or idiosyncratic use of words or phrases;

(d) lack of varied spontaneous make-believe or (when young) social imitative play.

(3) Restricted, repetitive and stereotyped patterns of behaviour, interests and activities are manifest in at least one of the following areas:

(a) an encompassing preoccupation with one or more stereotyped and restricted patterns of interest that are abnormal in content or focus; or one or more interests that are abnormal in their intensity and circumscribed

⇒

nature, though not in their content or focus.

(b) apparently compulsive adherence to specific, non-functional routines or rituals;

(c) stereotyped and repetitive motor mannerisms that involve either hand or finger flapping or twisting, or complex whole-body movements;

(d) preoccupations with part-objects or non-functional elements of play materials (such as their odour, the feel of their surface, or the noise or vibration that they generate);

C. The clinical picture is not attributable to the other varieties of pervasive developmental disorder: specific developmental disorder of receptive language (F80.2) with secondary socioemotional problems; reactive attachment disorder (F94.1) or disinhibited attachment disorder (F94.2); mental retardation (F70–F72) with some associated emotional or behavioural disorder; schizophrenia (F20.–) of unusually early onset; and Rett's syndrome (F84.2).

F84.1 Atypical autism

A type of pervasive developmental disorder that differs from childhood autism either in age of onset or in failing to fulfil all three sets of diagnostic criteria. This subcategory should be used when there is abnormal and impaired development that is present only after age 3 years, and a lack of sufficient demonstrable abnormalities in one or two of the three areas of psychopathology required for the diagnosis of autism (namely, reciprocal social interactions, communication and restricted, stereotyped, repetitive behaviour) in spite of characteristic abnormalities in the other area(s). Atypical autism arises most often in profoundly retarded individuals and in individuals with a severe specific developmental disorder of receptive language.

Atypical childhood psychosis

Mental retardation with autistic features

Use additional code (F70–F79), if desired, to identify mental retardation.

DCR-10

A. Abnormal or impaired development is evident at or after the age of 3 years (criteria as for autism except for age of manifestation).

B. There are qualitative abnormalities in reciprocal social interaction or in communication, or restricted, repetitive and stereotyped patterns of behaviour, interests and activities. (Criteria as for autism, except that it is unnecessary to meet the criteria for number of areas of abnormality.)

C. The disorder does not meet the diagnostic criteria for autism (F84.0). Autism may be atypical in either age of onset (F84.0) or symptoms (F84.11); the two types are differentiated with a fifth character for research purposes. Syndromes that are atypical in both respects should be coded F84.12.

F84.10 Atypicality in age of onset

DCR-10

A. The disorder does not meet criterion A for autism (F84.0); that is, abnormal or impaired development is evident only at or after the age of 3 years.

⇒

B. The disorder meets criteria B and C for autism (F84.0).

F84.11 Atypicality in symptomatology

DCR-10

A. The disorder meets criterion A for autism (F84.0); that is abnormal or impaired development is evident before the age of 3 years.

B. There are qualitative abnormalities in reciprocal social interactions or in communication, or restricted, repetitive and stereotyped patterns of behaviour, interests and activities. (Criteria as for autism, except that it is unnecessary to meet the criteria for number of areas of abnormality.)

C. The disorder meets criterion C for autism (F84.0).

D. The disorder does not fully meet criterion B for autism (F84.0).

F84.12 Atypicality in both age of onset and symptomatology

DCR-10

A. The disorder does not meet criterion A for autism (F84.0); that is, abnormal or impaired development is evident only at or after the age of 3 years.

B. There are qualitative abnormalities in reciprocal social interactions or in com-

⇒

munication, or restricted, repetitive and stereotyped patterns of behaviour, interests and activities. (Criteria as for autism, except that it is unnecessary to meet the criteria for number of areas of abnormality.)

C. The disorder meets criterion C for autism (F84.0).

D. The disorder does not fully meet criterion B for autism (F84.0).

F84.2   Rett's syndrome

A condition, so far found only in girls, in which apparently normal early development is followed by partial or complete loss of speech and of skills in locomotion and use of hands, together with deceleration in head growth, usually with an onset between 7 and 24 months of age. Loss of purposive hand movements, hand-wringing stereotypies and hyperventilation are characteristic. Social and play development are arrested but social interest tends to be maintained. Trunk ataxia and apraxia start to develop by age 4 years and choreoathetoid movements frequently follow. Severe mental retardation almost invariably results.

DCR-10

A. There is an apparently normal prenatal and perinatal period and apparently normal psychomotor development through the first 5 months and normal head circumference at birth.

B. There is declaration of head growth between 5 months and 4 years and loss of acquired purposeful hand skills between 5 and 30 months of age that is associated with concurrent communication dysfunction and impaired social interactions and the appear-

⇒

ance of poorly coordinated/unstable gait and/or trunk movements.

C. There is severe impairment of expressive and receptive language, together with severe psychomotor retardation.

D. There are stereotyped midline hand movements (such as hand-wringing or 'hand-washing') with an onset at or after the time when purposeful hand movements are lost.

F84.3 Other childhood disintegrative disorder

A type of pervasive developmental disorder that is defined by a period of entirely normal development before the onset of the disorder, followed by a definite loss of previously acquired skills in several areas of development over the course of a few months. Typically, this is accompanied by a general loss of interest in the environment, by stereotyped repetitive motor mannerisms, and by autistic-like abnormalities in social interaction and communication. In some cases the disorder can be shown to be due to some associated encephalopathy, but the diagnosis should be made on the behavioural features.

Dementia infantilis

Disintegrative psychosis

Heller's syndrome

Symbiotic psychosis

Use additional code, if desired, to identify any associated neurological condition.

Excludes: Rett's syndrome (F84.2)

DCR-10

A. Development is apparently normal up to the age of at least 2 years. The presence of normal age-appropriate skills in communication, social relationships, play and adaptive behaviour at age 2 years or later is required for diagnosis.

B. There is a definite loss of previously acquired skills at about the time of onset of the disorder. The diagnosis requires a clinically significant loss of skills (not just a failure to use them in certain situations) in at least two of the following areas:

(1) expressive or receptive language

(2) play

(3) social skills or adaptive behaviour

(4) bowel or bladder control

(5) motor skills.

C. Qualitatively abnormal social functioning is manifest in at least two of the following areas:

(1) qualitative abnormalities in reciprocal social interaction (of the type defined for autism);

(2) qualitative abnormalities in communication (of the type defined for autism);

(3) restricted, repetitive and stereotyped patterns of behaviour, interests and activities, including motor stereotypies and mannerisms;

(4) a general loss of interest in objects and in the environment.

D. The disorder is not attributable to the other varieties of pervasive developmental disorder: acquired aphasia with epilepsy (F80.6); elective mutism (F94.0); Rett's syndrome (F84.2) or schizophrenia (F20.–).

F84.4 Overactive disorder associated with mental retardation and stereotyped movements

An ill-defined disorder of uncertain nosological validity. The category is designed to include a group of children with severe mental retardation (IQ below 50) who show major problems in hyperactivity and in attention, as well as stereotyped behaviours. They tend not to benefit from stimulant drugs (unlike those with an IQ in the normal range) and may exhibit a severe dysphoric reaction (sometimes with psychomotor retardation) when given stimulants. In adolescence, the overactivity tends to be replaced by underactivity (a pattern that is not usual in hyperkinetic children with normal intelligence). This syndrome is also often associated with a variety of developmental delays, either specific or global. The extent to which the behavioural pattern is a function of low IQ or of organic brain damage is not known.

DCR-10

A. Severe motor hyperactivity is manifest by at least two of the following problems in activity and attention:

(1) continuous motor restlessness, manifest in running, jumping and other movements of the whole body;

(2) marked difficulty in remaining seated: the child will ordinarily remain seated for a few seconds at most, except when engaged in a stereotypic activity (see criterion B);

(3) grossly excessive activity in situations where relative stillness is expected;

(4) very rapid changes of activity, so that activities generally last for less than a minute (occasional longer periods spent in highly favoured activities do not exclude this, and very long periods spent

⇒

in stereotypic activities can also be compatible with the presence of this problem at other times).

B. Repetitive and stereotyped patterns of behaviour and activity are manifest by at least one of the following:

(1) fixed and frequently repeated motor mannerisms: these may involve either complex movements of the whole body or partial movements such as handflapping;

(2) excessive and non-functional repetition of activities that are constant in form: this may be play with a single object (e.g. running water) or a ritual of activities (either alone or involving other people);

(3) repetitive self-injury.

C. IQ is less than 50.

D. There is no social impairment of the autistic type, i.e. the child must show at least three of the following:

(1) developmentally appropriate use of eye gaze, expression and posture to regulate social interaction;

(2) developmentally appropriate peer relationships that include sharing of interests, activities etc.;

(3) approaches to other people, at least sometimes, for comfort and affection;

(4) ability to share other people's enjoyment at times; other forms of social impairment, e.g. a disinhibited approach to strangers, are compatible with the diagnosis.

E. The disorder does not meet diagnostic criteria for autism (F84.0 and F84.1), child-

hood disintegrative disorder (F84.3), or
hyperkinetic disorders (F90.–).

F84.5 Asperger's syndrome

A disorder of uncertain nosological validity, characterized by the same type of qualitative abnormalities of
reciprocal social interaction that typify autism, together
with a restricted, stereotyped, repetitive repertoire of
interests and activities. It differs from autism primarily
in the fact that there is no general delay or retardation
in language or in cognitive development. This disorder
is often associated with marked clumsiness. There is a
strong tendency for the abnormalities to persist into
adolescence and adult life. Psychotic episodes occasionally occur in early adult life.

Autistic psychopathy

Schizoid disorder of childhood

DCR-10

A. There is no clinically significant general delay
    in spoken or receptive language or cognitive
    development. Diagnosis requires that single
    words should have developed by 2 years of age
    or earlier, and that communicative phrases be
    used by 3 years of age or earlier. Self-help
    skills, adaptive behaviour and curiosity about
    the environment during the first 3 years
    should be at a level consistent with normal
    intellectual development. However, motor
    milestones may be somewhat delayed and
    motor clumsiness is usual (although not a
    necessary diagnostic feature). Isolated special
    skills, often related to abnormal pre-
    occupations, are common, but are not
    required for diagnosis.

⇒

B. There are qualitative abnormalities in reciprocal social interaction (criteria as for autism).

C. The individual exhibits an unusually intense circumscribed interest or restricted, repetitive and stereotyped patterns of behaviour, interests and activities (criteria as for autism; however, it would be less usual for these to include either motor mannerisms or preoccupations with part-objects or non-functional elements of play materials).

D. The disorder is not attributable to the other varieties of pervasive developmental disorder: simple schizophrenia (F20.6); schizotypal disorder (F21); obsessive–compulsive disorder (F42.–); anankastic personality disorder (F60.5); reactive and disinhibited attachment disorders of childhood (F94.1 and F94.2, respectively).

F84.8	Other pervasive developmental disorders

F84.9	Pervasive developmental disorder, unspecified

This is a residual diagnostic category that should be used for disorders that fit the general description for pervasive developmental disorders but in which contradictory findings or a lack of adequate information mean that the criteria for any of the other F84 codes cannot be met.

F88	Other disorders of psychological development

Developmental agnosia

F89 Unspecified disorder of psychological development

Developmental disorder NOS

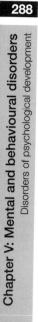

288

Chapter V: Mental and behavioural disorders
Disorders of psychological development

Behavioural and emotional disorders with onset usually occurring in childhood and adolescence (F90–F98)

289

Chapter V: Mental and behavioural disorders
Behavioural and emotional disorders with onset usually occurring in childhood and adolescence

F90 Hyperkinetic disorders

A group of disorders characterized by early onset (usually in the first 5 years of life), lack of persistence in activities that require cognitive involvement and a tendency to move from one activity to another without completing any one, together with disorganized, illregulated and excessive activity. Several other abnormalities may be associated. Hyperkinetic children are often reckless and impulsive, prone to accidents and find themselves in disciplinary trouble because of unthinking breaches of rules rather than deliberate defiance. Their relationships with adults are often socially disinhibited, with a lack of normal caution and reserve. They are unpopular with other children and may become isolated. Impairment of cognitive functions is common, and specific delays in motor and language development are disproportionately frequent. Secondary complications include dissocial behaviour and low self-esteem.

Excludes: anxiety disorders (F41.–)

mood [affective] disorders (F30–F39)

pervasive developmental disorders (F84.–)

schizophrenia (F20.–)

DCR-10

The research diagnosis of hyperkinetic disorder requires the definite presence of abnormal levels of inattention, hyperactivity and impulsivity that are pervasive across situations and persistent over time, and which are not caused by other disorders such as autism or affective disorders.

⇒

G1. *Inattention.* At least six of the following symptoms of inattention have persisted for at least 6 months, to a degree that is maladaptive and inconsistent with the developmental level of the child:

(1) often fails to give close attention to details, or makes careless errors in schoolwork, work or other activities;

(2) often fails to sustain attention in tasks or play activities;

(3) often appears not to listen to what is being said to him or her;

(4) often fails to follow through on instructions or to finish schoolwork, chores or duties in the workplace (not because of oppositional behaviour or failure to understand instructions);

(5) is often impaired in organizing tasks and activities;

(6) often avoids or strongly dislikes tasks, such as housework, that require sustained mental effort;

(7) often loses things necessary for certain tasks or activities, such as school assignments, pencils, books, toys or tools;

(8) is often easily distracted by external stimuli;

(9) is often forgetful in the course of daily activities.

G2. *Hyperactivity.* At least three of the following symptoms of hyperactivity have persisted for at least 6 months, to a degree that is maladaptive and inconsistent with the developmental level of the child:

(1) often fidgets with hands or feet or squirms on seat;

291

Chapter V: Mental and behavioural disorders
Behavioural and emotional disorders with onset usually occurring in childhood and adolescence

    (2) leaves seat in classroom or in other situations in which remaining seated is expected;

    (3) often runs about or climbs excessively in situations in which it is inappropriate (in adolescents or adults, only feelings of restlessness may be present);

    (4) is often unduly noisy in playing, or has difficulty in engaging quietly in leisure activities;

    (5) exhibits a persistent pattern of excessive motor activity that is not substantially modified by social context or demands.

G3. *Impulsivity.* At least one of the following symptoms of impulsivity has persisted for at least 6 months, to a degree that is maladaptive and inconsistent with the developmental level of the child:

    (1) often blurts out answers before questions have been completed;

    (2) often fails to wait in lines or await turns in games or group situations;

    (3) often interrupts or intrudes on others (e.g. butts into others' conversations or games);

    (4) often talks excessively without appropriate response to social constraints.

G4. Onset of the disorder is no later than the age of 7 years.

G5. *Pervasiveness.* The criteria should be met for more than a single situation, e.g. the combination of inattention and hyperactivity should be present both at home

$\Rightarrow$

and at school, or at both school and another setting where children are observed, such as a clinic (evidence for cross-situationality will ordinarily require information from more than one source; parental reports about classroom behaviour, for instance, are unlikely to be sufficient).

G6. The symptoms in G1–G3 cause clinically significant distress or impairment in social, academic or occupational functioning.

G7. The disorder does not meet the criteria for pervasive developmental disorders (F84.–) manic episode (F30.–), depressive episode (F32.–) or anxiety disorders (F41.–).

Diagnostic notes

Many authorities also recognize conditions that are sub-threshold for hyperkinetic disorder. Children who meet criteria in other ways but do not show abnormalities of hyperactivity/impulsiveness may be recognized as showing *attention deficit*; conversely, children who fall short of criteria for attention problems but meet criteria in other respects may be recognized as showing *activity disorder*. In the same way, children who meet criteria for only one situation (e.g. only the home or only the classroom) may be regarded as showing a *home-specific* or *classroom-specific disorder*. These conditions are not yet included in the main classification because of insufficient empirical predictive validation, and because many children with subthreshold disorders show other syndromes (such as oppositional defiant disorder, F91.3) and should be classified in the appropriate category.

F90.0 Disturbance of activity and attention

Attention deficit:

• disorder with hyperactivity

- hyperactivity disorder
- syndrome with hyperactivity

Excludes: hyperkinetic disorder associated with conduct disorder (F90.1)

> **DCR-10**
>
> The general criteria for hyperkinetic disorder (F90) must be met, but not those for conduct disorders (F91.–)

F90.1 Hyperkinetic conduct disorder

Hyperkinetic disorder associated with conduct disorder.

> **DCR-10**
>
> The general criteria for both hyperkinetic disorder (F90) and conduct disorders (F91.–) must be met.

F90.8 Other hyperkinetic disorders

F90.9 Hyperkinetic disorder, unspecified

Hyperkinetic reaction of childhood or adolescence NOS

Hyperkinetic syndrome NOS

> **DCR-10**
>
> This residual category is not recommended and should be used only when there is a lack of differentiation between F90.0 and F90.1 but the overall criteria for F90.– are fulfilled.

F91   Conduct disorders

Disorders characterized by a repetitive and persistent pattern of dissocial, aggressive or defiant conduct. Such behaviour should amount to major violations of age-appropriate social expectations; it should therefore be more severe than ordinary childish mischief or adolescent rebelliousness, and should imply an enduring pattern of behaviour (6 months or longer). Features of conduct disorder can also be symptomatic of other psychiatric conditions, in which case the underlying diagnosis should be preferred.

Examples of the behaviours on which the diagnosis is based include excessive levels of fighting or bullying, cruelty to other people or animals, severe destructiveness to property, fire-setting, stealing, repeated lying, truancy from school and running away from home, unusually frequent and severe temper tantrums, and disobedience. Any one of these behaviours, if marked, is sufficient for the diagnosis, but isolated dissocial acts are not.

Excludes: mood [affective] disorders (F30–F39)

pervasive developmental disorders (F84.–)

schizophrenia (F20.–)

when associated with:

- emotional disorders (F92.–)
- hyperkinetic disorders (F90.1)

DCR-10

G1.   There is a repetitive and persistent pattern of behaviour in which either the basic rights of others or major age-appropriate societal norms or rules are violated, lasting at least 6 months, during which some of the following symptoms are present (see individual sub-categories for rules or numbers of symptoms). **Note:** The symptoms in 11, 13, 15, 16, 20, 21 and 23 need only have occurred once for the criterion to be fulfilled.

⇒

295

Chapter V: Mental and behavioural disorders
Behavioural and emotional disorders with onset usually occurring in childhood and adolescence

The individual:

   (1) has unusually frequent or severe
       temper tantrums for his or her
       developmental level;

   (2) often argues with adults;

   (3) often actively refuses adults' requests
       or defies rules;

   (4) often, apparently deliberately, does
       things that annoy other people;

   (5) often blames others for his or her own
       mistakes or misbehaviour;

   (6) is often 'touchy' or easily annoyed by
       others;

   (7) is often angry or resentful;

   (8) is often spiteful or vindictive;

   (9) often lies or breaks promises to obtain
       goods or favours or to avoid
       obligations;

   (10) frequently initiates physical fights
        (this does not include fights with
        siblings);

   (11) has used a weapon that can cause
        serious physical harm to others (e.g.
        bat, brick, broken bottle, knife, gun);

   (12) despite parental prohibition, often
        stays out after dark (beginning before
        13 years of age);

   (13) exhibits physical cruelty to other
        people (e.g. ties up, cuts or burns a
        victim);

   (14) exhibits physical cruelty to animals;

   (15) deliberately destroys the property of
        others (other than by fire-setting);

⇒

(16) deliberately sets fire with a risk or intention of causing serious damage;

(17) steals objects of non-trivial value without confronting the victim either within the home or outside (e.g. shoplifting, burglary, forgery);

(18) is frequently truant from school, beginning before 13 years of age;

(19) has run away from parental or parental surrogate home at least twice, or has run away once for more than a single night (this does not include leaving to avoid physical or sexual abuse);

(20) commits a crime involving confrontation with the victim (including purse-snatching, extortion, mugging);

(21) forces another person into sexual activity;

(22) frequently bullies others (e.g. deliberate infliction of pain or hurt, including persistent intimidation, tormenting or molestation);

(23) breaks into someone else's house, building or car.

G2. The disorder does not meet the criteria for dissocial personality disorder (F60.2), schizophrenia (F20.–), manic episode (F30.–), depressive episode (F32.–), pervasive developmental disorders (F84.–), or hyperkinetic disorder (F90.–). (If the criteria for emotional disorder (F93.–) are met, the diagnosis should be mixed disorder of conduct and emotions, F92.–.)

⇒

It is recommended that the age of onset be specified:

– *childhood-onset type*: onset of at least one conduct problem before the age of 10 years;

– *adolescent-onset type*: no conduct problems before the age of 10 years.

Specification for possible subdivisions

Authorities differ on the best way of subdividing the conduct disorders, although most agree that the disorders are heterogeous. For determining prognosis, the severity (indexed by number of symptoms) is a better guide than the precise type of symptomatology. The best-validated distinction is that between socialized and unsocialized disorders, defined by the presence or absence of lasting peer friendships. However, it seems that disorders confined to the family context may also constitute an important variety, and a category is provided for this purpose. It is clear that further research is needed to test the validity of all proposed subdivisions of conduct disorder.

In addition to these categorizations, it is recommended that cases be described in terms of their scores on three dimensions of disturbance:

(1) hyperactivity (inattentive, restless behaviour);

(2) emotional disturbance (anxiety, depression, obsessionality, hypochondriasis);

(3) severity of conduct disorder:

    (a) *mild*: few if any conduct problems are in excess of those required to make the diagnosis, *and* conduct problems cause only minor harm to others;

    (b) *moderate*: the number of conduct problems and the effects on others are intermediate between 'mild' and 'severe';

297

Chapter V: Mental and behavioural disorders
Behavioural and emotional disorders with onset usually occurring in childhood and adolescence

(c) *severe*: there are many conduct problems in excess of those required to make the diagnosis, *or* the conduct problems cause considerable harm to others, e.g. severe physical injury, vandalism or theft.

F91.0 Conduct disorder confined to the family context

Conduct disorder involving dissocial or aggressive behaviour (and not merely oppositional, defiant, disruptive, behaviour), in which the abnormal behaviour is entirely, or almost entirely, confined to the home and to interactions with members of the nuclear family or immediate household. The disorder requires that the overall criteria for F91.– be met; even severely disturbed parent–child relationships are not of themselves sufficient for diagnosis.

DCR-10

A. The general criteria for conduct disorder (F91) must be met.

B. Three or more of the symptoms listed for F91 criterion G1 must be present, with at least three from items (9)–(23).

C. At least one of the symptoms from items (9)–(23) must have been present for at least 6 months.

D. Conduct disturbance must be limited to the family context.

F91.1 Unsocialized conduct disorder

Disorder characterized by the combination of persistent dissocial or aggressive behaviour (meeting the overall criteria for F91.– and not merely comprising oppositional, defiant, disruptive behaviour) with significant pervasive abnormalities in the individual's relationships with other children.

Conduct disorder, solitary aggressive type

Unsocialized aggressive disorder

299

Chapter V: Mental and behavioural disorders
Behavioural and emotional disorders with onset usually occurring in childhood and adolescence

---

DCR-10

A. The general criteria for conduct disorder (F91) must be met.

B. Three or more of the symptoms listed for F91 criterion G1 must be present, with at least three from items (9)–(23).

C. At least one of the symptoms from items (9)–(23) must have been present for at least 6 months.

D. There must be definitely poor relationships with the individual's peer group, as shown by isolation, rejection or unpopularity, and by a lack of lasting close reciprocal friendships.

F91.2   Socialized conduct disorder

Disorder involving persistent dissocial or aggressive behaviour (meeting the overall criteria for F91.– and not merely comprising oppositional, defiant, disruptive behaviour) occurring in individuals who are generally well integrated into their peer group.

Conduct disorder, group type

Group delinquency

Offences in the context of gang membership

Stealing in company with others

Truancy from school

DCR-10

A. The general criteria for conduct disorder (F91) must be met.

B. Three or more of the symptoms listed for F91 criterion G1 must be present, with at least three from items (9)–(23).

C. At least one of the symptoms from items (9)–(23) must have been present for at least 6 months.

D. Conduct disturbance must include settings outside the home or family context.

E. Peer relationships are within normal limits.

| F91.3 | Oppositional defiant disorder |

Conduct disorder, usually occurring in younger children, primarily characterized by markedly defiant, disobedient, disruptive behaviour that does not include delinquent acts or the more extreme forms of aggressive or dissocial behaviour. The disorder requires that the overall criteria for F91.– be met; even severely mischievous or naughty behaviour is not in itself sufficient for diagnosis. Caution should be employed before using this category, especially with older children, because clinically significant conduct disorder will usually be accompanied by dissocial or aggressive behaviour that goes beyond mere defiance, disobedience or disruptiveness.

DCR-10

A. The general criteria for conduct disorder (F91) must be met.

B. Four or more of the symptoms listed for F91 criterion G1 must be present, but with no

more than two symptoms from items (9)–
(23).

C.   The symptoms in criterion B must be mal-
     adaptive and inconsistent with the devel-
     opmental level.

D.   At least four of the symptoms must have been
     present for at least 6 months.

301

Chapter V: Mental and behavioural disorders
Behavioural and emotional disorders with onset usually occurring in childhood and adolescence

| F91.8 | Other conduct disorders |

| F91.9 | Conduct disorder, unspecified |

Childhood;

* behavioural disorder NOS
* conduct disorder NOS

DCR-10

This residual category is not recommended and
should be used only for disorders that meet the
general criteria for F91 but that have not been
specified as to subtype or that do not fulfil the
criteria for any of the specified subtypes.

| F92 | Mixed disorders of conduct and emotions |

A group of disorders characterized by the combination
of persistently aggressive, dissocial or defiant behaviour
with overt and marked symptoms of depression, anxiety
or other emotional upsets. The criteria for both conduct
disorders of childhood (F91.–) and emotional disorders
of childhood (F93.–), or an adult-type neurotic diagnosis (F40–F48) or a mood disorder (F30–F39) must
be met.

F92.0 Depressive conduct disorder

This category requires the combination of conduct disorder (F91.–) with persistent and marked depression of mood (F32.–), as demonstrated by symptoms such as excessive misery, loss of interest and pleasure in usual activities, self-blame and hopelessness; disturbances of sleep or appetite may also be present.

Conduct disorder in F91.– associated with depressive disorder in F32.–.

DCR-10

A. The general criteria for conduct disorders (F91.–) must be met.

B. Criteria for one of the mood [affective] disorders (F30–39) must be met.

F92.8 Other mixed disorders of conduct and emotions

This category requires the combination of conduct disorders (F91.–) with persistent and marked emotional symptoms such as anxiety, obsessions or compulsions, depersonalization or derealization, phobias or hyponchondriasis.

Conduct disorder in F91.– associated with:

- emotional disorder in F93.–
- neurotic disorder in F40–F48

DCR-10

A. The general criteria for conduct disorders (F91.–) must be met.

B. Criteria for one of the neurotic, stress-related and somatoform disorders (F40–F48) or childhood emotional disorders (F93.–) must be met.

| F92.9 | Mixed disorder of conduct and emotions, unspecified |

| F93 | **Emotional disorders with onset specific to childhood** |

Mainly exaggerations of normal developmental trends rather than phenomena that are qualitatively abnormal in themselves. Developmental appropriateness is used as the key diagnostic feature in defining the difference between these emotional disorders, with onset specific to childhood, and the neurotic disorders (F40–F48).

Excludes: when associated with conduct disorder (F92.–)

Diagnostic notes

Phobic anxiety disorder of childhood (F93.1), social anxiety disorder of childhood (F93.2) and general anxiety disorder of childhood (F93.80) have obvious similarities to some of the disorders in F40–F48, but current evidence and opinion suggest that there are sufficient differences in the ways that anxiety disorders present in children for additional categories to be provided. Further studies should show whether descriptions and definitions can be developed that can be used satisfactorily for both adults and children, or whether the present distinction should be preserved.

| F93.0 | Separation anxiety disorder of childhood |

Should be diagnosed when fear of separation constitutes the focus of the anxiety and when such anxiety first arose during the early years of childhood. It is differentiated from normal separation anxiety when it is of a degree (severity) that is statistically unusual (including an abnormal persistence beyond the usual age period), and when it is associated with significant problems in social functioning.

Excludes: mood [affective] disorders (F30–F39)

neurotic disorders (F40–F48)

phobic anxiety disorder of childhood (F93.1)

social anxiety disorder of childhood (F93.2)

DCR-10

A. At least three of the following must be present:

(1) unrealistic and persistent worry about possible harm befalling major attachment figures or about the loss of such figures (e.g. fear that they will leave and not return, or that the child will not see them again), or persistent concerns about the death of attachment figures;

(2) unrealistic and persistent worry that some untoward event will separate the child from a major attachment figure (e.g. the child getting lost, being kidnapped, admitted to hospital or killed);

(3) persistent reluctance or refusal to go to school because of fear over separation from a major attachment figure, in order to stay at home (rather than for other reasons such as fear over events at school);

(4) difficulty in separating at night, as manifested by any of the following:

(a) persistent reluctance or refusal to go to sleep without being near an attachment figure;

(b) getting up frequently during the night to check on, or to sleep near, an attachment figure;

⇨

305

Chapter V: Mental and behavioural disorders
Behavioural and emotional disorders with onset usually occurring in childhood and adolescence

   (c) persistent reluctance or refusal to sleep away from home.

 (5) persistent inappropriate fear of being alone, or otherwise without the major attachment figure, at home during the day;

 (6) repeated nightmares involving themes of separation;

 (7) repeated occurrence of physical symptoms (such as nausea, stomach ache, headache or vomiting) on occasions that involve separation from a major attachment figure, such as leaving home to go to school or on other occasions involving separation (holidays, camps etc.);

 (8) excessive, recurrent distress in anticipation of, during or immediately following separation from a major attachment figure (as shown by anxiety, crying, tantrums, persistent reluctance to go away from home, excessive need to talk with parents or desire to return home, misery, apathy or social withdrawal).

B. The criteria for generalized anxiety disorder of childhood (F93.80) are not met.

C. Onset is before the age of 6 years.

D. The disorder does not occur as part of a broader disturbance of emotions, conduct or personality, or of a pervasive developmental disorder, psychotic disorder or psychoactive substance use disorder.

E. Duration of the disorder is at least 4 weeks.

F93.1 Phobic anxiety disorder of childhood

Fears in childhood that show a marked developmental phase specificity and arise (to some extent) in a majority of children, but which are abnormal in degree. Other fears that arise in childhood but which are not a normal part of psychosocial development (for example agoraphobia) should be coded under the appropriate category in section F40–F48.

Excludes: generalized anxiety disorder (F41.1)

DCR-10

A. The individual manifests a persistent or recurrent fear (phobia) that is developmentally phase-appropriate (or was so at the time of onset) but which is abnormal in degree and is associated with significant social impairment.

B. The criteria for generalized anxiety disorder of childhood (F93.80) are not met.

C. The disorder does not occur as part of a broader disturbance of emotions, conduct or personality, or of a pervasive developmental disorder, psychotic disorder or psychoactive substance use disorder.

D. Duration of the disorder is at least 4 weeks.

F93.2 Social anxiety disorder of childhood

In this disorder there is a wariness of strangers and social apprehension or anxiety when encountering new, strange or socially threatening situations. This category should be used only where such fears arise during the early years, and are both unusual in degree and accompanied by problems in social functioning.

Avoidant disorder of childhood or adolescence

DCR-10

A. Persistent anxiety in social situations in which the child is exposed to unfamiliar people, including peers, is manifested by socially avoidant behaviour.

B. The child exhibits self-consciousness, embarrassment or overconcern about the appropriateness of his or her behaviour when interacting with unfamiliar figures.

C. There is significant interference with social (including peer) relationships, which are consequently restricted; when new or forced social situations are experienced, they cause marked distress and discomfort as manifested by crying, lack of spontaneous speech or withdrawal from the social situation.

D. The child has satisfying social relationships with familiar figures (family members or peers that he or she knows well).

E. Onset of the disorder generally coincides with a developmental phase where these anxiety reactions are considered appropriate. The abnormal degree, persistence over time and associated impairment must be manifest before the age of 6 years.

F. The criteria for generalized anxiety disorder of childhood (F93.80) are not met.

G. The disorder does not occur as part of broader disturbances of emotions, conduct or personality, or of a pervasive developmental disorder, psychotic disorder or psychoactive substance use disorder.

H. Duration of the disorder is at least 4 weeks.

Some degree of emotional disturbance, usually following the birth of an immediately younger sibling, is shown by a majority of young children. A sibling rivalry disorder should be diagnosed only if the degree or persistence of the disturbance is both statistically unusual and associated with abnormalities of social interaction.

Sibling jealousy

DCR-10

A. The child has abnormally intense negative feelings towards an immediately younger sibling.

B. Emotional disturbance is shown by regression, tantrums, dysphoria, sleep difficulties, oppositional behaviour or attention-seeking behaviour with one or both parents (two or more of these must be present).

C. Onset is within 6 months of the birth of an immediately younger sibling.

D. Duration of the disorder is at least 4 weeks.

F93.8 | Other childhood emotional disorders

Identity disorder

Overanxious disorder

Excludes: gender identity disorder of childhood (F64.2)

F93.80 Generalized anxiety disorder of childhood

Diagnostic notes

In children and adolescents the range of complaints by which the general anxiety is manifest is often more limited than in adults (see F41.1), and the specific symptoms of autonomic arousal are often less prominent. For these individuals, the following alternative set of criteria can be used if preferred:

DCR-10

A. Extensive anxiety and worry (apprehensive expectation) occur on at least half of the total number of days over a period of at least 6 months, the anxiety and worry referring to at least several events or activities (such as work or school performance).

B. The individual finds it too difficult to control the worry.

C. The anxiety and worry are associated with at least three of the following symptoms (with at least two symptoms present on at least half of the total number of days):

   (1) restlessness, feeling 'keyed up' or 'on edge' (as shown, for example, by feelings of mental tension combined with an inability to relax);

   (2) feeling tired, 'worn out' or easily fatigued because of worry or anxiety;

   (3) difficulty in concentrating, or mind 'going blank';

   (4) irritability;

   (5) muscle tension;

   (6) sleep disturbance (difficulty in falling or

⇒

staying asleep, or restless, unsatisfying sleep) because of worry or anxiety.

D. The multiple anxieties and worries occur across at least two situations, activities, contexts or circumstances. Generalized anxiety does not present as discrete paroxysmal episodes (as in panic disorder), nor are the main worries confined to a single, major theme (as in separation anxiety disorder or phobic disorder of childhood). (When more focused anxiety is identified in the broader context of a generalized anxiety, generalized anxiety disorder takes precedence over other anxiety disorders.)

E. Onset occurs in childhood or adolescence (before the age of 18 years).

F. The anxiety, worry or physical symptoms cause clinically significant distress or impairment in social, occupational or other important areas of functioning.

G. The disorder is not due to the direct effects of a substance (e.g. psychoactive substances, medication) or a general medical condition (e.g. hyperthyroidism) and does not occur exclusively during a mood disorder, psychotic disorder or pervasive developmental disorder.

F93.9 Childhood emotional disorder, unspecified

F94 Disorders of social functioning with onset specific to childhood and adolescence

A somewhat heterogeneous group of disorders that have in common abnormalities in social functioning which begin during the developmental period, but which (unlike the pervasive developmental disorders) are not primarily characterized by an apparently constitutional social incapacity or deficit that pervades all areas of functioning. In many instances, serious environmental distortions or privations probably play a crucial role in aetiology.

F94.0 Elective mutism

Characterized by a marked, emotionally determined selectivity in speaking, such that the child demonstrates a language competence in some situations but fails to speak in other (definable) situations. The disorder is usually associated with marked personality features involving social anxiety, withdrawal, sensitivity or resistance.

Selective mutism

Excludes: pervasive developmental disorders (F84.–)

schizophrenia (F20.–)

specific developmental disorders of speech and language (F80.–)

transient mutism as part of separation anxiety in young children (F93.0)

DCR-10

A. Language expression and comprehension, as assessed on individually administered standardized tests, is within the 2 standard deviations limit for the child's age.

B. There is demonstrable evidence of a consistent failure to speak in specific social situations in which the child would be expected to speak (e.g. in school), despite speaking in other situations.

C. Duration of the elective mutism exceeds 4 weeks.

D. There is no pervasive developmental disorder (F84.–)

⇒

E. The disorder is not accounted for by a lack of knowledge of the spoken language required in the social situation in which there is a failure to speak.

312

Chapter V: Mental and behavioural disorders
Behavioural and emotional disorders with onset usually occurring in childhood and adolescence

F94.1 Reactive attachment disorder of childhood

Starts in the first 5 years of life and is characterized by persistent abnormalities in the child's pattern of social relationships which are associated with emotional disturbance and are reactive to changes in environmental circumstances (e.g. fearfulness and hypervigilance, poor social interaction with peers, aggression towards self and others, misery, and growth failure in some cases). The syndrome probably occurs as a direct result of severe parental neglect, abuse or serious mishandling.

Use additional code, if desired, to identify any associated failure to thrive or growth retardation.

Excludes: Asperger's syndrome (F84.5)

disinhibited attachment disorder of childhood (F94.2)

maltreatment syndromes (T74.–)

normal variation in pattern of selective attachment

sexual or physical abuse in childhood, resulting in psychosocial problems (Z61.4–Z61.6)

DCR-10

A. Onset is before the age of 5 years.

B. The child exhibits strongly contradictory or ambivalent social responses that extend across social situations (but which may show variability from relationship to relationship).

C. Emotional disturbance is shown by lack of emotional responsiveness, withdrawal reactions, aggressive responses to the child's own or others' distress, and/or fearful hypervigilance.

D. Some capacity for social reciprocity and responsiveness is evident in interactions with normal adults.

E. The criteria for pervasive developmental disorders (F84.–) are not met.

F94.2 Disinhibited attachment disorder of childhood

A particular pattern of abnormal social functioning that arises during the first 5 years of life and which tends to persist despite marked changes in environmental circumstances, e.g. diffuse non-selectively focused attachment behaviour, attention-seeking and indiscriminately friendly behaviour, poorly modulated peer interactions; depending on circumstances there may also be associated emotional or behavioural disturbance.

Affectionless psychopathy

Institutional syndrome

Excludes: Asperger's syndrome (F84.5)

hospitalism in children (F43.2)

hyperkinetic disorders (F90.–)

reactive attachment disorder of childhood (F94.1)

DCR-10

A. Diffuse attachments are a persistent feature during the first 5 years of life (but do not necessarily persist into middle childhood).

⇒

Diagnosis requires a relative failure to show selective social attachments manifest by:

(1) a normal tendency to seek comfort from others when distressed;

(2) an abnormal (relative) lack of selectivity in the people from whom comfort is sought.

B. Social interactions with unfamiliar people are poorly modulated.

C. At least one of the following must be present:

(1) generally clinging behaviour in infancy;

(2) attention-seeking and indiscriminately friendly behaviour in early or middle childhood.

D. The general lack of situation-specificity in the above features must be clear. Diagnosis requires that the symptoms in criteria A and B above are manifest across the range of social contacts experienced by the child.

F94.8	Other childhood disorders of social functioning

F94.9	Childhood disorder of social functioning, unspecified

F95 Tic disorders

Syndromes in which the predominant manifestation is some form of tic. A tic is an involuntary, rapid, recurrent, non-rhythmic motor movement (usually involving circumscribed muscle groups) or vocal production that is of sudden onset and that serves no apparent purpose.

Tics tend to be experienced as irresistible but usually they can be suppressed for varying periods of time, are exacerbated by stress and disappear during sleep. Common simple motor tics include eye-blinking, neck jerking, shoulder-shrugging and facial grimacing. Common simple vocal tics include throat-clearing, barking, sniffing and hissing. Common complex tics including hitting oneself, jumping and hopping. Common complex vocal tics include the repetition of particular words, and sometimes the use of socially unacceptable (often obscene) words (coprolalia), and the repetition of one's own sounds or words (palilalia).

F95.0	Transient tic disorder

Meets the general criteria for a tic disorder but the tics do not persist longer than 12 months. The tics usually take the form of eye-blinking, facial grimacing or head-jerking.

DCR-10

A. Single or multiple motor or vocal tic(s) or both occur many times a day, on most days, over a period of at least 4 weeks.

B. Duration of the disorder is 12 months or less.

C. There is no history of Tourette syndrome, and the disorder is not the result of physical conditions or the side-effects of medication.

D. Onset is before the age of 18 years.

F95.1	Chronic motor or vocal tic disorder

Meets the general criteria for a tic disorder in which there are motor or vocal tics (but not both) that may be either single or multiple (but usually multiple) and last for more than a year.

DCR-10

A.   Motor or vocal tics, but not both, occur many times a day, on most days, over a period of at least 12 months.

B.   No period of remission during that year lasts longer than 2 months.

C.   There is no history of Tourette syndrome, and the disorder is not the result of physical conditions of the side-effects of medication.

D.   Onset is before the age of 18 years.

| F95.2 | Combined vocal and multiple motor tic disorder [de la Tourette's syndrome] |

A form of tic disorder in which there are, or have been, multiple motor tics and one or more vocal tics, although these need not have occurred concurrently. The disorder usually worsens during adolescence and tends to persist into adult life. The vocal tics are often multiple, with explosive repetitive vocalizations, throat-clearing and grunting, and there may be the use of obscene words or phrases. Sometimes there is associated gestural echopraxia, which may also be of an obscene nature (copropraxia).

DCR-10

A.   Multiple motor tics and one or more vocal tics have been present at some time during the disorder, but not necessarily concurrently.

B.   The frequency of tics must be many times a day, nearly every day, for more than 1 year, with no period of remission during that year lasting longer than 2 months.

C.   Onset is before the age of 18 years.

| F95.8 | Other tic disorders |

| F95.9 | Tic disorder, unspecified |

Tic NOS

> **DCR-10**
>
> A non-recommended residual category for a disorder that fulfils the general criteria for a tic disorder but in which the specific subcategory is not specified or in which the features do not fulfil the criteria for F95.0, F95.1 or F95.2

| **F98** | **Other behavioural and emotional disorders with onset usually occurring in childhood and adolescence** |

A heterogeneous group of disorders that share the characteristic of an onset in childhood but otherwise differ in many respects. Some of the conditions represent well-defined syndromes but others are no more than symptom complexes that need inclusion because of their frequency and association with psychosocial problems, and because they cannot be incorporated into other syndromes.

Excludes: breath-holding spells (R06.8)

gender identity disorder of childhood (F64.2)

Klein–Levin syndrome (G47.8)

obsessive-compulsive disorder (F42.–)

sleep disorders due to emotional causes (F51.–)

F98.0 Non-organic enuresis

A disorder characterized by involuntary voiding of urine, by day and by night, which is abnormal in relation to the individual's mental age, and which is not a consequence of a lack of bladder control due to any neurological disorder, to epileptic attacks or to any structural abnormality of the urinary tract. The enuresis may have been present from birth or it may have arisen following a period of acquired bladder control. The enuresis may or may not be associated with a more widespread emotional or behavioural disorder.

Enuresis (primary) (secondary) of non-organic origin

Functional enuresis

Psychogenic enuresis

Urinary incontinence of non-organic origin

Excludes: enuresis NOS (R32)

DCR-10

A. The child's chronological and mental age is at least 5 years.

B. Involuntary or intentional voiding of urine into bed or clothes occurs at least twice a month in children aged under 7 years, and at least once a month in children aged 7 years or more.

C. The enuresis is not a consequence of epileptic attacks or of neurological incontinence, and not a direct consequence of structural abnormalities of the urinary tract or any other non-psychiatric medical condition.

D. There is no evidence of any other psychiatric disorder that meets the criteria for other ICD-10 categories.

E. Duration of the disorder is at least 3 months.

⇒

A fifth character may be used, if desired, for further specification:

    F98.00   nocturnal enuresis only

    F98.01   diurnal enuresis only

    F98.02   nocturnal and diurnal enuresis.

F98.1   Non-organic encopresis

Repeated, voluntary or involuntary passage of faeces, usually of normal or near-normal consistency, in places not appropriate for that purpose in the individual's own sociocultural setting. The condition may represent an abnormal continuation of normal infantile incontinence, it may involve a loss of continence following the acquisition of bowel control, or it may involve the deliberate deposition of faeces in inappropriate places in spite of normal physiological bowel control. The condition may occur as a monosymptomatic disorder, or it may form part of a wider disorder, especially an emotional disorder (F93.–) or a conduct disorder (F91.–).

Functional encopresis

Incontinence of faeces of non-organic origin

Psychogenic encopresis

Use additional code, if desired, to identify the cause of any coexisting constipation.

Excludes: encopresis NOS (R15)

DCR-10

A. The child repeatedly passes faeces in places that are inappropriate for the purpose (e.g. clothing, floor), either involuntarily or intentionally. (The disorder may involve overflow incontinence secondary to functional faecal retention.)

⇒

B. The child's chronological and mental age is at least 4 years.

C. There is at least one encopretic event per month.

D. Duration of the disorder is at least 6 months.

E. There is no organic condition that constitutes a sufficient cause for the encopretic events.

A fifth character may be used, if desired, for further specification:

F98.10 failure to acquire physiological bowel control

F98.11 adequate bowel control with normal faeces deposited in inappropriate places

F98.12 soiling associated with excessively fluid faeces (such as with retention with overflow).

F98.2 Feeding disorder of infancy and childhood

A feeding disorder of varying manifestations, usually specific to infancy and early childhood. It generally involves food refusal and extreme faddiness in the presence of an adequate food supply, a reasonably competent caregiver and the absence of organic disease. There may or may not be associated rumination (repeated regurgitation without nausea or gastrointestinal illness).

Rumination disorder of infancy

Excludes: anorexia nervosa and other eating disorders (F50.–)

feeding:

• difficulties and mismanagement (R63.3)

• problems of newborn (P92.–)

pica of infancy or childhood (F98.3)

DCR-10

A. There is persistent failure to eat adequately, or persistent rumination or regurgitation of food.

B. The child fails to gain weight, loses weight or exhibits some other significant health problem over a period of at least 1 month. (In view of the frequency of transient eating difficulties, researchers may prefer a minimum duration of 3 months for some purposes.)

C. Onset of the disorder is before the age of 6 years.

D. The child exhibits no other mental or behavioural disorder in the ICD-10 classification (other than mental retardation, F70–F79).

E. There is no evidence of organic disease sufficient to account for the failure to eat.

F98.3 Pica of infancy and childhood

Persistent eating of non-nutritive substances (such as soil, paint chippings etc.) It may occur as one of many symptoms that are part of a more widespread psychiatric disorder (such as autism), or as a relatively isolated psychopathological behaviour; only the latter is classified here. The phenomenon is most common in mentally retarded children and, if mental retardation is also present, F70–F79 should be selected as the main diagnosis.

DCR-10

A. There is persistent or recurrent eating of non-nutritive substances, at least twice a week.

B. Duration of the disorder is at least 1 month. ⇒

(For some purposes, researchers may prefer a minimum period of 3 months.)

C. The child exhibits no other mental or behavioural disorder in the ICD-10 classification (other than mental retardation, F70–F79).

D. The child's chronological and mental age is at least 2 years.

E. The eating behaviour is not part of a culturally sanctioned practice.

F98.4   Stereotyped movement disorders

Voluntary, repetitive, stereotyped, non-functional (and often rhythmic) movements that do not form part of any recognized psychiatric or neurological condition. When such movements occur as symptoms of some other disorder, only the overall disorder should be recorded. The movements, which are of a non-self-injurious variety, include body-rocking, head-rocking, hair-plucking, hair-twisting, finger-flicking mannerisms and hand-flapping. Stereotyped self-injurious behaviour includes repetitive head-banging, face-slapping, eye-poking and biting of hands, lips or other body parts. All the stereotyped movement disorders occur most frequently in association with mental retardation (when this is the case, both should be recorded). If eye-poking occurs in a child with visual impairment, both should be coded; eye-poking under this category and the visual condition under the appropriate somatic disorder code.

Stereotype/habit disorder

Excludes: abnormal involuntary movements (R25.–)

movement disorders of organic origin (G20–G25)

nail-biting (F98.8)

nose-picking (F98.8)

stereotypies that are part of a broader psychiatric condition (F00–F95) thumb-sucking (F98.8)

tic disorders (F95.–)

trichotillomania (F63.3)

DCR-10

A. The child exhibits stereotyped movements to an extent that either causes physical injury or markedly interferes with normal activities.

B. Duration of the disorder is at least 1 month.

C. The child exhibits no other mental or behavioural disorder in the ICD-10 classification (other than mental retardation, F70–F79).

A fifth character may be used, if desired, for further specification:

    F98.40   non-self-injurious

    F98.41   self-injurious

    F98.42   mixed.

| F98.5 | Stuttering [stammering] |

Speech that is characterized by frequent repetition or prolongation of sounds or syllables or words, or by frequent hesitations or pauses that disrupt the rhythmic flow of speech. It should be classified as a disorder only if its severity is such as to markedly disturb the fluency of speech.

Excludes: tic disorders (F95.–)

cluttering (F98.6)

DCR-10

A. Stuttering (i.e. speech characterized by frequent repetition or prolongation of sounds or syllables or words, or by frequent hesitations

⇒

> or pauses) is persistent or recurrent and sufficiently severe to cause marked disruption of the fluency of speech.
>
> B. Duration of the disorder is at least 3 months.

F98.6 Cluttering

A rapid rate of speech with breakdown in fluency, but no repetitions or hesitations, of a severity to give rise to diminished speech intelligiblity. Speech is erratic and dysrhythmic, with rapid jerky spurts that usually involve faulty phrasing patterns.

Excludes: stuttering (F98.5)

tic disorders (F95.–)

> **DCR-10**
>
> A. Cluttering (i.e. rapid speech with breakdown in fluency, but no repetitions or hesitations) is persistent or recurrent and sufficiently severe to reduce significantly the intelligibility of speech.
>
> B. Duration of the disorder is at least 3 months.

F98.8 Other specified behavioural and emotional disorders with onset usually occurring in childhood and adolescence

Attention deficit disorder without hyperactivity

Excessive masturbation

Nail-biting

Nose-picking

Thumb-sucking

| F98.9 | Unspecified behavioural and emotional disorders with onset usually occurring in childhood and adolescence |

| **F99** | **Mental disorder, not otherwise specified** |

Mental illness NOS

Excludes: organic mental disorder NOS (F06.9)

This is a non-recommended residual category, to be employed when no other code from F00–F98 can be used.

ANNEX 1 TO DCR-10
Provisional criteria for selected disorders

This annex contains criteria for a number of disorders whose clinical or scientific status is still best regarded as uncertain. The disorders have been suggested for inclusion by interested research groups, but it was considered that further research is indicated before they could be regarded as having sufficient international acceptance to merit inclusion in Chapter V(F) of ICD-10. It is hoped that their presence in this annex, with provisional criteria, will stimulate research to clarify their nature and status.

Seasonal affective disorder

(could be applied to mood [affective] disorder, categories F30.–, F31–, F32.– and F33.–)

A. Three or more episodes of mood [affective] disorder must occur, with onset within the same 90-day period of the year, for 3 or more consecutive years.

B. Remissions also occur within a particular 90-day period of the year.

C. Seasonal episodes substantially outnumber any non-seasonal episodes that may occur.

Bipolar II disorder

(could be applied to bipolar affective disorder, categories F31.0, F31.3–F31.5, F31.7)

A. There must be one or more episodes of depression (F32.–).

B. There must be one or more episodes of hypomania (F30.0).

C. There are no episodes of mania (F30.1–F30.2).

Rapid cycling bipolar disorder

(could be applied to bipolar affective disorder, categories F31.0–F31.7)

A. The criteria for bipolar affective disorder (F31.0–F31.7) must be fulfilled.

B. At least four episodes of bipolar affective disorder must occur within a 12-month period.

Note: Episodes are demarcated by a switch to an episode of opposite or mixed polarity or by a remission.

Narcissistic personality disorder

A. The general criteria for personality disorder (F60.–) must be fulfilled.

B. At least five of the following must be present:

(1) a grandiose sense of self-importance (e.g. the individual exaggerates achievements and talents, expects to be recognized as superior without commensurate achievements);

(2) preoccupation with fantasies of unlimited success, power, brilliance, beauty or ideal love;

(3) belief that he or she is 'special' and unique and can be understood only by, or should associate only with, other special or high-status people (or institutions);

(4) need for excessive admiration;

(5) a sense of entitlement; unreasonable expectations of especially favourable treatment or automatic compliance with his or her expectations;

(6) exploitation of interpersonal relationships, taking advantage of others to achieve his or her own ends;

(7) lack of empathy; unwillingness to recognize or identify with the feelings and needs of others;

(8) frequent envy of others or belief that others are envious of him or her;

(9) arrogant, haughty behaviour or attitudes.

Passive–aggressive (negativistic) personality disorder

A. The general criteria of personality disorder (F60.–) must be met.

B. At least five of the following must be present:

(1) procrastination and delay in completing essential, routine tasks, especially those that others seek to have completed;

(2) unjustified protestation that others make unreasonable demands;

(3) sulkiness, irritability or argumentativeness when the individual is asked to do something he or she does not want to do;

(4) unreasonable criticism of or scorn for people in positions of authority;

(5) deliberately slow or poor work on tasks that the individual really does not want to do;

(6) obstruction of the efforts of others by the individual failing to do his or her share of the work;

(7) avoidance of obligations by claiming to have forgotten.

ANNEX 2 TO DCR-10
Culture–specific
disorders

(Compiled by Dr Ruthbeth Finerman, Associate Professor, Department of Anthropology, Memphis State University, Memphis, TN, USA)

Culture-specific disorders have diverse characteristics but share two principal features:

(1) they are not easily accommodated by the categories in established and internationally used psychiatric classifications;

(2) they were first described in, and subsequently closely or exclusively associated with, a particular population or cultural area.

These syndromes have also been referred to as culture-bound or culture-reactive, and as ethnic or exotic psychoses. Some are rare and some may be comparatively common; many are acute and transient, which makes their systematic study particularly difficult.

The status of these disorders is controversial: many researchers argue that they differ only in degree from disorders already included in existing psychiatric classifications, such as anxiety disorders and reactions to stress, and that they are therefore best regarded as local variations of disorders that have long been recognized. Their exclusive occurrence in specific population or cultural areas has also been questioned.

There is a clear need for research that will help to establish reliable clinical descriptions of these disorders and clarify their distribution, frequency and course. In the hope of stimulating and facilitating such research, WHO has undertaken the development of a glossary containing lexical definitions of terms used in cross-cultural and anthropological psychiatric research. It is expected that this glossary will become available in 1994. In the meantime, 12 frequently described 'culture-specific' disorders have been included in this annex by way of example, together with their clinical characteristics – extracted from anthropological and medical literature – and suggestions concerning their placement in ICD categories.

No attempt has been made to list detailed diagnostic criteria for these disorders: it is hoped that this will become possible when more reliable clinical, anthropological, epidemiological and biological information is available.

Assignment of the disorders to categories in ICD-10, Chapter V(F) must be regarded as tentative. In certain instances, when available descriptions suggest that there is considerable variation in the clinical states covered by the term, more than one code has been given.

References 1976

Lebra WP (ed) *Culture-bound syndromes, ethnopsychiatry, and alternate therapies.* University of Hawaii, Honolulu

Simons RC, Hughes CC (eds) 1985. *The culture-bound syndromes.* Reidel, Dordrecht.

Yap Pow-Meng 1951 Mental diseases peculiar to certain cultures: a survey of comparative psychiatry. *Journal of Mental Science* **97**: 313–327

Amok (Indonesia; Malaysia)

An indiscriminate, seemingly unprovoked, episode of homicidal or highly destructive behaviour, followed by amnesia or fatigue. Many episodes culminate in suicide. Most events occur without warning, although some are precipitated by a period of intense anxiety or hostility. Some studies suggest that cases may derive from the traditional values placed on extreme aggression and suicidal attacks in warfare.

Suggested ICD-10 code

F68.8   Other specified disorders of adult personality and behaviour

Potentially related syndromes

ahade idzi be (the island of New Guinea)
benzi mazurazura (southern Africa (among Shona and affiliated groups)
berserkergang (Scandinavia)
cafard (Polynesia)
colerina (the Andes of Bolivia, Colombia, Ecuador and Peru)
hwa-byung (Korean peninsula)
iich'aa (indigenous peoples of southwestern USA)

References

Lin Keh-Ming 1983 Hwa-byung: a Korean culture-bound syndrome? *American Journal of Psychiatry*, **140**: 105–107

Newman P 1964 'Wild man' behavior in a New Guinea Highlands community. *American Anthropologist*, **66**: 1–9

Simons RC, Hughes CC (eds) 1985. *The culture-bound syndromes.* Reidel, Dordrecht, 197–264

Spores J 1988 *Running amok: an historical inquiry.* Southeast Asia Series, No. 82 University Center for International Studies, Athens, Ohio

Yap Pow-Meng 1969 The culture-bound reactive syndromes. In: Caudill W, Tsung-yi Lin (eds.) *Mental health research in Asia and the Pacific.* East–West Center Press, Honolulu 33–53

Dhat, dhatu, jiryan, shenk'uei, shen-kui (India; China

Anxiety and somatic complaints such as fatigue and muscle pain, related to a fear of semen loss in men or women (also thought to secrete semen). Precursors are said to include excess coitus, urinary disorders, imbalances in body humours and diet. The main symptom is a whitish discharge in urine, interpreted as semen loss. Traditional remedies focus on herbal tonics to restore semen or humoral balance.

Suggested ICD-10 codes

F48.8   Other specified neurotic disorders

F45.34 Somatoform autonomic dysfunction of the genitourinary system (may be used if autonomic anxiety symptoms are prominent)

Potentially related syndromes

koro (China)

rabt (Egypt)

References

Bhatia MS, Malik SC 1991 Dhat syndrome – a useful diagnostic entity in Indian culture. *British Journal of Psychiatry* **159**: 691–695

Malhotra M, Wig N 1975 Dhat syndrome: a culture-bound sex neurosis of the Orient. *Archives of Sexual Behavior* **4**: 519–528

Singh SP 1992 Is Dhat culture bound? *British Journal of Psychiatry* **160**: 280–281

Wen Jung-Kwang, Wang Ching-Lun 1981 Shen-k'uei syndrome: a culture-specific sexual neurosis in Taiwan. In: Kleinman A, Lin Tsung-yi, (eds) *Normal and abnormal behavior in Chinese cultures.* Reidel, Dordrecht: 357–369

Koro, jinjin bemar, suk yeong, suo-yang
(southeast Asia, south China, India)

Acute panic or anxiety reaction involving fear of genital retraction. In severe cases, men become convinced that the penis will suddenly withdraw into the abdomen; women sense that their breasts, labia or vulva will retract. Victims expect the consequences to be fatal. Studies cite factors such as illness, exposure to cold or excess coitus as precursors, but interpersonal conflict and socio-cultural demands reportedly exert greater influence on the condition. Onset is rapid, intense and unexpected. Responses vary, but include grasping of the genitals by the victim or a family member, application or splints or devices to prevent retraction, herbal remedies, massage or fellatio.

Suggested ICD-10 codes

F48.8   Other specified neurotic disorders

F45.34 Somatoform autonomic dysfunction of the genitourinary system (may be used if autonomic anxiety symptoms are present)

Potentially related syndromes

dhat (India)

rabt (Egypt)

References

Adityanjee, Zain AM, Subramaniam M 1991 Sporadic koro and marital disharmony. *Psychopathology* **24**: 49–52

Bernstein RL, Gaw AC 1990 Koro: proposed classification for DSM-IV. *American Journal of Psychiatry* **147**: 1670–1674

Nandi DN et al 1983 Epidemic koro in West Bengal, India. *International Journal of Social Psychiatry* **29**: 265–268

Simons RC, Hughes CC (eds) 1985 The culture-bound syndromes. Reidel, Dordrecht

Turnier L, Chouinard G 1990 Effet anti-koro d'un antidepresseur tricyclique. [The anti-koro effect of a tricyclic antidepressant.] *Canadian Journal of Psychiatry* **35**: 331–333

Latah (Indonesia, Malaysia)

Highly exaggerated responses to a fright or trauma, followed by involuntary echolalia, echopraxia or trance-like states. Studies variously interpret cases as a neurophysiological response, a hypersuggestible state or a mechanism for expressing low self-image. Onlookers usually find such imitative episodes amusing but victims feel humiliated.

Suggested ICD-10 codes

F48.8   Other specified neurotic disorders

F44.88   Other specified dissociative [conversion] disorders

Potentially related syndromes

amurakh (Siberia)
bah-tsi (Thailand)
imu (Ainu (indigenous people of Japan))
jumping frenchman (Canada)
Lapp panic (Lapps)
mali-mali (Philippines)
pibloktoq (Inuits living within the Arctic Circle)
susto (Mexico, Central and South America)
yaun (Myanmar (formerly Burma))

References

Jenner JA 1990 Latah as coping: a case study offering a new paradox to solve the old one. *International Journal of Social Psychiatry* **36** (3): 194–199

Jenner JA 1991 A successfully treated Dutch case of latah. *Journal of Nervous and Mental disease* **179** (10): 636–637

Murphy HBM 1976 Notes for a theory on latah. In: Lebra WP (ed) *Culture-bound syndromes, ethnopsychiatry, and alternate therapies.* University of Hawaii, Honolulu, 3–21

Simons RC, Hughes CC (eds) 1985. The culture-bound syndromes. Reidel, Dordrecht: 41–113

Nerfiza, nerves, nevra, nervios (Egypt, northern Europe, Greece, Mexico, Central and South America)

Common, often chronic, episodes of extreme sorrow or anxiety, inducing a complex of somatic complaints such as head and muscle pain, diminished reactivity, nausea, appetite loss, insomnia, fatigue and agitation. The syndrome is more common in women than in men. Research links the condition to stress, anger, emotional distress and low self-esteem. Cases are traditionally treated with herbal teas, 'nerve pills', rest, isolation and family support.

Suggested ICD-10 codes

F32.11 Moderate depressive episode with somatic syndrome (this is the most likely code)

F48.0 Neurasthenia

F45.1 Undifferentiated somatoform disorder

Potentially related syndromes

anfechtung (Hutterites (a religious group))
brain fag (Nigeria)
colerina, pension, bilis (Mexico, Central and South America)
hsieh-ping, xie-bing (China)
hwa-byung (Korean peninsula)
narahati-e a sab, maraz-e a sab (Islamic Republic of Iran)
qissaatuq (Inuits living within the Arctic Circle)

References

Historical and cross-cultural perspectives on nerves. *Social science and medicine* 1988, **26** (12): 1197–1259

Davis DL, Low SM (eds) 1989 Gender, health and illness: the case of nerves. Hemisphere, New York

Good B, Good MJD, Moradi R 1985 The interpretation of Iranian depressive illness and dysphoric affect. In: Kleinman A, Good B (eds) *Culture and depression*. University of California, Berkeley, 369–428

Low SM 1985 Culturally interpreted symptoms or culture-bound syndromes: a cross-cultural review of nerves. *Social Science and Medicine*, 21: 187–196

Pa-leng, frigophobia (China, southeast Asia)

Anxiety state characterized by obsessive fear of cold and winds, believed to produce fatigue, impotence or death. Victims compulsively dress in heavy or excessive clothing. Fears are reinforced by cultural views of the condition as a legitimate humoral disorder.

Suggested ICD-10 code

F40.2   Specific phobias

Potentially related syndromes

agua frio, aire frio, frio (Mexico, Central and South America)

References

Kiev: A 1972 Transcultural psychiatry. Free Press, New York

Lin Keh-Ming, Kleinman A, Lin Tsung-Yi 1981 Overview of mental disorders in Chinese cultures: review of epidemiological and clinical studies. In: Kleinman A, Lin Tsung-Yi (eds) *Normal and abnormal behavior in Chinese culture*. Reidel, Dordrecht: 237–272

Pibloktoq, Arctic hysteria (Inuits living within the Arctic Circle)

Prodromal fatigue, depression or confusion followed by a 'seizure' of disruptive behaviour, including stripping or tearing off clothes, frenzied running, rolling in snow, glossolalia or echolalia, echopraxia, property destruction and coprophagia. Most episodes last only minutes and are followed by loss of consciousness, amnesia and comlete remission. Injury is rare and, while some studies have related cause to hypocalcaemic tetany, most researchers link incidents to interpersonal anxieties and cultural stressors.

Suggested ICD-10 codes

F44.7   Mixed dissociative [conversion] disorders

F44.88   Other specified dissociative [conversion] disorders

Potentially related syndromes

amok (Indonesia; Malaysia)
banga, misala (Congo), Malawi (formerly Nyasaland)
ebenzi (southern Africa, among Shona and affiliated groups)
grisi siknis (Miskito (indigenous people of Honduras))
imu (Ainu (indigenous people of Japan))
latah (Indonesia; Malaysia)
mali-mali (Philippines)
nangiarpok, kayak angst, quajimaillituq (Inuits)
ufufuyane (southern Africa, especially among Bantu, Zulu and affiliated groups)

References

Parker S 1962 Eskimo psychopathology in the context of Eskimo personality and culture. *American Anthropologist* **64**: 76–96

Simons RC, Hughes CC (eds) 1985 The culture-bound syndromes. Reidel, Dordrecht: 267–326

Wallace A 1972 Mental illness, biology and culture. In: Hsu FLK (ed) *Psychological anthropology*. Schenkman, Cambridge, MA 363–402

Susto, espanto (Mexico, Central and South America)

Highly diverse, chronic complaints attributed to 'soul loss' induced by a severe, often supernatural, fright. In some cases, traumatic events are not personally experienced: individuals may be stricken when others (usually relatives) suffer a fright. Symptoms often include agitation, anorexia, insomnia, fever, diarrhoea, mental confusion and apathy, depression and introversion. Studies variously attribute cases to hypoglycaemia, non-specific organic disease, generalized anxiety and stress resulting from social conflict and low self-esteem.

Suggested ICD-10 codes

F45.1   Undifferentiated somatoform disorder

F48.8   Other specified neurotic disorders

Potentially related syndromes

lanti (Philippines)
latah (Indonesia; Malaysia)
malgri (aborigines of Australia)
mogo laya (the island of New Guinea)
narahati (Islamic Republic of Iran)
saladera (regions around Amazon river)

References

Good B, Good MJD 1982 Toward a meaning-centered analysis of popular illness categories: fright illness and heart distress in Iran. In: Marsella AJ, White GM (eds) *Cultural conceptions of mental health and therapy.* Reidel, Dordrecht: 150–158

Houghton A, Boersma F 1988 The grief–loss connection in susto. *Ethnology* 27: 145–154

Lipp F 1989 The study of disease in relation to culture – the sustocomplex among the Mixe of Oaxaca. *Dialectical Anthropology* 12: 435–443

Rubel AJ, O'Neill CW, Collado-Ardon R 1984 Susto, a folk illness. University of California Press, Berkeley

Simons RC, Hughes CC (eds) 1985 The culture-bound syndromes. Reidel, Dordrecht: 329–407

Taijin kyofusho, shinkeishitsu, anthropophobia (Japan)

Anxiety or phobia more common among men and young adults. Cases are marked by a fear of social contact (especially friends), extreme self-consciousness (concern about physical appearance, body odour, blushing), and a fear of contracting disease. Somatic symptoms include head, body and stomach aches, fatigue and insomnia. Victims, popularly regarded as highly intelligent and creative, may display perfectionist tendencies. Studies suggest that cultural values encourage 'oversocialization' of some children, producing feelings of inferiority and anxiety in social situations.

Suggested ICD-10 codes

F40.1   Social phobias

F40.8   Other phobic anxiety disorders
        (may be used if there are many other fears)

Potentially related syndromes

anfechtung (Hutterites (a religious group))
itiju (Nigeria)

References

Lock M 1980 East Asian medicine in urban Japan. University of California Press, Berkeley 222–224

Tanaka-Matsumi J. 1979 Taijin kyofusho. *Culture, medicine and psychiatry* 3: 231–245

Prince R, Techeng-Laroche F 1987 Culture-bound syndromes and international classification of disease. *Culture, Medicine and Psychiatry* 11: 3–20

Reynolds D 1976 Morita therapy. University of California Press, Berkeley

Ufufuyane, saka (southern Africa (among Bantu, Zulu and affiliated groups; Kenya)

An anxiety state popularly attributed to magical potions administered by rejected lovers, or spirit possession. Features include shouting, sobbing, repeated neologisms, paralysis, convulsions and a trance-like stupor or loss of consciousness. Most victims are young unmarried women. Some experience nightmares with sexual themes or rare episodes of temporary blindness. Attacks, which can continue for days or weeks, may be provoked by the sight of men or foreigners.

Suggested ICD-10 codes

F44.3   Trance and possession disorders

F44.7   Mixed dissociative [conversion] disorders

Potentially related syndromes

aluro (Nigeria)
phii pob (Thailand)
zar (Egypt, Ethiopia, Sudan)

References

Harris G 1957 Possession 'hysteria' in a Kenya tribe. *American Anthropologist* **59**: 1046–1066

Loudon JB 1959 Psychogenic disorder and social conflict among the Zulu. In: Opler MK (ed) *Culture and mental health.* Macmillan, New York: 351–369

Uqamairineq (Inuits living within the Arctic Circle)

Sudden paralysis associated with borderline sleep states, accompanied by anxiety, agitation or hallucinations. Prodromal indicators may include a detectable yet transient sound or smell. Although the condition is usually chronic and can prompt panic, most attacks last only minutes and are followed by complete remission. Cases are fairly common and traditionally alleged to result from soul loss, soul wandering or spirit possession. Studies describe the experience as a dissociative hysterical reaction and possible variant of the narcolepsy-category syndrome.

Suggested ICD-10 codes

F44.88   Other specified dissociative [conversion] disorders

G47.4   Narcolepsy and cataplexy

Includes: sleep paralysis

Potentially related syndromes

aluro (Nigeria)
old hag (Newfoundland)
phii pob (Thailand)

References

Hufford D 1982 The terror that comes in the night. University of Pennsylvania, Philadelphia

Parker S 1962 Eskimo psychopathology in the context of Eskimo personality and culture. *American Anthropologist* **64**: 76–96

Simons RC, Hughes CC (eds) 1985 The culture-bound syndromes. Reidel, Dordrecht: 115–148

Windigo (various spellings) (indigenous people of northeastern regions of North America)

Rare, historic accounts of cannibalistic obsession. Traditionally, cases were ascribed to possession, with victims (usually male) turning into cannibal monsters. Symptoms included depression, homicidal or suicidal thoughts, and a delusional compulsive wish to eat human flesh. Most victims were socially ostracized or put to death. Early research described episodes as hysterical psychosis, precipitated by chronic food shortages and cultural myths about starvation and windigo monsters. Some controversial new studies question the syndrome's legitimacy, claiming that cases were actually a product of hostile accusations invented to justify the victim's ostracism or execution.

Suggested ICD-10 code

The available information is too unreliable to suggest a likely code. If a code is needed, use:

F68.8   Other specified disorders of adult personality and behaviour

Potentially related syndromes

amok (Malaysia)
hsieh-ping (China (Province of Taiwan))
zar (Egypt, Ethiopia, Sudan)

References

Bishop C 1975 Northern Algonkian cannibalism and windigo psychosis. In: Williams T (ed) *Psychological anthropology*. Mouton, The Hague: 237–248

Hay T 1971 The windigo psychosis. *American Anthropologist* 73: 1–19

Parker S 1960 The wiitiko psychosis in the context of Ojibwa personality and culture. *American Anthropologist* 1985 **62**: 603–623

Simons RC Hughes CC (eds) 1985 The culture-bound syndromes. Reidel, Dordrecht: 409–465

Notes on unsolved problems

The reactions of the several hundred clinicians and researchers who participated in the field trials of both the *Clinical descriptions and diagnostic guidelines* (CDDG) and the *Diagnostic criteria for research* (DCR-10) of Chapter V of ICD-10 make it clear that the new classification is a great improvement on its predecessor. Nevertheless, many problems still remain to be addressed in future revisions, and in this section a selection of those problems that often gave rise to comments and debates during the process of development are briefly discussed. Most of the issues mentioned are also unsolved in other current national or regional psychiatric classifications, so to comment upon them here will remind the user that there is plenty of room for improvement in all existing psychiatric classifications.

Number and order of the main sections of the classification

Whether or not there is an optimal number of main sections is an interesting question that should be debated, but in the case of Chapter V the number of main sections is dictated by a general rule that has nothing to do with psychiatry. All chapters of the ICD can have no more than 10 major subdivisions because the ICD is a statistical classification containing a specified and therefore finite amount of classificatory space. There is no particular reason why all psychiatric disorders should fit neatly into ten groups, but in practice this restriction causes no serious problems.

The order that has been adopted is the same as that found in most textbooks of psychiatry and in most other psychiatric classifications. It probably reflects the desire of clinicians to give precedence to those disorders for which something is known about aetiology. The order also reflects a general hierarchy of 'severity' and likelihood of a comparatively poor outcome. The placing of disorders of development and those usually limited to childhood and adolescence at the end is probably a reflection of the later development of child psychiatry as a discipline in its own right. Future versions of this and other psychiatric classifications would be likely to benefit from an overt discussion of their structure and presentation (Cooper 1988).

Chapter V as a descriptive classification

In the earliest stages of development of Chapter V it was agreed that, because of the incomplete and often controversial state of knowledge about the aetiology of most psychiatric disorders, the classification would be, as far as possible, worked out on a descriptive basis. Strictly speaking, this implies that the disorders should be grouped by means of similarities and differences evident only in their symptoms and signs, and that a disorder so described should occur in only one place in the classification. However, when this is attempted it soon becomes clear that a classification arrived at as a result of a strict adherence to these principles would be very unlikely to appeal to clinicians, who like to be able to give prominence to aetiology whenever it is known. For this reason, broad types of aetiology (organic causes, substance use and stress) are built into the groupings of the disorders in several sections, rather than being reserved for a separate statement on another axis.

The result of this is that Chapter V is a mixed classification combining two aspects or axes, although it is often assumed that it has only one. Fortunately, these rule violations do not cause many problems, since it is usually possible to describe specific clinical pictures to justify the groups that are used (for instance, although stress reactions include depressive symptoms that are also found in depressive episodes, the pattern and severity of the depressive symptoms are different in the two types of disorder). This is not so, however, for Section F06: 'Mental disorders, not involving cognitive impairment, due to brain disease, damage or dysfunction, or to physical disease'. This contains a miniature or 'nested' version of several other categories, in that categories F06.0–F06.5 are not clinically distinguishable from their counterparts in other sections, and differ only in that they are known to have an organic aetiology. Another example is F02.4: Dementia in HIV infection: strictly speaking, this should be included in F02.8: Dementia in other specified conditions, but its current importance in public health statistics was thought to justify a separate category enabling it to be retrieved by using only one code instead of two.

The presence of these anomalies means that Chapter V is impure from a taxonomic point of view, but it is much more likely to be used by clinicians than if the rules of classification had been followed strictly.

Organic aetiology

Recent advances in the technology of brain imaging (such as CT, PET and MRI) have shown that we no longer know what to call 'organic'. When used to indicate obvious loss of, or damage to, brain tissue, the aetiological implications of this term are clear, but it is not justified to use it also to cover, for instance, minimal ventricular enlargement on an MRI brain image of an otherwise normal person. The fact that a similar finding exists in a proportion of subjects who also have a psychiatric syndrome does not allow the general conclusion that there is a direct causal link between the syndrome and the minor abnormality. All we can say at the moment is that it is increasingly possible to detect a variety of brain abnormalities in both normal subjects and patients, whose significance is as yet uncertain.

The terms 'symptomatic' and 'cognitive' were considered as other options for a general title in place of 'organic', but both of these have additional problems. A conservative decision was finally made to retain the familiar and still widely accepted 'organic'.

Definition of boundaries

Reliance on description of emotions, experience and behaviour inevitably means that there are likely to be many problems in defining the boundaries between different disorders, and between mild and severe degrees of the same disorder. The classification of mood (affective) disorders in this and in all other current psychiatric classifications is beset with many problems of this type, the most common instances being the distinction between different grades of severity of depressive states. The differentiation of bipolar disorder from cyclothymia, and the differentiation of dysthymia from other recurrent and chronic states of depression and anxiety, also present difficulties.

In spite of these problems, there is no better alternative at present than to continue to rely upon these descriptive categories, since useful and consistent subgroupings of patients with mood disorders has not yet been achieved by independent biochemical or neurophysiological measurements. It seems likely that the present unsatisfactory state of knowledge about how to subdivide mood disorders (and many others) will not improve until new techniques of investigations and new concepts are developed. Detailed clinical description of signs and symptoms, as now represented in the standardized interviewing and rating procedures closely linked to ICD-10 Chapter V (such as SCAN and CIDI – see page 401), have probably now been taken to the limits of tolerance of both the subjects and the interviewers, and it is difficult to see how this line of investigation can be developed further.

Neurosis and psychosis

An important feature of the new classification that surprises clinicians in many countries is the absence of the traditional distinction between neurosis and psychosis. This distinction was retained in ICD-9, but with a warning that these were terms of convenience rather than precision. In ICD-10, this distinction has now been abandoned in favour of the grouping of disorders by common descriptive characteristics or themes, as already noted above. This carries with it some problems, but at least they are largely practical; they are certainly less difficult to deal with than the theoretical and conceptual problems that appear to be inherent in the concepts of neurosis and psychosis. Attempts to agree on definitions of neurosis and psychosis that would be sufficiently precise to be useful in the construction of a classification are usually frustrated by the introduction of complicated concepts such as 'insight' and 'reality testing', and by the involvement of hypothetical psychological defence mechanisms that are far from universally accepted, even in the cultures in which they originated. Nevertheless, in spite of these problems it is clear that many clinicians find neurosis and psychosis to be useful as general descriptive terms. This has therefore been recognized in ICD-10 by their retention as adjectives. The great majority of the disorders associated with the concept of neurosis will be found in Section F4: Neurotic, stress-related and somatoform disorders, and most of the disorders often referred to as functional psychoses will be found in Section F2: Schizophrenia, schizot~ and delusional disorders. The following guid~

the meaning of psychotic is provided: 'Its use does not involve assumptions about psychodynamic mechanisms, but simply indicates the presence of hallucinations, delusions, or a limited number of severe abnormalities of behaviour, such as gross excitement and overactivity, marked psychomotor retardation, and catatonic behaviour.' (WHO 1992).

Use of diagnostic criteria

The idea of specifying diagnostic criteria for research purposes is not new (e.g. Cooper 1967, Feighner et al 1972, Spitzer et al 1977) but their use in comprehensive classifications is more recent. The policy of the World Health Organization with respect to Chapter V of ICD-10 (Sartorius 1991) has been to provide 'clinical guidelines' for general psychiatric use (WHO 1992) and a separate but compatible set of diagnostic criteria for the purposes of research (WHO 1993). To list the essential characteristics of a disorder in comparatively precise terms gives some obvious advantages, but some basic problems about the use of such 'criteria' have not yet been resolved. A critical debate is now required about what are the essential characteristics of the criteria themselves, since the lists that have been appearing in the research literature over the last decade or so bring with them a number of problems due to their heterogeneity. Under the general label of 'diagnostic criteria' there can now be found, apart from the expected symptoms and items of abnormal behaviour, statements about the age and sex of the patient, the duration of symptoms and behaviour, and the personal and social consequences of the disorders. Statements about what other diagnoses must not be present are also commonly included. In other words, what are currently called diagnostic criteria are a mixed bag of items, some of which give the diagnosis of the disorder present, some of which describe the most commonly encountered type of patient, some of which describe the likely consequences of the disorder, and some of which describe the relative priorities of disorders in a hierarchy of diagnostic importance.

We would probably learn more about both the strong and the weak points of psychiatric diagnoses if, for each disorder, these different types of information were clearly labelled as such, rather than being lumped together. One useful consequence of doing this would probably be a much wider agreement that, as far as possible, it is not appropriate to include the social consequences of a disorder among the defining features of the disorder itself. This is particularly important for an internationally used classification such as the ICD, because the social environment of individuals varies widely from one culture to another. The same symptoms and behaviour that are tolerated in one culture may cause severe social problems in another culture, and it is clearly undesirable for diagnostic decisions to be determined by cultural and social differences.

To develop the discussion of diagnostic criteria in this way has the consequence of immediately highlighting another fundamental but insufficiently debated issue: what is the nature of the objects of classification in current psychiatric classifications? It is easy to forget that only a small proportion of psychiatric diagnoses refers to concepts that are comparable to those upon which the practice of general medicine is based. Many psychiatric diagnoses, as currently defined, have no correlates in disturbed anatomy or physiology, and many (particularly those used in the psychiatry of childhood and adolescence) are dependent for their recognition upon a complex of disturbed emotions and behaviour in more than one person.

Faced with the awkward task of putting such a mixture into some sort of order, it is not surprising that the organizers of Chapter V of ICD-10 (and of DSM-3 and DSM-3-R) decided to use the term 'disorder' to describe what is being classified. This has the advantage of avoiding the need to debate the meaning and usefulness of terms such as 'disease', 'illness' and 'sickness', but is almost tantamount to saying that a psychiatric classification should contain anything that psychiatrists and other mental health professionals want it to contain; in Chapter V of ICD-10, 'disorder' is used 'to imply the existence of a clinically recognizable set of symptoms or behaviour associated in most cases with distress and with interference with personal functions' (WHO 1992). Further guidance is given to the effect that 'social deviance or conflict alone, without personal dysfunction, should not be included in mental disorder as defined here'. The increase in clinical usefulness resulting from such a wide definition of what is being classified is offset by a decrease in the taxonomic and scientific characteristics of the classification, but perhaps this is a fair reflection of the current state of clinical psychiatry.

Problems of duration

Compilers of either clinical guidelines or diagnostic criteria for research are faced with many frustrating problems when trying to decide what to specify (if anything) about how long disorders should be expected to last. Problems tend to fall into two different types; the more important is the conceptual problem attached to the nature of the particular concept in question – for instance, how acute is an 'acute psychotic disorder' and when does it turn into schizophrenia or some other more long-lasting disorder? These and other problems of duration with respect to schizophrenia are discussed in the 'Notes on selected categories in the classification of mental and behavioural disorders of ICD-10' that accompany the volume *Clinical descriptions and diagnostic guidelines* (WHO 1992, p 9–12). The second type of duration problem is inherent in the idea of criteria for research: however artificial it may seem from a clinical point of view, it is necessary for purposes of comparison to choose durations of symptoms and behaviour that must be achieved before a disorder can be said to be present. Similar arbitrary decisions have to be made about how long is an episode, and what constitute a remission between relapses. Clinicians may well view the suggestions made for research purposes with interest, but they would be ill-advised to apply them in clinical settings with the same rigidity that is required in many types of research. Urgent decisions may be necessary in clinical practice that cannot wait for the duration criteria appropriate for research to be fulfilled.

Special needs of the psychiatry of childhood

The abandoning of the distinction between neurosis and psychosis as a major principle of classification has allowed a much more satisfactory presentation of the disorders with onset specific to childhood and adolescence. Two large sections, F80–89 and F90–98, are now devoted to these topics, and they contain plenty of unallocated categories to deal with future developments and changes.

The general rule in ICD-10 is that disorders in the other parts of the classification should be used for children and adolescents when they fit the clinical picture, but it is recognized that it is appropriate to specify various forms of morbid anxiety and related emotions that occur in children only. For instance, F93.1: Phobic anxiety disorder of childhood, and F93.2: Social anxiety disorder of childhood, are both considered to have a pattern and course of symptoms significantly different from their adult equivalents. The status of F93.80: Generalized anxiety disorder of childhood, is less certain, so this category is placed only in the Diagnostic criteria for research, for the moment.

The comparatively complicated and socially interactive nature of many disorders of childhood and adolescence has already been noted, but the range and variety of symptoms and abnormal behaviour seen are narrow compared with adult disorders. These characteristics have resulted in the production of comprehensive multiaxial systems of description and classification for use by clinicians in child psychiatry in the past. Similar systems centred around Chapter V of ICD-10 are now in preparation together with one for the assessment of persons with mental retardation.

Equivalence between categories in Chapters V of ICD-9 and ICD-10

In the great majority of instances the equivalences indicated in the conversion table (pages 379–400) are quite clear. Nevertheless, two types of problem affect a small number of categories, first, because there are more categories in ICD-10 than in ICD-9, and second, because different clinical traditions in different centres and countries may lead to dissimilar interpretations of the same terms and categories.

Problems of the first type are evident from the relative numbers of categories placed opposite to each other in the table, and are commented upon in the 'Notes for users' placed immediately before the table. Problems of the second type will have to be resolved by users themselves, since space does not allow the inclusion of the debates and comments that might be justified in more lengthy documents.

References

Cooper JE 1967 Diagnostic change in a longitudinal study of psychiatric patients. *British Journal of Psychiatry* 113: 129–142

Cooper JE 1988 The structure and presentation of contemporary Psychiatric classifications with special reference to ICD-9 and 10. In: (eds) Sartorius N, Jablensky JE, Cooper JE, Burke JD, Psychiatric classifications in an international perspective: *British Journal of Psychiatry* 152: Supplement 1, 21–28

Feighner JP, Robins E, Guze SB, Woodruff RA, Winokur G, Munoz R 1972 Diagnostic criteria for use in psychiatric research. *Archives of General Psychiatry* 26: 57–63

Sartorius N 1991 The classification of mental disorders in the Tenth revision of the International classification of diseases. *European Journal of Psychiatry* 6: 315–322

Spitzer RL, Endicott J, Robins E 1977 Research diagnostic criteria (RDC) for a selected group of functional disorders (3rd edn). New York State Psychiatric Institute, New York

WHO 1992 *The ICD-10 Classification of Mental and Behavioural Disorders: Clinical descriptions and diagnostic guidelines.* World Health Organization, Geneva

WHO 1993 *The ICD-10 Classification of Mental and Behavioural Disorders: Diagnostic criteria for research.* World Health Organization, Geneva

Other conditions from ICD-10 often associated with mental and behavioural disorders

This appendix contains a list of conditions in other chapters of ICD-10 that are often found in association with the disorders in Chapter V(F) itself. They are provided here so that psychiatrists recording diagnoses by means of the *Clinical descriptions and diagnostic guidelines* have immediately to hand the ICD terms and codes that cover the associated diagnoses most likely to be encountered in ordinary clinical practice. The majority of the conditions covered are given only at the three-character level, but four-character codes are given for a selection of those diagnoses that will be used most frequently.

Chapter I
Certain infectious and parasitic diseases (A00–B99)

A50 Congenital syphilis
A50.4 Late congenital neurospyhilis [juvenile neurospyhilis]

A52 Late syphilis
A52.1 Symptomatic neurosyphilis

Includes: tabes dorsalis

A81 Slow virus infections of central nervous system
A81.0 Creutzfeldt–Jakob disease
A81.1 Subacute sclerosing panencephalitis
A81.2 Progressive multifocal leukoencephalopathy

B22 Human immunodeficiency virus (HIV) disease resulting in other specified diseases
B22.0 HIV disease resulting in encephalopathy

Includes: HIV dementia

Chapter II
Neoplasms (C00–D48)

C70.– Malignant neoplasm of meninges

C71.– Malignant neoplasm of brain

C72.– Malignant neoplasm of spinal cord, cranial nerves and other parts of central nervous system

D33.– Benign neoplasm of brain and other parts of central nervous system

D42.– Neoplasm of uncertain and unknown behaviour of meninges

D43.– Neoplasm of uncertain and unknown behaviour of brain and central nervous system

Chapter IV
Endocrine, nutritional and metabolic diseases (E00–E90)

E00.– Congenital iodine-deficiency syndrome

E01.– Iodine deficiency-related thyroid disorders and allied conditions

E02 Subclinical iodine-deficiency hypothyroidism

E03 Other hypothyroidism
    E03.2 Hypothyroidism due to medicaments and other exogenous substances
    E03.5 Myxoedema coma

E05.– Thyrotoxicosis [hyperthyroidism]

E15 Non-diabetic hypoglycaemic coma

E22 Hyperfunction of pituitary gland
    E22.0 Acromegaly and pituitary gigantism
    E22.1 Hyperprolactinaemia

    Includes: drug-induced hyperprolactinaemia

E23.– Hypofunction and other disorders of pituitary gland

E24.– Cushing's syndrome

E30   Disorders of puberty, not elsewhere classified
E30.0   Delayed puberty
E30.1   Precocious puberty

E34   Other endocrine disorders
E34.3   Short stature, not elsewhere classified

E51   Thiamine deficiency
E51.2   Wernicke's encephalopathy

E64.– Sequelae of malnutrition and other nutritional deficiencies

E66.– Obesity

E70   Disorders of aromatic amino-acid metabolism
E70.0   Classical phenylketonuria

E71   Disorders of branched-chain amino-acid metabolism and fatty-acid metabolism
E71.0   Maple-syrup urine disease

E74.– Other disorders of carbohydrate metabolism

E80.– Disorders of porphyrin and bilirubin metabolism

Chapter VI
Diseases of the nervous system (G00–G99)

G00.– Bacterial meningitis, not elsewhere classified

Includes: haemophilus, pneumococcal, streptococcal, staphylococcal and other bacterial meningitis

G02.– Meningitis in other infectious and parasitic diseases classified elsewhere

G03.– Meningitis due to other and unspecified causes

G04.– Encephalaitis, myelitis and encephalomyelitis

G06 Intracranial and intraspinal abscess and granuloma
G06.2 Extradural and subdural abscess, unspecified

G10 Huntington's disease

G11.– Hereditary ataxia

G20 Parkinson's disease

G21 Secondary parkinsonism
G21.0 Malignant neuroleptic syndrome
G21.1 Other drug-induced secondary parkinsonism
G21.2 Secondary parkinsonism due to other external agents
G21.3 Postencephalitic parkinsonism

G24 Dystonia

Includes: dyskinesia

G24.0 Drug-induced dystonia
G24.3 Spasmodic torticollis
G24.8 Other dystonia

Includes: tardive dyskinesia

G25.– Other extrapyramidal and movement disorders

Includes: restless legs syndrome, drug-induced tremor, myoclonus, chorea, tics

G30 Alzheimer's disease
G30.0 Alzheimer's disease with early onset
G30.1 Alzheimer's disease with late onset
G30.8 Other Alzheimer's disease
G30.9 Alzheimer's disease, unspecified

G31 Other degenerative diseases of nervous system, not elsewhere classified
G31.0 Circumscribed brain atrophy

Includes: Pick's disease

G31.1 Senile degeneration of brain, not elsewhere classified

G31.2 Degeneration of nervous system due to alcohol

Includes: alcoholic cerebellar ataxia and degeneration, cerebral degeneration and encephalopathy, dysfunction of the autonomic nervous system due to alcohol

G31.8 Other specified degenerative diseases of the nervous system

Includes: Subacute necrotizing encephalopathy [Leigh], grey-matter degeneration [Alpers]

G31.9 Degenerative disease of nervous sytem, unspecified

G32.– Other degenerative disorders of nervous system in diseases classified elsewhere

G35 Multiple sclerosis

G37 Other demyelinating diseases of central nervous system
G37.0 Diffuse sclerosis

Includes: periaxial encephalitis, Schilder's disease

G40 Epilepsy
G40.0 Localization-related (focal) (partial) idiopathic epilepsy and epileptic syndromes with seizures of localized onset

Includes: benign chldhood epilepsy with centrotemporal EEG spikes or occipital EEG paroxysms

G40.1 Localization-related (focal) (partial) symptomatic epilepsy and epileptic syndromes with simple partial seizures

Includes: attacks without alteration of consciousness

G40.2 Localization-related (focal) (partial) symptomatic epilepsy and epileptic syndromes with complex partial seizures

Includes: attacks with alteration of consciousness, often with automatisms

G40.3 Generalized idiopathic epilepsy and epileptic syndromes
G40.4 Other generalized epilepsy and epileptic syndromes

Includes: salaam attacks

G40.5 Special epileptic syndromes

Includes: epileptic seizures related to alcohol, drugs and sleep deprivation

G40.6 Grand mal seizures, unspecified (with or without petit mal)
G40.7 Petit mal, unspecified, without grand mal seizures

G41.– Status epilepticus

G43.– Migraine

G44.– Other headache syndromes

G45.– Transient cerebral ischaemic attacks and related syndromes

G47 Sleep disorders
G47.2 Disorders of the sleep–wake schedule
G47.3 Sleep apnoea
G47.4 Narcolepsy and cataplexy

G70 Myasthenia gravis and other myoneural disorders
G70.0 Myasthenia gravis

G91.– Hydrocephalus

G92 Toxic encephalopathy

G93 Other disorders of brain

G93.1 Anoxic brain damage, not elsewhere classified

G93.3 Postviral fatigue syndrome

Includes: benign myalgic encephomyelitis

G93.4 Encephalopathy, unspecified

G97 Postprocedural disorders of nervous system, not elsewhere classified
G97.0 Cerebrospinal fluid leak from spinal puncture

Chapter VII
Diseases of the eye and adnexa (H00–H59)

H40 Glaucoma
H40.6 Glaucoma secondary to drugs

Chapter VIII
Diseases of the ear and mastoid process (H60–H95)

H93 Other disorders of ear, not elsewhere classified
H93.1 Tinnitus

Chapter IX
Diseases of the circulatory system (I00–I99)

I10 Essential (primary) hypertension

I60.– Subarachnoid haemorrhage

I61.– Intracerebral haemorrhage

I62 Other nontraumatic intracranial haemorrhage
I62.0 Subdural haemorrhage (acute) (nontraumatic)
I62.1 Non-traumatic extradural haemorrhage

I63.– Cerebral infarction

I64   Stroke, not specified as haemorrhage or infarction

I65.– Occlusion and stenosis of precerebral arteries, not resulting in cerebral infarction

I66.– Occlusion and stenosis of cerebral arteries, not resulting in cerebral infarction

I67   Other cerebrovascular diseases
  I67.2   Cerebral atherosclerosis
  I67.3   Progressive vascular leukoencephalopathy

  Includes: Binswanger's disease

  I67.4   Hypertensive encephalopathy

I69.– Sequelae of cerebrovascular disease

I95   Hypotension
  I95.2   Hypotension due to drugs

Chapter X
Diseases of the respiratory system (J00–J99)

J10   Influenza due to identified influenza virus
  J10.8   Influenza with other manifestations, influenza virus identified

J11   Influenza, virus not identified
  J11.8   Influenza with other manifestations, virus not identified

J42   Unspecified chronic bronchitis

J43.– Emphysema

J45.– Asthma

Chapter XI
Diseases of the digestive system (K00–K93)

K25   Gastric ulcer

K26   Duodenal ulcer

K27 **Peptic ulcer, site unspecified**

K29 **Gastritis and duodenitis**
K29.2 Alcoholic gastritis

K30 **Dyspepsia**

K58.– **Irritable bowel syndrome**

K59.– **Other functional intestinal disorders**

K70.– **Alcoholic liver disease**

K71.– **Toxic liver disease**
Includes: drug-induced liver disease

K86 **Other diseases of pancreas**
K86.0 Alcohol-induced chronic pancreatitis

Chapter XII
Diseases of the skin and subcutaneous tissue (L00–L99)

L20.– **Atopic dermatitis**

L98 **Other disorders of skin and subcutaneous tissue, not elsewhere classified**
L98.1 Factitial dermatitis

Includes: neurotic excoriation

Chapter XIII
Diseases of the musculoskeletal system and connective tissue (M00–M99)

M32.– **Systemic lupus erythematosus**

M54.– **Dorsalgia**

Chapter XIV
Diseases of the genitourinary system (N00–N99)

N48 **Other disorders of penis**
N48.3 Priapism
N48.4 Impotence of organic origin

N91.– **Absent, scanty and rare menstruation**

N94 **Pain and other conditions associated with female genital organs and menstrual cycle**
  N94.3 Premenstrual tension syndrome
  N94.4 Primary dysmenorrhoea
  N94.5 Secondary dysmenorrhoea
  N94.6 Dysmenorrhoea, unspecified

N95 **Menopausal and other perimenopausal disorders**
  N95.1 Menopausal and female climacteric states
  N95.3 States associated with artificial menopause

Chapter XV
Pregnancy, childbirth and the puerperium (O00–O99)

O04 **Medical abortion**

O35 **Maternal care for known or suspected fetal abnormality and damage**
  O35.4 Maternal care for (suspected) damage to fetus from alcohol
  O35.5 Maternal care for (suspected) damage to fetus by drugs

O99 **Other maternal diseases classifiable elsewhere but complicating pregnancy, childbirth and puerperium**
  O99.3 Mental disorders and diseases of the nervous system complicating pregnancy, childbirth and the puerperium

  Includes: conditions in F00–F99 and G00–G99

Chapter XVII
Congenital malformations, deformations and chromosomal abnormalities (Q00–Q99)

Q02 **Microcephaly**

Q03.– Congenital hydrocephalus

Q04.– Other congenital malformations of brain

Q05.– Spina bifida

Q75.– Other congenital malformations of skull and face bones

Q85 **Phakomatoses, not elsewhere classified**
Q85.0   Neurofibromatosis (non-malignant)
Q85.1   Tuberous sclerosis

Q86 **Congenital malformation syndromes due to known exogenous causes, not elsewhere classified**
Q86.0   Fetal alcohol syndrome (dysmorphic)

Q90 **Down's syndrome**
Q90.0   Trisomy 21, meiotic non-disjunction
Q90.1   Trisomy 21, mosaicism (mitotic non-disjunction)
Q90.2   Trisomy 21, translocation
Q90.9   Down's syndrome, unspecified

Q91.– Edwards' syndrome and Patau's syndrome

Q93 **Monosomies and deletions from the autosomes, not elsewhere classified**
Q93.4   Deletion of short arm of chromosome 5
Includes: cri-du-chat syndrome

Q96.– Turner's syndrome

Q97.– Other sex chromosome abnormalities, female phenotype, not elsewhere classified

Q98 **Other sex chromosome abnormalities, male phenotype, not elsewhere classified**
Q98.0   Klinefelter's syndrome karyotype 47,XXY
Q98.1   Klinefelter's syndrome, male with more than two X chromosomes

Chapter XVIII
**Symptoms, signs and abnormal clinical and
laboratory findings, not elsewhere classified
(R00–R99)**

R90.– Abnormal findings on diagnostic imaging of central nervous system

R94 Abnormal results of function studies

R94.0 Abnormal results of function studies of central nervous system

Includes: abnormal electroencephalogram [EEG]

Chapter XIX
Injury, poisoning and certain other consequences of external causes (S00–T98)

S06 Intracranial injury

S06.0 Concussion

S06.1 Traumatic cerebral oedema

S06.2 Diffuse brain injury

S06.3 Focal brain injury

S06.4 Epidural haemorrhage

S06.5 Traumatic subdural haemorrhage

S06.6 Traumatic subarachnoid haemorrhage

S06.7 Intracranial injury with prolonged coma

Chapter XX
External causes of morbidity and mortality (V01–Y98)

Intentional self-harm (X60–X84)

Includes: purposely self-inflicted poisoning or injury, suicide

X60 Intentional self-poisoning by and exposure to non-opioid analgesics, antipyretics and antirheumatics

X61 Intentional self-poisoning by and exposure to antiepileptic, sedative–hypnotic, antiparkinsonism and psychotropic drugs, not elsewhere classified

Includes: antidepressants, barbiturates, neuroleptics, psychostimulants

X62 Intentional self-poisoning by and exposure to narcotics and psychodysleptics [hallucinogens], not elsewhere classified

Includes: cannabis (derivatives), cocaine, codeine, heroin, lysergide [LSD], mescaline, methadone, morphine, opium (alkaloids)

X63 Intentional self-poisoning by and exposure to other drugs acting on the autonomic nervous systems

X64 Intentional self-poisoning by and exposure to other and unspecified drugs and biological substances

X65 Intentional self-poisoning by and exposure to alcohol

X66 Intentional self-poisoning by and exposure to organic solvents and halogenated hydrocarbons and their vapours

X67 Intentional self-poisoning by and exposure to other gases and vapours

Includes: carbon monoxide, utility gas

X68 Intentional self-poisoning by and exposure to pesticides

X69 Intentional self-poisoning by and exposure to other and unspecified chemicals and noxious substances

Includes: corrosive aromatics, acids and caustic alkalis

X70 Intentional self-harm by hanging, strangulation and suffocation

X71 Intentional self-harm by drowning and submersion

X72 Intentional self-harm by handgun discharge

X73 Intentional self-harm by rifle, shotgun and larger firearm discharge

X74 Intentional self-harm by other and unspecified firearm discharge

X75 Intentional self-harm by explosive material

X76 Intentional self-harm by fire and flames

X77 Intentional self-harm by steam, hot vapours and hot objects

X78 Intentional self-harm by sharp object

X79 Intentional self-harm by blunt object

X80 Intentional self-harm by jumping from a high place

X81 Intentional self-harm by jumping or lying before moving object

X82 Intentional self-harm by crashing of motor vehicle

X83 Intentional self-harm by other specified means

> *Includes:* crashing of aircraft, electrocution, caustic substances (except poisoning)

X84 Intentional self-harm by unspecified means

Assault (X85–Y09)

> *Includes:* homicide, injuries inflicted by another person with intent to injure or kill, by any means

X93 Assault by handgun discharge

X99 Assault by sharp object

Y00 Assault by blunt object

Y04   **Assault by bodily force**

Y05   **Sexual assault by bodily force**

Y06.- **Neglect and abandonment**

Y07.- **Other maltreatment syndromes**

> *Includes:* mental cruelty, physical abuse, sexual abuse, torture

Drugs, medicaments and biological substances causing adverse effects in therapeutic use (Y40–Y59)

Y46   **Antiepileptics and antiparkinsonism drugs**
     Y46.7   Antiparkinsonism drugs

Y47.- **Sedatives, hypnotics and antianxiety drugs**

Y49   **Psychotropic drugs, not elsewhere classified**
     Y49.0   Tricyclic and tetracyclic antidepressants
     Y49.1   Monoamine-oxidase-inhibitor antidepressants
     Y49.2   Other and unspecified antidepressants
     Y49.3   Phenothiazine antipsychotics and neuroleptics
     Y49.4   Butyrophenone and thioxanthene neuroleptics
     Y49.5   Other antipsychotics and neuroleptics
     Y49.6   Psychodysleptics [hallucinogens]
     Y49.7   Psychostimulants with abuse potential
     Y49.8   Other psychotropic drugs, not elsewhere classified
     Y49.9   Psychotropic drug, unspecified

Y50.- **Central nervous system stimulants, not elsewhere classified**

Y51.- **Drugs primarily affecting the autonomic nervous system**

Y57.– **Other and unspecified drugs and medicaments**

Chapter XXI
Factors influencing health status and contact with health services (Z00–Z99)

Z00 **General examination and investigation of persons without complaint and reported diagnosis**
Z00.4 General psychiatric examination, not elsewhere classified

Z02 **Examination and encounter for administrative purposes**
Z02.3 Examination for recruitment to armed forces
Z02.4 Examination for driving licence
Z02.6 Examination for insurance purposes
Z02.7 Issue of medical certificate

Z03 **Medical observation and evaluation for suspected diseases and conditions**
Z03.2 Observation for suspected mental and behavioural disorders

Includes: observation for dissocial behaviour, fire-setting, gang activity and shoplifting, without manifest psychiatric disorder

Z04 **Examination and observation for other reasons**

Includes: examination for medicolegal reasons
Z04.6 General psychiatric examination, requested by authority

Z50 **Care involving use of rehabilitation procedures**
Z50.2 Alcohol rehabilitation
Z50.3 Drug rehabilitation
Z50.4 Psychotherapy, not elsewhere classified
Z50.7 Occupational therapy and vocational rehabilitation, not elsewhere classified

Z50.8   Care involving use of other specified
         rehabilitation procedures

Includes: tobacco abuse rehabilitation, training
         in activities of daily living [ADL]

Z54   Convalescence
Z54.3   Convalescence following psychotherapy

Z55.– Problems related to education and literacy

Z56.– Problems related to employment and unemployment

Z59.– Problems related to housing and economic circumstances

Z60   Problems related to social environment
Z60.0   Problems of adjustment to life-cycle
         transitions
Z60.1   Atypical parenting situation
Z60.2   Living alone
Z60.3   Acculturation difficulty
Z60.4   Social exclusion and rejection
Z60.5   Target of perceived adverse
         discrimination and persecution
Z60.8   Other specified problems related to
         social environment

Z61   Problems related to negative life events in childhood
Z61.0   Loss of love relationship in childhood
Z61.1   Removal from home in childhood
Z61.2   Altered pattern of family relationships
         in childhood
Z61.3   Events resulting in loss of self-esteem in
         childhood
Z61.4   Problems related to alleged sexual abuse
         of child by person within primary
         support group
Z61.5   Problems related to alleged sexual abuse
         of child by person outside primary
         support group
Z61.6   Problems related to alleged physical
         abuse of child

	Z61.7	Personal frightening experience in childhood
	Z61.8	Other negative life events in childhood

Z62 Other problems related to upbringing

	Z62.0	Inadequate parental supervision and control
	Z62.1	Parental overprotection
	Z62.2	Institutional upbringing
	Z62.3	Hostility towards and scapegoating of child
	Z62.4	Emotional neglect of child
	Z62.5	Other problems related to neglect in upbringing
	Z62.6	Inappropriate parental pressure and other abnormal qualities of upbringing
	Z62.8	Other specified problems related to upbringing

Z63 Other problems related to primary support group, including family circumstances

	Z63.0	Problems in relationship with spouse or partner
	Z63.1	Problems in relationship with parents and in-laws
	Z63.2	Inadequate family support
	Z63.3	Absence of family member
	Z63.4	Disappearance and death of family member
	Z63.5	Disruption of family by separation and divorce
	Z63.6	Dependent relative needing care at home
	Z63.7	Other stressful life events affecting family and household
	Z63.8	Other specified prolems related to primary support group

Z64 Problems related to certain psychosocial circumstances

	Z64.0	Problems related to unwanted pregnancy
	Z64.2	Seeking and accepting physical, nutritional and chemical interventions known to be hazardous and harmful

Z64.3 Seeking and accepting behavioural and
       psychological interventions known to
       be hazardous and harmful
Z64.4 Discord with counsellors

Includes: probation officer, social worker

Z65   Problems related to other psychosocial
          circumstances
Z65.0 Conviction in civil and criminal
       proceedings without imprisonment
Z65.1 Imprisonment and other incarceration
Z65.2 Problems related to release from prison
Z65.3 Problems related to other legal
       circumstances

Includes: arrest
            child custody or support proceedings

Z65.4 Victim of crime and terrorism
       (including torture)
Z65.5 Exposure to disaster, war and other
       hostilities

Z70.– Counselling related to sexual attitude,
          behaviour and orientation

Z71   Persons encountering health services for
          other counselling and medical advice, not
          elsewhere classified
Z71.4 Alcohol abuse counselling and
       surveillance
Z71.5 Drug abuse counselling and
       surveillance
Z71.6 Tobacco abuse counselling

Z72   Problems relating to lifestyle
Z72.0 Tobacco use
Z72.1 Alcohol use
Z72.2 Drug use
Z72.3 Lack of physical exercise
Z72.4 Inappropriate diet and eating habits
Z72.5 High-risk sexual behaviour
Z72.6 Gambling and betting
Z72.8 Other problems related to lifestyle

Includes: self-damaging behaviour

Z73 **Problems related to life-management difficulty**

Z73.0 Burnout
Z73.1 Accentuation of personality traits

Includes: type A behaviour pattern

Z73.2 Lack of relaxation or leisure
Z73.3 Stress, not elsewhere classified
Z73.4 Inadequate social skills, not elsewhere classified
Z73.5 Social role conflict, not elsewhere classified

Z75 **Problems related to medical facilities and other health care**

Z75.1 Person awaiting admission to adequate facility elsewhere
Z75.2 Other waiting period for an investigation and treatment
Z75.5 Holiday relief care

Z76 **Persons encountering health services in other circumstances**

Z76.0 Issue of repeat prescription
Z76.5 Malingerer [conscious simulation]

Includes: persons feigning illness with obvious motivation

Z81 **Family history of mental and behavioural disorders**

Z81.0 Family history of mental retardation
Z81.1 Family history of alcohol abuse
Z81.3 Family history of other psychoactive substance abuse
Z81.8 Family history of other mental and behavioural disorders

Z82 **Family history of certain disabilities and chronic diseases leading to disablement**

Z82.0 Family history of epilepsy and other diseases of the nervous system

Z85.– **Personal history of malignant neoplasm**

Z86 **Personal history of certain other diseases**

Z86.0 Personal history of other neoplasms

Z86.4 Personal history of psychoactive substance abuse

Z86.5 Personal history of other mental and behavioural disorders

Z86.6 Personal history of diseases of the nervous system and sense organs

Z87 Personal history of other diseases and conditions

Z87.7 Personal history of congenital malformations, deformations and chromosomal abnormalities

Z91 Personal history of risk factors, not elsewhere classified

Z91.1 Personal history of non-compliance with medical treatment and regimen

Z91.4 Personal history of psychological trauma, not elsewhere classified

Z91.5 Personal history of self-harm

Includes: parasuicide, self-poisoning, suicide attempt

Conversion Table between Chapter V (Mental Disorders) of the ICD-9, and Chapter V (Mental and Behavioural Disorders) of the ICD-10

Notes for users

In the left-hand column (ICD-9) some inclusion terms are listed in italics. The right-hand column (ICD-10) shows their equivalent (or nearest equivalent) ICD-10 code.

Chapter V of ICD-10 contains more codes than that of ICD-9, so an ICD-9 code may have several options for conversion into ICD-10. Information in addition to the ICD code may be available which indicates the exact equivalent in ICD-10, but if not, then the ICD-10 code which is listed first should be used. For instance, the code 290.1 in ICD-9, Presenile dementia, may be accompanied by additional information which indicates that the ICD-10 equivalent is F02.0, Pick's disease. However, if only the code and/or the title are available then F00.0, Dementia in Alzheimer's disease, early onset, should be used, as this is the most common type of presenile dementia.

Acknowledgements

This conversion table is based upon the set of conversion tables between ICD-8, ICD-9 and ICD-10 prepared for the Division of Mental Health, WHO, Geneva, by Dr J van Drimmelen (Internal Document Reference WHO/MNH 92:16), with assistance and guidance from Mr A. L'Hours (technical officer: Strengthening of Epidemiological and Statistical Services, WHO), Dr A Bertelsen (Director of the ICD-10 Field Trial Coordinating Centre, Aarhus) and the directors of the other Field Trial Coordinating Centres listed in the WHO publications containing the CDDG and the DCR-10 of Chapter V of ICD-10 (WHO 1992, WHO 1993).

ICD-9		ICD-10	
290	Senile and presenile organic psychotic conditions		
290.0	Senile dementia, simple type	F00.1*	Dementia in Alzheimer's disease, late onset (G30.1 +)

ICD-9		ICD-10	
290.1	Presenile dementia	F00.0*	Dementia in Alzheimer's disease, early onset (G30.0+)
	Dementia in:		
	• *Jakob–Creutzfeldt disease*	F02.1*	Dementia in Creutzfeldt–Jakob disease (A81.0+)
	• *Pick's disease*	F02.0*	Dementia in Pick's disease (G31.0+)
290.2	Senile dementia, depressed or paranoid type	F00.1*	Dementia in Alzheimer's disease, late onset
			.13 with other predominantly depressive symptoms
			.11 with other predominantly delusional symptoms
		F00.2*	Dementia in Alzheimer disease, atypical or mixed type (G30.8+)
			.23 with other predominantly depressive symptoms
			.21 with other predominantly delusional symptoms
290.3	Senile dementia with acute confusional state	*Use two codes:*	
		F05.1	Delirium, superimposed on dementia
		plus:	
		F00.1*	Dementia in Alzheimer's disease, late onset (G30.1+) or
		F00.2*	Dementia in Alzheimer's disease, atypical or mixed type (F30.8+)
290.4	Arteriosclerotic dementia	F01.1	Multi-infarct dementia
		F01.0	Vascular dementia of acute onset
		F01.2	Subcortical vascular dementia
		F01.3	Mixed cortical and subcortical vascular dementia
		F01.8	Other vascular dementia

ICD-9		ICD-10	
290.8 Other		F00.24	Dementia in Alzheimer's disease, atypical or mixed type with other mixed symptoms
		F01.8	Other vacular dementia
		F02.8	Dementia in other diseases classified elsewhere
290.9 Unspecified		F03	Unspecified dementia
291	**Alcoholic psychoses**		
291.0 Delirium tremens		F10.4	Withdrawal state with delirium due to use of alcohol
291.1 Korsakov's psychosis, alcoholic		F10.6	Amnesic syndrome due to use of alcohol
291.2 Other alcoholic dementia		F10.73	Dementia due to use of alcohol
291.3 Other alcoholic hallucinosis		F10.52	Psychotic disorder due to use of alcohol, predominantly hallucinatory
291.4 Pathologic drunkenness		F10.07	Pathological intoxication due to use of alcohol
291.5 Alcoholic jealous		F10.51	Psychotic disorder due to use of alcohol, predominantly delusional
291.8 Other alcoholic psychoses		F10.8	Other mental and behavioural disorders due to use of alcohol
		F10.56	Psychotic disorder due to use of alcohol, mixed
		F10.75	Late-onset psychotic disorder due to use of alcohol
	Alcoholic withdrawal syndrome	F10.3	Withdrawal state due to use of alcohol
291.9 Unspecified		F10.9	Unspecified mental and behavioural disorder due to use of alcohol
	Alcoholic:		
	• Mania NOS	F10.55	Psychotic disorder due to use of alcohol, predominantly manic
	• psychosis NOS	F10.56	Psychotic disorder due to use of alcohol, mixed

ICD-9		ICD-10	
292	**Drug psychoses**		
292.0	Drug withdrawal syndrome	F1x.3	Withdrawal state due to psychoactive substance use
		F1x.4	Withdrawal state with delirium due to psychoactive substance use
292.1	Paranoid and/or hallucinatory states induced by drugs	F1x.5	Psychotic disorder due to psychoactive substance use, .51 predominantly delusional .52 predominantly hallucinatory
292.2	Pathological drug intoxication	F1x.07	Pathological intoxication due to psychoactive substance use
292.8	Other	F1x.5	Psychotic disorder due to psychoactive substance use .50 schizophrenia-like .53 predominantly polymorphic .54 predominantly depressive symptoms .55 predominantly manic symptoms .56 mixed
		F1x.7	Residual and late-onset psychotic disorder due to use of psychoactive substance use
292.9	Unspecified	F1x.9	Unspecified mental and behavioural disorder due to psychoactive substance use
293	**Transient organic psychotic conditions**		
293.0	Acute confusional state	F05.0	Delirium, not superimposed on dementia, so described *Consider also:*
		F05.8	Other delirium
		F05.9	Unspecified delirium

ICD-9		ICD-10	
293.0	*Epileptic twilight state*	F06.5	Organic dissociative disorder
293.1	Subacute confusional state	F05.8	Other delirium
			Consider also:
		F05.0	Delirium, not superimposed on dementia, so described
		F05.9	Unspecified delirium
293.8	Other	F06.8	Other specified mental disorders due to brain damage and dysfunction and to physical disease
		F06.0	Organic hallucinosis
		F06.1	Organic catatonic disorder
		F06.2	Organic delusional disorders
		F06.3	Organic mood disorders
293.9	Unspecified	F06.9	Unspecified mental disorders due to brain damage and dysfunction and to physical disease
		F05.9	Delirium, unspecified
		F09	Unspecified organic or symptomatic mental disorder

294	**Other organic psychotic conditions (chronic)**		
294.0	Korsakov's psychosis or syndrome (non-alcoholic)	F04	Organic amnesic syndrome, not induced by alcohol and other psychoactive substances
		F1x.6	Amnesic syndrome due to psychoactive substances, other than alcohol
294.1	Dementia in conditions classified elsewhere	F02.*	Dementia in other diseases classified elsewhere
294.8	Other	F06.0	Organic hallucinosis
		F06.1	Organic catatonic disorder
		F06.2	Organic delusional disorder
		F06.3	Organic mood [affective] disorder
		F06.8	Other specified mental disorders due to brain

ICD-9	ICD-10	
294.8		damage and dysfunction and to physical disease
294.9 Unspecified	F06.9	Unspecified mental disorder, due to brain damage and dysfunction and to physical disease
	F09	Unspecified organic or symptomatic mental disorder

295	**Schizophrenic psychoses**		
295.0 Simple type	F20.6	Simple schizophrenia
295.1 Hebephrenic type	F20.1	Hebephrenic schizophrenia
295.2 Catatonic type	F20.2	Catatonic schizophrenia
295.3 Paranoid type	F20.0	Paranoid schizophrenia
295.4 Acute schizophrenic episode	F23.2	Acute schizophrenia-like psychotic disorder
	F23.1	Acute polymorphic psychotic disorder with symptoms of schizophrenia
	F20.8	Other schizophrenia
295.5 Latent schizophrenia	F21	Schizotypal disorder
295.6 Residual schizophrenia	F20.5	Residual schizophrenia
295.7 Schizoaffective type	F25.–	Schizoaffective disorders
295.8 Other	F20.8	Other schizophrenia
295.9 Unspecified *Schizophrenic reaction* *Schizophreniform psychosis NOS*	F20.9	Schizophrenia, unspecified
	F23.2	Acute schizophrenia-like psychotic disorder
	F23.1	Acute polymorphic psychotic disorder with symptoms of schizophrenia *Consider also:*
	F20.8	Other schizophrenia

ICD-9	ICD-10
296 Affective psychoses	
296.0 Manic–depressive psychosis, manic type	F30.– Manic episode (single episode)
	F31.1 Bipolar affective disorder, current episode manic without psychotic symptoms
	F31.2 Bipolar affective disorder, current episode manic with psychotic symptoms
	F31.8 Other bipolar affective disorder
296.1 Manic–depressive psychosis, depressed type	F32.11 Moderate depressive episode with somatic symptoms
	F32.2 ⎫ Severe depressive episode, F32.3 ⎭ all types
	F33.11 Recurrent depressive disorder, current episode moderate, with somatic symptoms
	F33.2 ⎫ Recurrent depressive F33.3 ⎭ disorder, current episode severe, all types
296.2 Manic–depressive psychosis, circular type but currently manic	F31.0 Bipolar affective disorder, current episode hypomanic
	F31.1 Bipolar affective disorder, current episode manic without psychotic symptoms
	F31.2 Bipolar affective disorder, current episode manic with psychotic symptoms
296.3 Manic–depressive psychosis, circular type but currently depressed	F31.3 Bipolar affective disorder, current episode mild or moderate depression
	F31.4 Bipolar affective disorder current episode severe depression without psychotic symptoms
	F31.5 Bipolar affective disorder, current episode severe depression with psychotic symptoms

ICD-9		ICD-10	
296.4	Manic–depressive psychosis, circular type, mixed	F31.6	Bipolar affective disorder, current episode mixed
		F38.00	Mixed affective episode (single)
296.5	Manic–depressive psychosis, circular type, current condition not specified	F31.9	Bipolar affective disorder, unspecified
296.6	Manic–depressive psychosis, other and unspecified	F31.8	Other bipolar affective disorder
		F31.9	Bipolar affective disorder, unspecified
296.8	Other	F30.8	Other manic episodes
		F31.8	Other bipolar affective disorders
		F32.8	Other depressive episodes
		F33.8	Other recurrent depressive disorders
		F38.8	Other mood [affective] disorders
296.9	Unspecified	F39	Unspecified mood [affective] disorder
297	**Paranoid states**		
297.0	Paranoid state, simple	F22.0	Delusional disorder
297.1	Paranoia	F22.0	Delusional disorder
297.2	Paraphrenia *Involutional paranoid state*	F22.0	Delusional disorder
		F22.8	Other persistent delusional disorders
297.3	Induced psychosis	F24	Induced delusional disorder
297.8	Other	F22.8	Other persistent delusional disorders
	Sensitiver Beziehungswahn	F22.0	Delusional disorder
297.9	Unspecified	F22.0	Persistent delusional disorder, unspecified

ICD-9	ICD-10

298 Other non-organic psychosis

298.0 Depressive type	F32.11 Moderate depressive episode, with somatic symptoms
	F32.2 / F32.3 Severe depressive episode, all types
	F33.11 Recurrent depressive disorder, current episode moderate, with somatic symptoms
	F33.2 / F33.3 Recurrent depresive disorder, current episode severe, all types
298.1 Excitative type	F23.81 Other acute and transient psychotic disorders, with associated acute stress
	F30.– Manic episode
298.2 Reactive confusion	F23.01 Acute polymorphic psychotic disorder without symptoms of schizophrenia with associated acute stress
	F23.81 Other acute and transient psychotic disorder, with associated acute stress
298.3 Acute paranoid reaction	F23.31 Other acute predominantly delusional psychotic disorders, with associated acute stress
298.4 Psychogenic paranoid psychosis	F23.31 Other acute predominantly delusional psychotic disorders, with associated acute stress
	F22.0 Delusional disorder
	F22.8 Other persistent delusional disorders
	F24 Induced delusional disorder
298.8 Other and unspecified reactive psychosis	F23.81 Other acute and transient psychotic disorders, with associated acute stress
	F23.91 Acute and transient psychotic disorder, with associated acute stress, unspecified

Conversion table between ICD-9 and ICD-10

ICD-9		ICD-10	
298.9	Unspecified psychosis	F29	Unspecified non-organic psychosis
		F99	Unspecified mental disorder
299	**Psychoses with origin specific to childhood**		
299.0	Infantile autism	F84.0	Childhood autism
		F84.1	Atypical autism
		F84.2	Rett's syndrome
299.1	Disintegrative psychosis	F84.3	Other childhood disintegrative disorder
299.8	Other	F84.5	Asperger's syndrome
		F84.8	Other pervasive developmental disorder
299.9	Unspecified	F84.9	Pervasive developmental disorder, unspecified
	Schizophrenia, childhood type	F20.8	Other schizophrenia
300	**Neurotic disorders**		
300.0	Anxiety states	F41.–	Other anxiety disorders, all types. Specify type if possible. Consider also F40.01, Agoraphobia with panic disorder
		F43.22	Mixed anxiety and depressive reaction
	Panic attack or disorder	F41.0	Panic disorder
300.1	Hysteria	F44.–	Dissociative disorders Consider also:
		F43.23	Adjustment reaction with predominant disturbance of other emotions
	Compensation neurosis	F68.0	Elaboration of physical symptoms for psychological reasons
300.2	Phobic state *Anxiety hysteria*	F40.–	Phobic anxiety disorders, all types except F40.1, Agoraphobia with panic disorder
	Anxiety hysteria	F41.8	Other specified anxiety disorders

ICD-9		ICD-10	
300.3	Obsessive–compulsive disorders	F42.–	Obsessive–compulsive disorder, all types
300.4	Neurotic depression	F34.1	Dysthymia
		F32.0	Mild depressive episode
		F33.0	Recurrent depressive disorder, current episode mild
		F43.21	Adjustment reaction, prolonged depressive reaction
	Anxiety depression	F41.2	Mixed anxiety and depressive disorder
	Depressive reaction ⎫	F32.0	Mild depressive episode
	Reactive depression ⎭	F32.8	Other depressive episodes
		F33.0	Recurrent depressive disorder, current episode mild
		F43.20	Brief depressive reaction
		F43.21	Prolonged depressive reaction
300.5	Neurasthenia	F48.0	Neurasthenia
300.6	Depersonalization syndrome	F48.1	Depersonalization–derealization syndrome
300.7	Hypochondriasis	F45.2	Hypochondriacal disorder
300.8	Other neurotic disorders	F48.8	Other specified neurotic disorders
300.9	Unspecified	F48.9	Neurotic disorder, unspecified
		F99	Mental disorder, not otherwise specified
301	**Personality disorders**		
301.0	Paranoid personality disorder	F60.0	Paranoid personality disorder
	Paranoid traits	Z73.1	Accentuated personality traits
301.1	Affective personality disorder	F34.0	Cyclothymia
		F34.1	Dysthymia
301.1		F60.8	Other specific personality disorders
301.2	Schizoid personality disorder	F60.1	Schizoid personality disorder

ICD-9		ICD-10	
301.3	Explosive personality disorder	F60.3	Emotionally unstable personality disorder
301.4	Anankastic personality disorder	F60.5	Anankastic personality disorder
301.5	Hysterical personality disorder	F60.4	Histrionic personality disorder
301.6	Asthenic personality disorder	F60.7	Dependent personality disorder
301.7	Personality disorder with predominantly sociopathic or asocial manifestion	F60.2	Dissocial personality disorder
301.8	Other personality disorders	F60.6	Anxious [avoidant] personality disorder
		F60.8	Other specific personality disorders
		F61	Mixed and other personality disorders
		F68.8	Other specified disorders of adult personality and behaviour
301.9	Unspecified	F60.9	Personality disorder, unspecified
302	**Sexual deviations and disorders**		
302.0	Homosexuality	No equivalent code	
302.1	Bestiality	F65.8	Other disorder of sexual preference
302.2	Paedophilia	F65.4	Paedophilia
302.3	Transvestism	F65.1	Fetishistic transvestism
		F64.1	Dual-role transvestism
302.4	Exhibitionism	F65.2	Exhibitionism
302.5	Transsexualism	F64.0	Transsexualism
302.6	Disorders of psychosexual identity	F64.2	Gender identity disorder of childhood
		F64.8 and .9	Gender identity disorder, other and unspecified

ICD-9		ICD-10	
302.7	Fridigity and impotence *Dyspareunia, psychogenic*	F52.0 F52.2 F52.6 F52.5	Lack or loss of sexual desire Failure of genital response Non-organic dyspareunia Non-organic vaginismus
302.8	Other	F64.8	Other gender identity disorders
		F65.8	Other disorders of sexual preference
		F52.8	Other sexual dysfunction, not caused by organic disorder or disease
	Fetishism	F65.0	Fetishism
	Masochism/sadism	F65.5	Sadomasochism
302.9	Unspecified	F64.9	Gender identity disorder, unspecified
		F65.9	Disorder of sexual preference, unspecified
		F52.9	Unspecified sexual dysfunction not caused by organic disorder or disease
303	**Alcohol dependence syndrome**	F10.2	Dependence syndrome due to use of alcohol
304	**Drug dependence**		
304.0	Morphine type	F11.2	Dependence syndrome due to use of opioids
304.1	Barbiturate type	F13.2	Dependence syndrome due to use of sedatives or hypnotics
304.2	Cocaine	F14.2	Dependence syndrome due to use of cocaine
304.3	Cannabis	F12.2	Dependence syndrome due to use of cannabinoids
304.4	Amphetamine-type and other psychostimulants	F15.2	Dependence syndrome due to use of other stimulants, including caffeine
304.5	Hallucinogens	F16.2	Dependence syndrome due to use of hallucinogens
304.6	Other	F18.2	Dependence syndrome due to use of volatile solvents

ICD-9		ICD-10	
304.6		F19.2	Dependence syndrome due to multiple drug use and use of other psychoactive substances
304.7	Combinations of morphine type drug with any other	F19.2	Dependence syndrome due to multiple drug use and use of other psychoactive substances
304.8	Combinations excluding morphine type drug		
304.9	Unspecified		
305	**Non-dependent abuse of drugs**		
305.0	Alcohol	F10.1	Harmful use of alcohol
		F10.0	Acute intoxication due to use of alcohol
305.1	Tobacco *Tobacco dependence* Note: although contradictory to the title of 305, ICD-9 includes tobacco dependence here.	F17.1	Harmful use of tobacco
		F17.2	Dependence syndrome due to use of tobacco
305.2	Cannabis	F12.1	Harmful use of cannabinoids
		F12.0	Acute intoxication due to use of cannabinoids
305.3	Hallucinogens	F16.1	Harmful use of hallucinogens
		F16.0	Acute intoxication due to use of hallucinogens
305.4	Barbiturates and tranquillizers	F13.1	Harmful use of sedatives or hypnotics
		F13.0	Acute intoxication due to use of sedatives or hypnotics
305.5	Morphine type	F11.1	Harmful use of opioids
		F11.0	Acute intoxication due to use of opioids
305.6	Cocaine type	F14.1	Harmful use of cocaine
		F14.0	Acute intoxication due to use of cocaine

ICD-9		ICD-10	
305.7	Amphetamine type	F15.1	Harmful use of other stimulants,
		F15.0	Acute intoxication due to use of other stimulants
305.8	Antidepressants	F55	Abuse of substances, not producing dependence
305.9	Other, mixed or unspecified	F19.1	Abuse of multiple or other psychoactive substances
		F55	Abuse of substances, not producing dependence
306	**Physiological malfunction arising from mental factors**		
306.0	Musculoskeletal	F45.8	Other somatoform disorders
306.1	Respiratory	F45.33	Somatoform autonomic dysfunction of respiratory system
306.2	Cardiovascular	F45.30	Somatoform autonomic dysfunction of heart and cardiovascular system
306.3	Skin	F45.8	Other somatoform disorders
306.4	Gastrointestinal	F45.31	Somatoform autonomic dysfunction of upper gastrointestinal tract
		F45.32	Somatoform autonomic dysfunction of lower gastrointestinal tract system
	Psychogenic cyclical vomiting	F50.5	Vomiting associated with other psychological disturbances
306.5	Genitourinary	F45.3	Somatoform autonomic dysfunction of genitourinary system
	Psychogenic dysmenorrhoea	F45.8	Other somatoform disorders
306.6	Endocrine	Use two codes:	
		F54	Psychological and behavioural factors associated with disorders

06.6		or diseases classified elsewhere plus a code from Chapter IV for specific endocrine disorder
06.7 Organs of special sense	F45.8	Other somatoform disorders
06.8 Other	F45.8	Other somatoform disorders
06.9 Unspecified	F45.9	Somatoform disorders, unspecified
07	**Special symptoms or syndromes not elsewhere classified**	
07.0 Stammering and stuttering	F98.5	Stuttering
Cluttering	F98.6	Cluttering
07.1 Anorexia nervosa	F50.0	Anorexia nervosa
	F50.1	Atypical anorexia nervosa
07.2 Tics	F95.–	Tic disorders
07.3 Stereotyped repetivive movements	F98.4	Stereotyped movement disorders
07.4 Specific disorders of sleep	F51.–	Non-organic sleep disorders
07.5 Other and unspecified disorders of eating	F50.1	Atypical anorexia nervosa
	F50.2	Bulimia nervosa
	F50.3	Atypical bulimia nervosa
	F50.4	Overeating associated with other psychological disturbances
	F50.5	Vomiting associated with other psychological disturbances
	F50.8	Other eating disorders
	F50.9	Eating disorder, unspecified
Infantile feeding disturbances	F98.2	Feeding disorder of infancy
Pica (in children)	F98.3	Pica of infancy and chilhood
07.6 Enuresis	F98.0	Non-organic enuresis
07.7 Encopresis	F98.1	Non-organic encopresis

ICD-9		ICD-10	
307.8	Psychalgia	F45.4	Persistent somatoform pain disorder
	Tension headache	G44.2	Tension headache
307.9	Other and unspecified	F98.8	Other specified behavioural and emotional disorders with onset usually occurring in childhood and adolescence
		F98.9	Unspecified behavioural and emotional disorders with onset usually occurring in childhood and adolescence
	Lalling	F80.0	Specific speech articulation disorder
308	**Acute reaction to stress**		
308.0	Predominant disturbance of emotions	F43.0	Acute stress reaction
308.1	Predominant disturbance of consciousness	F43.0	Acute stress reaction *consider also:*
		F44.1	Elective mutism
308.2	Predominant psychomotor disturbance	F43.0	Acute stress reaction
308.3	Other	F43.8	Other reactions to severe stress
308.4	Mixed	F43.0	Acute stress reaction
308.9	Unspecified	F43.9	Reaction to severe stress, unspecified
309	**Adjustment reaction**	F43.2	Adjustment disorders
309.0	Brief depressive reaction		.20 brief depressive reaction
309.1	Prolonged depressive reaction		.21 prolonged depressive reaction
309.2	With predominant disturbance of other emotions		.23 with predominant disturbance of other emotions
	Abnormal separation anxiety	F93.0	Separation anxiety disorder of childhood

396

Conversion table between ICD-9 and ICD-10

CD-9		ICD-10	
309.3	With predominant disturbance of conduct	F43.2 .24	Adjustment disorders with predominant disturbance of conduct
309.4	With mixed disturbance of emotions and conduct	.25	with mixed disturbance of emotions and conduct
309.8	Other	.28	other specified adjustment disorders *Consider also:*
		F94.0	Elective mutism
309.9	Unspecified	F43.2	Adjustment disorders
310	**Specific non-psychotic mental disorders following organic brain damage**		
310.0	Frontal lobe syndrome	F07.0	Organic personality disorder
310.1	Cognitive or personality change of other type	F06.7	Mild cognitive disorder
		F07.8	Other organic personality and behaviour disorders
		F06.6	Organic emotionally labile [asthenic] disorder
310.2	Postconcussional syndrome	F07.2	Postconcussional syndrome
310.8	Other	F07.1	Postencephalitic syndrome
		F07.8	Other organic personality and behavioural disorders
		F06.4	Organic anxiety disorder
		F06.5	Organic dissociative disorder
310.9	Unspecified	F07.9	Organic personality and behaviour disorder, unspecified
311	**Depressive disorder, not elsewhere classified**	F32.9	Depressive episode, unspecified
		F33.9	Recurrent depressive disorder, unspecified
		F38.10	Recurrent brief depressive disorder

ICD-9		ICD-10	
312	**Disturbance of conduct not elsewhere classified**		
312.0	Unsocialized disturbance of conduct	F91.1	Unsocialized conduct disorder
312.1	Socialized disturbance of conduct	F91.2	Socialized conduct disorde
312.2	Compulsive conduct disorder	F63.–	Habit and impulse disorders
312.3	Mixed disturbance of conduct and emotions	F92.–	Mixed disorders of conduct and emotions
312.8	Other	F91.0	Conduct disorder confined to the family context
		F91.3	Oppositional defiant disorder
		F91.8	Other conduct disorders
312.9	Unspecified	F91.9	Conduct disorder, unspecified
313	**Disturbance of emotions specific to childhood and adolescence**		
313.0	With anxiety and fearfulness	F93.1	Phobic anxiety disorder of childhood
		F93.2	Social anxiety disorder of childhood
		F93.0	Separation anxiety disorder of childhood
			Consider also:
	Overanxious reaction of childhood	F94.0	Elective mutism
		F93.8	Other childhood emotional disorders
313.1	With misery and unhappiness	F32.0	Mild depressive episode
		F32.8	Other depressive episodes
		F43.20	Brief depressive reaction
		F43.21	Prolonged depressive reaction
		F92.0	Depressive conduct disorder

CD-9		ICD-10	
13.2	With sensitivity, shyness and social withdrawal	F93.2	Social anxiety disorder of childhood
			consider also:
		F94.0	Elective mutism
13.3	Relationship problems	F93.3	Sibling rivalry disorder
		F94.1	Reactive attachment disorder of childhood
		F94.2	Disinhibited attachment disorder of childhood
13.8	Other or mixed	F93.8	Other childhood emotional disorders
13.9	Unspecified	F93.9	Childhood emotional disorder, unspecified
314	**Hyperkinetic syndrome of childhood**		
314.0	Simple disturbance of activity and attention	F90.0	Disturbance of activity and attention
314.1	Hyperkinesis with developmental delay	F90.0	Disturbance of activity and attention <u>plus</u> additional code from <u>F80–F83</u> for specific developmental disorder
314.2	Hyperkinetic conduct disorder	F90.1	Hyperkinetic conduct disorder
314.8	Other	F90.8	Other hyperkinetic disorders
314.9	Unspecified	F90.9	Hyperkinetic disorder, unspecified
315	**Specific delays in development**		
315.0	Specific reading retardation	F81.0	Specific reading disorder
315.1	Specific arithmetical retardation	F81.2	Specific disorder of arithmetical skills
315.2	Other specific learning difficulties	F81.8	Other developmental disorders of scholastic skills

ICD-9		ICD-10	
315.3	Developmental speech or language disorder	F80.–	Specific developmental disorders of speech and language
315.4	Specific motor retardation	F82	Specific developmental disorder of motor function
315.5	Mixed developmental disorder	F83	Mixed specific developmental disorders
315.8	Other	F88	Other disorders of psychological development
315.9	Unspecified	F89	Unspecified disorder of psychological development
316	**Psychic factors associated with diseases classified elsewhere**	F54	Psychological and behavioural factors associated with disorders or diseases classified elsewhere
317	**Mild mental retardation**	F70	Mild mental retardation
318	**Other specified mental retardation**		
318.0	Moderate mental retardation	F71	Moderate mental retardation
318.1	Severe mental retardation	F72	Severe mental retardation
318.2	Profound mental retardation	F73	Profound mental retardation
319	**Unspecified mental retardation**	F79	Unspecified mental retardation

Conversion table between ICD-9 and ICD-10

Diagnostic instruments and publications associated with ICD-10 Chapter V

The Schedule for Clinical Assessment in Neuropsychiatry (SCAN), the Composite International Diagnostic Interview (CIDI), and the International Personality Disorder Examination (IPDE) have been developed within the framework of the WHO/ADAMHA Joint Project on Diagnosis and Classification of Mental Disorders, Alcohol- and Drug-related Problems. More information about these instruments can be obtained from the Division of Mental Health, World Health Organization, 1211 Geneva 27, Switzerland.

Training in the use of these instruments can at present be obtained in the following languages: Chinese, Danish, English, French, German, Greek, Hindi, Kannada, Portuguese, Spanish, Tamil and Turkish.

1. Jablensky A, Sartorius N, Hirschfeld R, Pardes H et al 1983 Diagnosis and classification of mental disorders and alcohol- and drug-related problems: a research agenda for the 1980s. *Psychological Medicine* **13**: 907–921

2. Mental disorders, alcohol- and drug-related problems: international perspectives on their diagnosis and classification. 1985. *Excerpta Medica* (International Congress Series, No. 669) Amsterdam

3. Sartorius N et al (eds) 1988 Psychiatric classification in an international perspective. *British Journal of Psychiatry* **152**: (Suppl. 1)

4. Robins L et al 1989 The composite international diagnostic interview. *Archives of General Psychiatry* **45**: 1069–1077

5. WHO 1994 *Lexicon of psychiatric and mental health terms.* 2nd edn. World Health Organization, Geneva

6. Wing J K et al 1990 SCAN: Schedules for clinical assessment in neuropsychiatry. *Archives of General Psychiatry* **47**: 589–593

7. Sartorius N et al (eds) 1990 Sources and traditions of classification in psychiatry. Hogrefe and Huber, Toronto

8. Sartorius N 1991 The classification of mental disorders in the Tenth Revision of The International Classification of Diseases. *European Journal of Psychiatry* **6**: 315–322

9. Loranger A W et al 1991 The WHO/ADAMHA International Pilot Study of Personality Disorders: background and purpose. *Journal of Personality Disorders* **5**: 296–306

10. WHO 1992 *The ICD-10 Classification of Mental and Behavioural Disorders: Conversion tables between ICD-8, ICD-9 and ICD-10.* World Health Organization, Geneva (unpublished WHO document WHO/MNH/92/16, available on request from Division of Mental Health, World Health Organization, 1211 Geneva 27, Switzerland)

11. WHO 1992, 1993, 1994 *International Statistical Classification of Diseases and Related Health Problems.* Tenth Revision. Vol. 1: Tabular list, 1992. Vol. 2: Instruction manual, 1993. Vol. 3: Alphabetical Index. World Health Organization, Geneva

12. WHO 1992 *The ICD-10 Classification of Mental and Behavioural Disorders. Clinical descriptions and diagnostic guidelines.* World Health Organization, Geneva

13. Composite International Diagnostic Interview 1.1 1993. American Psychiatric Press, Washington, DC

14. Sartorius N et al 1993 Progress towards achieving a common language in psychiatry: results from the field trials of the clinical guidelines accompanying the WHO Classification of Mental and Behavioural Disorders in ICD-10. *Archives of General Psychiatry* **50**: 115–124

15. WHO 1993 *The ICD-10 Classification of Mental and Behavioural Disorders: Diagnostic criteria for research.* World Health Organization, Geneva

16. WHO 1994 (in preparation) *Psychiatric Adaptation of ICD-10.* World Health Organization, Geneva

INDEX

Index

Index